PRAISE FOR BEYO[...]

D0069104

"*Beyond Valor* is an inspiring true story of heroism aboard a B-29 Superfortress in the skies over Japan during World War II. In a swift moment of instinctive reaction, Red Erwin selflessly saved the lives of many, and for his courage and sacrifice he was awarded the congressional Medal of Honor, inspiring generations to come. Red's grandson Jon Erwin, along with William Doyle, recaptures this amazing story with the depth and care that a hero deserves. This is a thrilling and poignant story of patriotism that all Americans can be stirred, moved, and encouraged by."

—Gary Sinise, actor, veterans advocate, founder of the Gary Sinise
Foundation, and author of *Grateful American*

"The human heart is moved by great stories. Each of us yearns for our lives to be connected to a larger purpose. That's why stories inspire us. We see reflections of our own lives in the stories of others. My friend Jon Erwin is a master storyteller who has inspired millions with his movies. *Beyond Valor* is a story of heroism, love, and devotion that will inspire you to believe there is a grand purpose for your own life, larger than you can see, greater than you can imagine."

—Greg Laurie, senior pastor of Harvest Christian Fellowship and
author of *Johnny Cash: The Redemption of an American Icon*

BEYOND VALOR

BEYOND VALOR

A World War II Story of Extraordinary Heroism,
Sacrificial Love, and a Race Against Time

JON ERWIN & WILLIAM DOYLE

NELSON
BOOKS
An Imprint of Thomas Nelson

Published in Nashville, Tennessee, by Nelson Books, an imprint of Thomas Nelson. Nelson Books and Thomas Nelson are registered trademarks of HarperCollins Christian Publishing, Inc.

Thomas Nelson titles may be purchased in bulk for educational, business, fundraising, or sales promotional use. For information, please e-mail SpecialMarkets@ThomasNelson.com.

Unless otherwise noted, Scripture quotations taken from The Holy Bible, New International Version®, NIV®. Copyright © 1973, 1978, 1984, 2011 by Biblica, Inc.® Used by permission of Zondervan. All rights reserved worldwide. www.Zondervan.com. The "NIV" and "New International Version" are trademarks registered in the United States Patent and Trademark Office by Biblica, Inc.®

Scripture quotations marked KJV are taken from the King James Version. Public domain.

Any internet addresses, phone numbers, or company or product information printed in this book are offered as a resource and are not intended in any way to be or to imply an endorsement by Thomas Nelson, nor does Thomas Nelson vouch for the existence, content, or services of these sites, phone numbers, companies, or products beyond the life of this book.

ISBN: 978-1-4002-1686-4 (TP)

Library of Congress Cataloging-in-Publication Data

Names: Erwin, Jon, 1982- author.
Title: Beyond valor : a World War II story of extraordinary heroism, sacrificial love, and a race against time / Jon Erwin and William Doyle.
Description: Nashville : Thomas Nelson, 2020. | Includes bibliographical references. | Summary: "A miraculous true story of a soldier's unspeakable heroism, a teenage woman's unfailing love, and the faith that secured them all"--Provided by publisher.
Identifiers: LCCN 2020001894 | ISBN 9781400216833 (hardcover) | ISBN 9781400216840 (ebook)
Subjects: LCSH: Erwin, Henry Eugene, 1921-2002. | United States. Army Air Forces. Bombardment Squadron, 29th--Biography. | Flight radio operators--United States--Biography. | City of Los Angeles (Bomber) | World War, 1939-1945--Pacific Area--Aerial operations, American. | World War, 1939-1945--Regimental histories--United States. | Veterans Administration Hospital (Birmingham, Ala.)--Employees--Biography. | Disabled veterans--United States--Biography. | Burns and scalds--Patients--United States--Biography. | Aircraft accidents--United States--History--20th century. | Birmingham (Ala.)--Biography.
Classification: LCC D790.263 29th .E79 2020 | DDC 940.54/4973092 [B]--dc23
LC record available at https://lccn.loc.gov/2020001894

Printed in the United States of America

21 22 23 24   LSC   10 9 8 7 6 5 4 3 2 1

To the men and women who have given the ultimate sacrifice for our freedom, and to those who dedicate their lives to our country knowing they may give the same sacrifice.

"I am not a hero. The real heroes are those who have given the ultimate sacrifice for this country, those who have given their lives. They're the ones who deserve the medals. I am only a survivor. I don't wear the Medal of Honor for what I did, I wear it for *everyone* who served."

—Red Erwin

I sought the LORD, and he heard me, and delivered me from all my fears.

—PSALM 34:4 KJV

Greater love hath no man than this, that a man lay down his life for his friends.

—JOHN 15:13 KJV

We have a lot of problems in this country, but we should never forget how fortunate we really are. I thank God I was born an American. We have been blessed in so many ways. It reminds me of that passage in the Bible: "For unto whomsoever much is given, of him shall be much required."

—RED ERWIN

Henry Eugene "Red" Erwin, 1944
(Erwin Family Collection)

CONTENTS

PROLOGUE

SATURDAY, JANUARY 19, 2002. FREEZING RAIN beating down on me.

This is what I remember as I stepped out of a limousine filled with relatives and set foot on the wet grass of Elmwood Cemetery in Birmingham, Alabama. Occasional gusts of wind blew the water beneath my umbrella and soaked my suit. To this day I still remember the bone-chilling feeling of cold—and sadness.

We had come to bury my grandfather, with full military honors. The funeral procession extended for a half mile, and law-enforcement agencies throughout Birmingham sealed off roads and highways for the caravan. Police cars and motorcycles with flashing lights guided the hearse in front of us. I was nineteen years old.

Winter in Alabama is wet and gray, and this day was no exception. The grass was anything but green, and the occasional oak tree had lost all color. Elmwood is a vast cemetery, the largest in the city of Birmingham, my hometown. Crypts and gravestones stretch into the distance, farther than the eyes can see. It's the final resting place of many renowned people, among them the legendary football coach Paul "Bear" Bryant and several congressmen and governors.

We made the long walk from the cars to a couple of tents in the distance that covered an opening in the ground on a family plot containing several other Erwin graves. As we followed the flag-covered casket, carried by a detachment of air force enlisted personnel, I realized this was no ordinary day and no ordinary funeral. Not many civilians made it to the outdoor burial service because it was raining so hard, but the US military showed up. And in strength. To my surprise, there was a small army of generals, officers, and enlisted men and women in dress uniforms to pay their respects and honor our family.

I watched in awe as the flag covering the casket was folded with solemn reverence and machinelike precision. Then the air force officer in charge, dripping wet, knelt down next to my grandmother, Betty, and then my father, Henry Erwin Jr., and repeated the same words: "On behalf of the president of the United States and a grateful nation, I present this flag as a token of appreciation for your father's faithful service." He stood and saluted my father, my grandmother, and then the casket of my grandfather.

Other military personnel followed suit, saluting and standing perfectly still. They held that salute for the longest time while they were pounded with sheets of rain. After a twenty-one-gun salute, as the coffin was being lowered into the ground, a squadron of aircraft from my grandfather's old outfit, the Twentieth Air Force, joined a squadron of C-130s from the 314th Air Wing out of Arkansas, and flew low, beneath the clouds, and tipped their wings to a brother airman. One by one, as they emerged from the low clouds, the hum and power of their engines shook me to my core. The sound was deafening. The message was clear.

Finally, two buglers played "Taps," standing a hundred feet apart and on either side of the proceeding, as if they were guardian angels. For the longest time they had been standing perfectly still and without rain gear, looking like frozen statues in the rainstorm. Now their time had come. They echoed each other, creating a beautiful and melancholy sound, which resonated even more in the vastness of the cemetery.

When the ceremony concluded and the downpour tapered off, I went over to the rain-drenched buglers and offered an apology. "We're so sorry you had to stand out here in the cold rain to do this for our family."

One of them replied directly and emphatically, "No, sir, your grandfather was one of our nation's heroes. It is our honor to be here."

With those simple words, a deep question suddenly lodged in my brain: *Who was my grandfather?*

I walked toward his grave amid the other Erwin family members, aware of the fact I was treading on my legacy. I looked at Red's simple gravestone, no bigger than a yard sign, sitting horizontally in the ground. It simply read "Henry E. Erwin Sr., Medal of Honor." I stared at it and wondered, *Who was this man I took for granted? What had he accomplished that merited such awe-inspiring recognition?* I wished I could turn back the clock and have another day with him so I could ask him all the questions that were unanswerable now.

The intermittent rain was accompanied by feelings of guilt, and a powerful realization washed over me. I did not know Red Erwin as a hero, only as a grandfather. I stared down at his gravestone and at the words *Medal of Honor*, and memories of him began to flood my mind.

I remembered when I was no older than seven or eight, sitting in the basement of his house in Bessemer, Alabama, eating my grandmother's fresh-baked cookies.

Downstairs was an office and a den with a comfortable couch, lots of books, flags set in wooden mounts, plaques, awards, certificates, and clippings. I didn't register this at the time, but they were all about my grandfather, about ceremonies and buildings that were named in his honor. On this day, Red ducked into the closet of his office and reappeared with a mahogany box in his hand. He sat me down at his desk and opened the box. Inside was a light blue silk neck ribbon attached to a beautiful gold medal. It was the Medal of Honor awarded to him in April 1945, when he was on what everyone assumed was his deathbed.

I had no idea I was holding America's highest military honor, reserved only for extraordinary acts "above and beyond the call of duty." I looked it over curiously, clueless to the significance of its every detail. On top, just beneath the blue ribbon, was an American eagle clutching an olive branch in its right wing, a symbol of mercy, and arrows in its left, a symbol of strength. The eagle sat atop the word *Valor*, which was connected to an inverted five-point star, surrounded by an open, circular wreath, representing victory. Inside the star was a circle bearing the inscription "United States of America" and an etched profile of Minerva, the Roman goddess of wisdom and war.

But to my eyes as a child, it was a simple gold medal with a blue ribbon. I had no idea what I held in my hands. Slowly my grandfather leaned over my shoulders and said, "Freedom isn't free." I didn't understand the words then, but they reverberated in my mind now as I stared down at his gravestone, looking at an engraving of the same symbol above his name. I closed my eyes, remembering his face, remembering the moments we shared together.

My grandfather had many distinguishing features, such as honesty, gentleness, kindness, humor, strength of character, a quiet but firm set of religious beliefs, curiosity, and affection for people. He considered pretty much everybody to be his friend.

But if you met my grandfather for the first time, you would probably be startled, if not shocked. He looked very different from other people. Your first reaction upon seeing him might be to think, *Oh, my God, what happened to this man? Something terrible happened to him!*

Hundreds of times I saw people have this reaction when my grandfather was out in public. He had been severely wounded, especially in the visible areas of the head, eyes, face, arm, and hand. His right arm was fused into one position and largely immobile. His fingers were visibly and severely disfigured, and he only had minor movement of three of his fingers. The right side of his face was incredibly burned. His nose, ears, lips, eyelids, and facial skin had clearly been reconstructed after a terrible mangling.

But to me, the way he looked wasn't a big deal; it was just the way he looked. I loved him, not as a hero or a historical figure, but as my granddad. The trouble is, I had every opportunity to know him as a hero, but I was never listening as I should have.

INTRODUCTION

ON APRIL 12, 1945, A YOUNG MAN WAS SET ON FIRE.

The conflagration occurred inside a speeding aircraft at an altitude of 1,500 feet over the ocean near the coast of Japan.

The man was Henry Eugene Erwin. He was a staff sergeant in the US Army Air Force, and his buddies called him Red because of his thick red hair.

He was my grandfather.

What happened inside the airplane took about twenty-two seconds, and it resulted in Red Erwin being awarded the Medal of Honor, the highest military award in the United States. It changed his life, and it deeply affected my own.

Red Erwin was twenty-three years old. He had brown eyes, stood five foot ten, and weighed 165 pounds. He was a former Boy Scout, steelworker, and Methodist church volunteer. He was a passionate history buff and a devoted baseball fan. His crew commander, Tony Simeral, called him "a country boy, quiet, unassuming, religiously devout," and the best radioman in the squadron.

Red came from a little town near Birmingham, Alabama. He was described by those who knew him as cheerful, humble, reliable, and highly intelligent. He loved his new wife of three months, and he loved his family, his church, and his country.

Erwin was the radio operator on board a B-29 Superfortress, a strategic heavy bomber, nicknamed the *City of Los Angeles* and manned by a crew of twelve airmen. This was their eleventh combat mission. Their unit was based on the Pacific island of Guam, and it was part of the Fifty-Second Bombardment Squadron, Twenty-Ninth Bombardment Group of the Twenty-First Bomber Command, led by the legendary Maj. Gen. Curtis E. LeMay.

The *City of Los Angeles* was the lead plane (the pathfinder) in an airborne task force of eighty-five B-29s preparing for a low-level attack on a military chemical production complex north of Tokyo.

Erwin and the thousands of American airmen and support crew personnel in the B-29 force were in the process of trying to end World War II in the Pacific by burning the cities, factories, and military bases of the Japanese Empire to the ground and forcing its government to surrender unconditionally to the Allies. It was a horrible calculus of fire and death that consumed tens of thousands of Japanese civilians, but it seemed the only way to force a surrender that would potentially save many more multitudes of Japanese and American lives.

At 9:30 a.m., on a signal from the pilot, my grandfather, whom I'll simply call Red, positioned himself over a small chute near his feet in the deck of the plane and released a series of three smoke bombs to signal the following planes to swarm together in a broad formation to prepare to attack their target.

Then, as a final marker signal, Red placed a cylindrical object the size of a large rolling pin into the chute. It was a 20-pound phosphorus bomb, which resembled a small rocket, and it produced a massive fused explosion of white-yellow fire and smoke in the sky that could be seen from dozens of miles away. It was a maneuver he had performed dozens of times before in training and in combat.

Only this time something went terribly wrong.

Instead of dropping several hundred feet into the sky below, for some reason the bomb jammed, detonated inside the chute, and shot a ball of fire up and onto my grandfather, coating him in phosphorus, which was burning at over 1,400 degrees Fahrenheit, more than six and a half times the temperature of boiling water.

The plane filled with smoke. The pilot could not see the controls. And the gigantic bomber began to plummet toward the ocean. The aircraft would slam into the sea in a matter of seconds.

Red Erwin was blind and on fire. The flames incinerated his head, arms, and upper body. He was a human torch.

His brain and body registered infinite waves of pain, but he also clearly sensed the bomb somewhere nearby, flopping around on the floor and spewing mountains of billowing fire and smoke. It was just a few feet from the bomb bay, which contained 8 tons of incendiary and demolition bombs. If the burning phosphorus fell among the bombs, it would touch off a spectacular explosion that could engulf the other B-29s in the formation.

Red Erwin had a split-second choice to make. He could resign himself to his fate and die along with the eleven other souls on board the plane, or he could try to alter that fate.

The first thing he did was pray. He was a quiet, intensely religious young man, and prayer came naturally to him.

Lord, I need Your help now.

What Red Erwin did next was so courageous and so mind-blowingly difficult that it defies belief. For many years, I wanted to distance myself from thinking about it because I thought I could never measure up to it.

Red's choice triggered a series of events that shaped his life, my life, the lives of many others, and the history of the highest award for military valor the United States can bestow upon a warrior: the Medal of Honor. Red Erwin decided he would find the burning bomb, pick it up with his bare hands, embrace it with his body, and find a way to get it out of the aircraft and into space—with the help of God.

An instant after he prayed, Red stopped feeling any pain. He could hear voices calling out to him, *Go! Go! Go! You can do it!* Only he sensed these weren't human voices, and they weren't coming from inside the plane. They came from somewhere else.

He leaned down and frantically felt around the floor.

He found the bomb, still burning ferociously and spewing columns of smoke, scooped it into his arms, and hugged it to the side of his chest like a running back cradling a football.

Then Red moved through the plane, blind and completely on fire.

———

Since 1862 more than forty million men and women have served in the armed forces of the United States. So far, only 3,506 of them have been awarded the Medal of Honor, a distinction reserved for only the most extraordinary displays of courage and valor and awarded by the president on behalf of the US Congress.

My grandfather is one of them.

For some years, as a young man, I felt as if I lived in the shadow of my grandfather. And I tried to run away from it.

This book is the story of my grandfather and his Medal of Honor and my journey to discover who he was and how his life shaped mine.

This is a story of war and of one American's journey through a cataclysm that engulfed millions of human beings in a clash that would define the destiny of the twentieth century and shape the world we live in today.

This is a story of love. Of one man's love for his country and his brothers in arms and how it gave him the power to perform an act of supreme courage. It is the story of the love of one woman and how it gave that man the power to struggle through impossible odds and unbearable pain on a journey from the flames of hell toward a life of love and peace.

And it is a story of how a horribly wounded young man decided to honor his country and his fellow wounded veterans by devoting the rest of his life to serving them.

This is a story of one man's journey from ultimate despair to a place beyond service, beyond honor, and beyond valor to a life illuminated by the light of God's love.

Chapter One

THE MAKING OF A MAN

RED ERWIN GREW UP IN POVERTY ON THE EDGE of a magic city.

For decades the city of Birmingham was such a boomtown it was called the Magic City and the Pittsburgh of the South for its access to iron ore, coal, and limestone—the main materials used to produce steel. When Red was born, Birmingham was a top twenty US city in size, and it was home to over 30 percent of the state's population. But his day-to-day reality was one of grinding poverty.

"I came from a poor family in Alabama, had no high school education, no college, and no money," Red recalled, in one of a series of letters, notes, articles, and oral histories I discovered after he died.

He was born May 8, 1921, to Walter and Pearl Erwin and grew up in a small mining village in Jefferson County, Alabama, near Birmingham. His father was a coal miner in northern Alabama. One of Red's grandfathers was a Confederate veteran of the Civil War who fought under Thomas J. "Stonewall" Jackson. He had come to Alabama from Texas and died in 1928, when Red was seven years old. Red was the oldest of six brothers and one sister. His mother called him Gene, and his brothers called him Eugene. Everyone else called him Red.

The family lived in a little house in Docena, a community just west of Birmingham, in the heart of coal-mining country. It was a planned community built and managed by the Tennessee Coal, Iron and Railroad Company, designed to help their employees care for their families while they worked. The company built small frame houses and rented them to the employees. They also built grade schools and dry goods stores.

Red's father, Walter, had a dirty, dusty job at the coal mine. He was a coal washer, and he rinsed off the seemingly endless supply of coal that was harvested from the ground. Eventually, the coal dust killed Red's father, as it did countless others who slaved away in the coal mines scattered across Appalachia.

The family struggled to survive while Walter was alive. His tiny salary barely covered food and clothing. But they were a happy house, echoing with childhood laughter and mischief.

"When I was five," Red confessed, "my younger brother Howard and I dragged my father's shotgun out of the house, propped it up against a tree, and pulled the trigger. The concussion from the blast knocked both of us down! It scared us so bad, we took the gun back and never told a soul."

Despite the constant financial pressures felt by the family, Red grew up as a laughing, outgoing, confident boy. He often looked to the sky to admire the aircraft passing to and from the new Birmingham airport, and he dreamed of someday being a pilot.

Red grew up in a flashpoint of American social, political, and economic history. Ever since the devastation of the Civil War, poverty was the constant companion of many Alabamans, white and black, who were shackled to the brutal financial realities of tenant farming, often for unscrupulous landowners.

Poor people, regardless of race, had it bad, but the suffering of African Americans in Alabama was multiplied by generations of repression and racial segregation by both law and social custom. Their rights as American citizens were systematically stripped away through segregated public accommodations, voting restrictions, limited employment opportunities, and a host of other repressive measures. In 1896, the US Supreme Court's *Plessy v. Ferguson* decision upheld the legality of segregation throughout the nation, and Alabama's 1901 constitution sanctified white supremacy as the foundation of the state government and society.

As a mine worker, Walter was a small cog in the machine of rapid industrialization that washed over Alabama in the early twentieth century. But in 1930 the Great Depression hit Alabama extremely hard, and it happened at the same time a tragedy befell Red's family and plunged it toward the abyss of destitution.

"My father passed away at the age of fifty-two, when I was ten years old," recalled Red. "My mother, Pearl, faced the greatest test of her religious faith. She faced the world alone with seven young children and no income. The mining company let us stay in our rented home without pay while friends and relatives sustained the family with food and clothes. Pearl began washing and ironing neighbors' laundry for extra money. She worked around the clock without complaint. In the midst of her pain and loneliness, she would comfort us children by saying, 'We'll just trust the Lord.' But in order to survive, she had to resort to some painful actions. Some of the children were sent to live with relatives. We experienced the agony of separation. Those days would follow us for the rest of our lives."

According to journalist Robert St. John, who interviewed my grandfather in 1946, "Red grew up strong and straight." He "firmly believed that a just God watched over the Erwin destinies," and he "carried his faith, then and later, as a shining shield."

At the age of ten, Red Erwin was the man of the house, and he soon took a crash course in hard work and personal responsibility.

"We needed money," he explained. "So I went right to work. After school I worked in the coal company commissary, stocking shelves with groceries, getting between fifty cents and a dollar a night, which was a lot of money at that time. It helped us get along."

The mining company let the family stay in company housing for close to five years, and it allowed Red to bring bags of groceries home to sustain them. Every Friday night he brought a special treat home: a box or two of glazed donuts, which were savored by the whole family.

Starting in 1938, one of President Franklin D. Roosevelt's New Deal programs had a direct impact on Red's life. The Civilian Conservation Corps (CCC) was a national public works relief program for young unemployed men. At the age of seventeen, in July 1938, Red dropped out of high school and joined the CCC to earn money for his family.

"I was stationed first in northern Alabama, planting kudzu in raw red ditches to stop erosion," he remembered. "Then I traveled out west to Redwood National Forest in California to plant and cut trees, clear trails, fight fires, build outdoor amphitheaters, and work on soil conservation. I was paid thirty dollars a month in wages, and I sent twenty-one dollars home to my mother to help the family. I was promoted to first sergeant. We wore khakis and dungarees for work details. I had charge of 220 men when I was seventeen years of age."

Red's powerful work ethic, maturity, and leadership skills won him a strong recommendation letter from his CCC camp advisor: "It affords me much pleasure to commend Mr. Erwin to any who require the services of a fine, sober, Christian and upright young man." A devout Christian, Red never touched alcohol. He didn't want to disappoint his mother by drinking.

In late 1941 Red was back in Alabama, where he took a backbreaking job at the Fairfield Steel Works just outside of Birmingham.

"It was terrible work," Red recalled. "I was what you call a hooker, hooking hot bars of steel as they rolled off the line. Our job was to keep the rolling steel coming through these mills and making sure they didn't fall onto the floor. We wore facemasks. We would throw salt on the steel. I was getting ninety-three cents an hour, and I felt like I earned my living. It was white-hot steel, and the heat was pulverizing. Molten steel would flare up, sometimes it slinged off sparks of metal that flew in all directions. Sometimes the sparks would lodge in the protective clothes I wore, sending me into a furious dance to get rid of the burning embers."

But all of Red's hard work paid off. "At the age of nineteen," recalled my father, Hank Jr., "he bought his mother and family a small five-room wood-frame house close to the steel mill. To the family, it was as good as a castle. One of the greatest moments of his life was presenting the key to his mother. He took the place of his father, and he took care of the family. He had become a man."

When the United States entered World War II, Red recalled, "I felt like I had a responsibility to get into the military service even though I probably could have stayed home with a deferment, being the bread-winner in my family. But like most kids back at that time that Japan had attacked us, I felt like I would be shirking my duty if I didn't enlist like many of my cohorts did. Plus, all my brothers joined the military. In July 1942, I took a college-equivalency test as an entrance examination to join the army air force, and I scored very high. I qualified for the air corps and technical training. More than anything, I wanted to be a fighter pilot. I had these Buck Rogers dreams that I was going to be a pilot, shoot down the enemy, and that I was going to win the Medal of Honor, believe it or not!"

But his dream of becoming a pilot never came true. Red joined the army reserve at Bessemer, was called to active duty on February 3, 1943, as an aviation cadet, and went to the army pilot training facility at Taylor Field in Ocala, Florida, to prepare for flight training school. On a series of training flights in small aircraft, Red learned that, no matter how hard he tried, for whatever reason, he simply could not land a plane prop-erly. With Red at the controls, the plane's tail kept jumping up and down whenever he tried to land. He was rejected for further training due to what was described as a "flying deficiency."

"A monkey can take a plane off, but landing a plane can be a very dif-ficult proposition," explained retired US Air Force Lt. Col. Dan Hampton, a pilot, military historian, and combat veteran of the Gulf, Kosovo, and Iraq Wars. "You've got spatial relationships, depth perception, wind effects, managing speed, distance, and angle of approach. When you're coming down to the ground at 100 miles an hour, there's a lot that your brain has to take in, and to be honest, you either have it or you don't. If you don't have it, it can't be taught. As Erwin advanced in his training, he would have gone from small training planes to heavier, faster, more complex and more powerful aircraft, and things would have gotten progressively more difficult for him."

The death of Red's dream to become a pilot was a devastating blow. Fighter and bomber pilots were the dashing superheroes of the war, the stars of motion pictures and magazine articles. They were lords of the sky, taking on the enemy in high-speed combat in beautiful machines. Women treated them like stars, and men wanted to be like them. Red had come so close to his dream; he had actually entered the pilot training program. He was shattered by the rejection.

But he had no idea this unexpected setback would launch a series of events that would elevate him to the pantheon of America's great military heroes.

The army offered Red a seventeen-week assignment at Yale University to become a communications officer, but he turned down the offer, thinking it would delay him from entering combat.

In June 1943, Red enthusiastically accepted a reassignment for training as a radio operator and technician and what he hoped would be a faster path to combat. He yearned to get into the fight as fast as possible.

———

Then, on a summer day in 1943, Red Erwin fell in love.

Red was a Bible-believing, observant Christian. His mother was a devout Christian, and he followed in her footsteps, studying the scriptures, volunteering as a youth minister at church, and attending United Methodist Church events.

At twenty-two years of age, Red was a handsome man, and his physical appearance had been sharpened by many months of rugged outdoor work in the California forest and in a blazing steel mill. These two things—his faith and his good looks—combined to change his life.

It happened on a Sunday, at a church fellowship event in Minor Heights, Alabama. A young woman spotted him, and she was startled. Her name was Martha Elizabeth Starnes, and everyone called her Betty. She was seventeen years old and in her last year of high school. And she eventually became my grandmother.

"I just saw him there," she told me decades later. "I thought he was the best-looking thing I'd ever seen. I reckon he thought I was too. I can still remember what he had on. It was a casual green suit. I can still remember that. He was the handsomest thing I'd ever seen in a suit. And he had the prettiest red hair. I loved the way he wore his cap at an angle. I thought he was really good-looking. He was real smart, and he just looked wonderful. He was just real friendly. I wished he'd come over and say hello."

To her disappointment, it didn't happen that day, but the following Sunday, as they were leaving church, Red came over to chat with Betty, and they agreed to go out on a date.

"I thought he was the best-looking thing I'd ever seen. I reckon he thought I was too." (Erwin Family Collection)

Betty was a sweet, shy country girl from a close-knit, churchgoing family of three sisters and one brother. Her father was a mine worker, just like Red's dad, and she grew up not far from where Red's family lived.

Like Red's family, hers was greatly influenced by their faith in divine power and their belief that God would pull them through the tough times. At age seventeen, Betty was maturing into an attractive young woman. She was annoyed by the wolf whistles she sometimes attracted from male admirers, but soon she was even more irritated by the commotion caused among her girlfriends when her handsome boyfriend Red, whom she called Gene, after his middle name, came to visit her.

On their first date in late 1943, they rode the bus and trolley to the Alabama Theater in downtown Birmingham to see the movie *A Guy Named Joe*, about a star-crossed romantic triangle between two airmen and a female pilot. This time, Red, who traveled down from his base at Pratt, Kansas, wore his army uniform, which sent Betty into an even deeper swoon.

"I thought he just looked wonderful!" she recalled.

Soon he was racing home on weekend furloughs by train from his base to Birmingham, and then taking a bus 20 miles south to the town of Calera, in Shelby County, and then hitchhiking 5 miles to the Alabama State College for Women at Montevallo, where, beginning in the fall of 1944, Betty was a freshman. After a few hours together, he would have to do a reverse mad dash back to Kansas.

As they courted through 1943 and 1944, Red poured out his heart to Betty in letters from training bases and aviation complexes in Alabama, Mississippi, New Mexico, Florida, South Dakota, Wisconsin, Texas, and Kansas, while he was training to become a radio operator on the army's B-17 Flying Fortress bomber.

"He wrote the best letters," Betty told me sixty years later. "And his penmanship was so neat and artistic. I still cherish those letters."

When I discovered the letters, I was amazed at the strength of their feelings for each other and how letters can be such a powerful way of expressing your love for someone. In those letters, he told her:

> I've been thinking of you all evening, so I'm going to try at least to say hello beautiful, what's cookin'?

I wonder as I watch the moon, up in the sky so far.

Are you watching too, or is it dank and raining where you are? And when I twirl a radio dial and hear some song that's new, I wonder if off where you are you might be listening too?

Do you daydream as I daydream and miss me too, My Dear?

Am hoping and praying I get a letter from you tomorrow. Good night and pleasant dreams, darling.

I really felt miserable that night when I had to leave and you cried. I felt like cutting out my heart.

Darling, you're so good and wonderful and I love you truly. You're the one who means all the world to me. I'd give anything in the world to be near you.

I miss you very much and I love you with all of my heart. Every night before I go to bed I look at your picture and whisper "Goodnight, Darling." Looking at your picture and thinking of you makes you feel very close to me. I'd give anything to be there tonight.

From the moment I saw you I've never cared about being with anyone but you. And the last time I was home was the most wonderful thing which ever happened in my life. Then I knew what life was really for. I'm so very happy knowing that you love me, knowing that I have everything in the world to live for and something to come home to.

I lie awake at night thinking of you and my heart aches. I love you, darling. If my letters make you happy then I'm happy because yours make me happy knowing I have such a sweetheart as you.

My belief has always been if anything is worth doing then do your best because I believe there's a silver cloud ahead. Like a motto I once heard "To strive, to seek, to find and not to yield."

Words can't express how I care for you, Bet. It's something beyond that. It's like a hunger in my heart and deep yearning. I can see you all the time (daydreaming habit) and I think to myself, "you're a lucky guy, Mr. Erwin" with a girl like her.

Since I started writing you I've been the happiest man in the Army.

I close my eyes and there you are. I know it sounds like a fairy tale.

The letters worked. Red gathered up the courage to ask Betty's parents for permission to marry her. At first they thought she was too young, but they soon warmed to Red and gave their blessing.

On December 6, 1944, Red and Betty were married in a simple, small ceremony at her family's house, performed by the local Methodist minister and attended by family and a few friends. A neighbor played the piano. Betty was eighteen and wore a Sunday dress instead of a wedding gown. Red was twenty-three and wore his army air force uniform.

He didn't have much money, so the diamond he bought her was a small one, which was fine with her.

———

While Red and Betty were courting, Red had decided to volunteer for a highly dangerous, experimental new military program that would take him into the thick of combat.

It was a project that would strike a direct blow at the very heart of the enemy—and possibly end the war.

Chapter Two

TO END THIS BUSINESS OF WAR

LATE IN 1943, RED ERWIN HEARD A FANTASTIC rumor: the United States was building the ultimate long-range weapons platform, a gigantic high-tech battleship in the sky. It was an aircraft called the B-29. And when the opportunity came, he jumped at the chance to volunteer to join it.

Red explained in a letter to Betty, "The B-29 is the latest super-deluxe bomber of the army, better than the B-17. The B-29 carries 8 tons of bombs and the guns on it are radar-controlled. Very little is known about it. It's very secretive. My inner sense tells me Tokyo is where they'll do their baptism because they're capable of flying 8,000 miles non-stop. I'd like to see 500 or 1,000 over Tokyo and end this business of war." His hunch was right. The B-29 was specifically designed to blast the military might of Japan from the face of the earth.

By early 1944, Red had achieved excellent ratings in his radio operator training at the technical school in Sioux Falls, South Dakota, and the advanced class at Truax Field, Wisconsin. After a short time in B-17s, Red joined a B-29 crew of the Fifty-Second Bombardment Squadron (Very Heavy) that was being mustered in June 1944 for combat training at Dalhart Army Air Base in Texas. Later they were posted to Pratt Army Airfield in Kansas.

The B-29 was nicknamed the Superfortress. It was a very heavy long-range strategic bomber, the largest combat aircraft up to that time ever to go into full production. It had the potential to strike a death blow on the Japanese Empire and end World War II without the need for the Allies to invade Japan, without the possibly apocalyptic civilian and military casualties that such an invasion would trigger. The plane could carry a 16,000-pound bombload a distance of more than 3,000 miles, and a crew of eleven men: pilot (usually called the air commander), copilot (called the pilot), navigator, bombardier, radar bombardier, radio operator, flight engineer, central fire control gunner, and right, left, and tail gunners.

When Red first laid eyes on a B-29, he was stunned at how big it was, as many other servicemen were. "Whew, it's some ship," he explained to Betty in a letter. "The nose of the plane looks like a dirigible itself. We have to have a pass to get into the airfield itself and then another pass to get into the Radio School. Lots of radar equipment and it's really guarded. We also have a pass to get on and off the air base itself which makes three passes altogether."

When pilot Ernest Pickett saw one of the planes, he recalled, "We could hardly believe our eyes. It was huge, twice the size of a B-24. We stood on the ground looking at it, absolutely awestruck."

Someone muttered, "That thing'll never fly."

Pickett was especially struck by the "enormous Plexiglas greenhouse which comprised the nose of the craft [and] took some getting used to." He explained, "We were up higher and back farther from the nose than we had ever been before. Instead of the co-pilot sitting right next to the pilot, it felt as if the seats were across a room from one another."

Since the pilot's seat was so unusually far off to the left of center, on early practice flights he brought a man along to sit between him and the copilot and holler instructions back and forth to keep the nosewheel on the center line during taxiing and takeoff, until they got used to the feel of the behemoth.

Another airman recalled, "The first impression of a B-29 is, and I'm sure most B-29ers will recite the same words, 'I can't believe it will fly. It's too big!' The second thought was how beautiful it was. That airplane was almost aerodynamically perfect. It was a beautiful sight to behold. It truly was."

This feeling extended to Japanese observers too, including Emperor Hirohito's wife, Nagako, who in 1945 wrote to a friend about the awesome sight of the sleek, gleaming aluminum plane: "Every day from morning to night, B-29s, naval bombers and fighters freely fly over the palace making an enormous noise. As I sit at my desk writing and look up at the sky, countless numbers are passing over." She concluded, "Unfortunately, the B-29 is a splendid plane."

When Japanese combat ace 1st Lt. Isamu Kashiide first spotted a B-29 in the glare of searchlights over Japan, he was amazed. "I was scared! It was known that the B-29 was a huge plane, but when I saw my opponent it was much larger than I ever expected."

———

As 1944 drew to a close, Red's plane was designated as part of the Fifty-Second Bombardment Squadron, Twenty-Ninth Bombardment Group, Twenty-First Bomber Command, Twentieth Air Force. Most of his crew were in their early twenties. They hailed from all over the United States. And from the start, they meshed very well together.

"We were regular guys," remembered Red. "We took pride in how we functioned as a crew, and we were as close as family."

The plane's pilot was Capt. George "Tony" Simeral, a cool Californian whose boyhood dream was to be an army officer. The copilot was Lt. LeRoy "Roy" Stables. The plane's navigator, Capt. Pershing Youngkin, came from Texas, where much of his family was involved in the oil business. When the war started, Sgt. Vern Schiller, the flight engineer, was working at the Florence Stove Company in Kankakee, Illinois, wondering if his dream of becoming an aviation engineer would ever come true.

The war came, and his dream became a reality. First Lt. William "Bill" Loesch was managing a finance office in Cleveland when Pearl Harbor was attacked. He decided to get married, joined the army air force, and wound up as the highly skilled bombardier aboard this B-29.

Crew of the City of Los Angeles *in Kansas, prior to deployment to Guam. Back row, left to right: Pershing Youngkin (navigator), Roy Stables (pilot), William Loesch (bombardier), Leo D. Connors (radar-bombardier), and George A. Simeral (air commander). Front row, left to right: Vern W. Schiller (flight engineer), Herbert Schnipper (right gunner), Kenneth E. Young (tail gunner), Vernon G. Widemeyer (left gunner), Henry E. "Red" Erwin (radio operator), and Howard Stubstad (central fire control gunner).* (Alabama Department of Archives and History, http://digital.archives.alabama.gov/cdm/ref/collection/photo/id/5922)

Radar operator–bombardier 1st Lt. Leo D. Connors was a low-key, quiet man from Wisconsin who had a talent for sleeping soundly through those parts of long missions when his job wasn't needed. Like radio operator Red Erwin, Connors dreamed of becoming a pilot but washed out during training, in his case for a weak stomach. He was happily married to a woman who told him, "You're the nicest guy in a million."

Rounding out the crew were the four gunners: New Yorker Sgt. Herbert Schnipper; Ohio-born Sgt. Kenneth E. Young; Sgt. Vernon G. Widemeyer, who grew up with ten siblings on a North Dakota farm;

and Sgt. Howard Stubstad, a wiry, beaming former Minnesota millworker who was so beloved by the other crewmen that they came to him for advice and encouragement. He had a wife and a newborn son back home.

The B-29 program was the most expensive military project of World War II, costing about $3 billion, compared to the $2 billion spent on the Manhattan Project (the development of the atomic bomb). It was a colossal gamble since the plane went into mass production before it was fully flight-tested. Early B-29s were so buggy that as soon as they came off the assembly line they were rushed to maintenance facilities for extensive repairs and rebuilding. Major mechanical problems, some fatal, plagued the aircraft throughout the war. The engines overheated and shut down during takeoff. Propeller speeds were volatile. Fuel consumption was unpredictable. Bomb bay doors got stuck. Bombs jammed in their racks. And electrical systems malfunctioned.

An early flight was aborted due to a major engine fire. On February 18, 1943, a prototype at Boeing Field in Seattle caught fire and crashed, killing test pilot Edmund Allen, the ten-man crew, twenty workers at a nearby meat-packing plant, and one firefighter.

By the summer of 1944, the Allied victory seemed increasingly inevitable in the wake of a series of strategic battlefield turning points, including the D-day landings at Normandy, the American victories in the Pacific at the Coral Sea, Guadalcanal and the Solomons, and Midway and the Philippine Sea, and Soviet victories at the battles of Moscow, Stalingrad, and Kursk. The only questions were how soon the end would come in the form of the surrender of the Axis powers and how many people would die before that happened. The B-29 was built to make that surrender happen as fast as possible. Nearly four thousand were built.

Red's B-29 aircraft, serial number 42–65302, was first christened *Snatch Blatch* by pilot Tony Simeral. This was an esoteric, bawdy reference to a witch who appeared in the satire *Gargantua and Pantagruel* by the French Renaissance satirist François Rabelais. It was in the tradition of risqué names for bombers across all the war theaters, such as *Hore-zontal Dream*, *Filthy Fay*, *Hump Happy Mammy*, *Ready Betty*, *Mrs. Tittymouse*, *Ramp Tramp*, and *Urgin' Virgin*. The aircraft sometimes also had suggestive pinup-style artwork painted on the fuselage.

There was a rumor that the first lady, Eleanor Roosevelt, was distressed by the bawdy aircraft artwork during her morale-boosting tours of military installations, and word of the randy nicknames filtered back to the ladies' aid societies in the States, who also objected. An order came down that the salacious references should be scrubbed. Henceforth, B-29s were named after US cities, which some B-29ers thought was a dull idea. Nonetheless, the *Snatch Blatch* became the *City of Los Angeles*, named after Captain Simeral's hometown. In practice, however, the original nicknames lingered. A compromise was reached: a plane's nickname was painted on the left side of the nose and the city name was painted on the right. Official photos would only be taken of the right side.

The B-29 was both a masterpiece of advanced engineering and a mind-bogglingly complex aircraft, requiring lead contractor Boeing and thousands of subcontractors to develop tens of thousands of design plans. The technical challenge was to build an aircraft that could strike Japan from long distance, requiring round trips of 3,000 miles, and deliver its bombload on various Japanese targets. No less than six hundred thousand rivets were needed to bolt the plane together.

The man in charge of the problematic megaproject was the commander of the US Army Air Force, Gen. Henry H. "Hap" Arnold, the only five-star general in the air force. General Arnold was a bulldozer of a man, temperamental and aggressive, a West Point graduate who by late 1943 was fighting a losing battle with the Boeing assembly line, which was overwhelmed with delays and bottlenecks. Arnold himself was beset by health crises; he had five heart attacks during the war. An anxious President Roosevelt was breathing down his neck, wanting B-29s to be stationed in China and India and put into action immediately against Japanese targets. But in January 1944, Boeing cranked out just ninety-seven aircraft, and only sixteen were serviceable.

An uneasy Arnold visited the main production facilities in Kansas and found a situation "so chaotic that it was obvious upon my arrival that schedules could not possibly be met." In his eyes, the program was "void of organization, management, and leadership," constituting a "disgrace to the Army Air Force." He launched a crash program to get 150 B-29s deployed to the China-Burma-India (CBI) theater by mid-April. Arnold's confrontation with Boeing became known as the Battle of Kansas—and it worked. Arnold established the first B-29 force as the Twentieth Air Force, an independent command that reported directly to him at the Pentagon, as a member of the joint chiefs of staff. This gave the project an unusual degree of power, prestige, and autonomy.

General Arnold had the authority to reject requests for support from titanic personalities such as Allied theater commanders Adms. Chester W. Nimitz and Louis Mountbatten and Gens. Douglas MacArthur and Joseph W. Stilwell. At the same time, however, he could demand they support B-29 operations. It was an unusual, highly effective, bureaucratic structure.

Red Erwin described the B-29 bomber as "big, heavy, and fast. It had beautiful, unbroken nose contours. For practical purposes it was divided into two halves, with part of the crew forward of the bomb bay, the other part aft, connected by a [pressurized] crawl tunnel above the bay. As the radio operator, I sat with my back to the bulkhead in the rear of the front half, looking forward at the flight engineer, the two pilots, and, in the very front, the bombardier, who had the best view in the house."

The B-29 was first conceived as a hemisphere-defense weapon to prevent Axis forces from establishing bases in Latin America, and then it was seen as a successor to the smaller workhorse B-17 Flying Fortress and B-24 Liberator bombers in the Allied arsenals, which were doing major service in Europe. In 1936, Boeing started working on an experimental long-range bomber dubbed the XB-15, which anticipated some aspects of the B-29 design, including four engines, tricycle landing gear, and an all-glass nose. Around the same time Germany was also working on a surprisingly similar ultra-long-range heavy bomber dubbed the Me-264 Amerika Bomber, which was intended to hit targets on the East Coast of the United States and return to Germany. But only three buggy prototypes were ever built. The Germans abandoned the program, but the Americans pressed on and, in a big way, eventually built four thousand Superfortresses.

The B-29 was a quantum leap beyond anything in the Allied or Axis arsenals, a high-tech marvel that also was the biggest and most expensive aircraft of World War II. It was the world's first mass-production long-range heavy bomber. It featured the first computer-assisted remote-control weapons system, and pressurized compartments that enabled the crew to work in shirtsleeves rather than have to wear bulky clothing and oxygen masks. The aircraft had a maximum range of more than 3,000 miles, a cruising speed between 200 and 250 miles per hour, a maximum speed of 375 miles per hour, and could fly at nearly 32,000 feet, which was beyond the reach of most Axis fighters and antiaircraft fire.

Once perfected, the B-29 was an aircraft that bristled with superlatives. It was the biggest and heaviest aircraft that had ever been mass-produced. It was the largest operational aircraft of World War II. The colossal aircraft had a wingspan of 141 feet, was 99 feet long, and weighed 133,500 pounds when fully loaded. It carried up to 10 tons of bombs, four times more than the capacity of the B-17.

The plane was powered by four temperamental, turbo-supercharged 2,200-horsepower Wright R-3350 Duplex-Cyclone 18-cylinder radial engines, which had an alarming habit of catching fire. The engines were the most powerful force in aviation, and they turned the largest propellers, sixteen and a half feet in diameter.

One of Red's crewmates, Robert Bigelow, explained the aircraft's cutting-edge design: "Although it replaced the B-17, the B-29 was a radically different airplane, featuring significant aerodynamic innovations." The fuel tanks were self-sealing, and later models featured bomb bay doors that snapped open in seven-tenths of a second and closed in three seconds.

The B-29 featured what was by far the most advanced high-tech defensive gunnery system in the air, featuring as many as twelve air-cooled Browning M2/AN .50-caliber machine guns mounted in four remotely operated, powered turrets as well as a 20-millimeter M2 cannon in the tail. The gunner stations were mounted in Plexiglas bubbles, or blisters, on the exterior of the aircraft; the gunners worked from these remote sighting stations, and a first-of-its-kind analog computer-assisted system enabled them to operate their weapons independently or to hand off control of multiple guns to each other, depending on the nature of the threat and which crewman had the best view and position. The computer calculated and corrected for gravity, temperature, humidity, lead, deflection, range, elevation, and size of attacking aircraft, and also accounted for the B-29's altitude, airspeed, and wind speed.

Ed Shahinian, a B-29 gunner based on Saipan, explained, "The B-29 was the best airplane made at the time. It had remote control gun sights. It wasn't handheld like a B-17, where it's 65 below zero and you've got this heavy suit on and you're freezing to death. We were air-conditioned and heated. My guns were 40 feet away from me. I never touched a machine gun. I had control. As long as I kept [the enemy aircraft] in the reticle of the gun sight, theoretically the computer would track it and would shoot it down."

———

During the first weeks of 1945, Red Erwin received the news he'd anxiously awaited for almost two years: he was going to war, to the very front line of combat.

The *City of Los Angeles* was being sent from Kansas to the western Pacific to strike targets on the Japanese home islands.

A B-29 Superfortress. (US Air Force)

In February 1945, a thirty-eight-year-old general sat at a desk on an island in the western Pacific, smoked his pipe, thumbed through various military manuals, and scribbled numbers down on paper. He was thinking about bombs, guns, bullets, gravity, wind speeds, explosions, weather, timetables, and fires. He was thinking about mathematics. And he was thinking about death. His name was Curtis E. LeMay. He was Red Erwin's commander, the chief of the Twenty-First Bomber Command.

LeMay held much of the destiny of World War II in his hands, and he knew it. If he could just figure out the math. But no matter how many times he ran the numbers, he couldn't get them to work. He was only a few weeks into his job, and he knew he was on the verge of being fired. After months of combat, the B-29 project was, thus far, a spectacular failure.

When LeMay was hired, he was told by Brig. Gen. Lauris Norstad, chief of staff for the Twentieth Air Force, "You go ahead and get results with the B-29. If you don't get results, you'll be fired. If you don't get results, also, there'll never be any strategic Air Force of the Pacific." Norstad added, "If you don't get results, it will mean eventually a mass amphibious invasion of Japan, to cost probably half a million more American lives."

Based in a corrugated-steel Quonset hut at North Field on the island of Guam that housed the US Army Air Force operations center, Maj. Gen. Curtis LeMay was in a race against time.

For nearly seven months, B-29s flying from India, China, and from the recently captured Marianas Islands of Guam, Saipan, and Tinian had pounded away at Japanese targets on two thousand missions, dropping millions of tons of bombs at military complexes, airfields, factories, docks, refineries, and chemical plants in Japan and occupied Southeast Asia.

Since the campaign began in June 1944, almost a hundred B-29s had been lost in action to enemy fighters, antiaircraft fire, severe weather, and equipment malfunctions. And thus far the Superfortresses hadn't fully destroyed a single strategic target. The campaign was, by any measure, a fiasco and a colossal waste of resources.

LeMay's predecessor, Gen. Heywood S. Hansell, who was considered by General Norstad as suffering from an "utter absolute complete and irreversible lack of competence," was fired in January 1945. LeMay had been based in China as Hansell's deputy, and then he was sent to Guam, where the main bombing effort was now based, and named as Hansell's replacement and told to salvage the mess. But he couldn't figure out the logistics.

LeMay had been nicknamed "Old Iron Pants" by his soldiers, and he was the youngest two-star general in the army. A big-game hunter, he had a brilliant, ruthless intellect, just the kind you need when you're trying to win a war. At the same time, he suffered from Bell's palsy, a condition that partially froze the muscles of his mouth into a permanent frown, so he constantly chomped on a pipe or cigar to distract from the effect. He was as blunt as a blowtorch, and he inspired fear and awe in allies and enemies alike. "After working with that man," recalled an officer, "he seems almost like a machine—or a god. Fire a thousand questions at him in an hour. If he'll answer you, you can bet that 99 percent of the answers will be right. He doesn't open his mouth often, but when he does you better damn well listen—and act. He means every single syllable."

Robert Morgan, an experienced bomber pilot, offered a vivid description of General LeMay: "With his jowly, scowling face, his thick dark hair, and smoldering gaze, he gave many the impression that running a bombing campaign wasn't quite stimulating enough for him, that he wouldn't mind taking apart a few Quonset huts with his bare hands. His speaking style—barely audible sentence fragments murmured through clenched teeth—reinforced his aura as a borderline sociopath."

Curtis LeMay had guts to spare. A career military man who had grown up in Ohio, he personally led a series of hazardous B-17 bombing missions over Europe as a colonel and commander of the 305th Bombardment Group of the Eighth Air Force, including an epic mission against the Nazi's largest Messerschmitt aircraft factory at Regensburg, for which the bombers launched from bases in England and landed at bases in North Africa to avoid fighter attacks during the return leg.

He was promoted to brigadier general in September 1943 and to major general in March 1944, and then he was sent to the China-Burma-India theater in August 1944. But B-29 operations from China were very hard to resupply by air over the Himalayan Mountains, and they could only hit targets in southern Japan.

In the summer of 1944, after weeks of intense combat, the US Marines and Army finally captured a staging point from which the B-29s could effectively strike all of Japan: the Marianas Islands. This included Guam, a kidney bean–shaped coral island of jungle hills and ravines, measuring 10 miles wide by 30 miles long. Construction crews hardened and expanded the Japanese military runways on Guam and neighboring Saipan and Tinian Islands to accommodate the massive amount of B-29 traffic: 180 planes for each of five runways. By late 1944, the B-29s were gearing up to strike the enemy in force.

"Hell," said LeMay, "I'm not here to win friends. I'm here to win a war. And the only way to do that is for my men to drop the max weight of bombs on the target." So far, it just wasn't working.

LeMay had tried, it seemed, almost everything. He sent B-29s over

Japan at midday, at night, in small groups, and in two-hundred-plane formations, but reconnaissance photos always showed only minor damage.

"I sat up nights," LeMay remembered, "fine-tooth combing all the pictures we had of every target which we had attacked or scouted."

For days, LeMay huddled with his staff to come up with new approaches that might accomplish their goal.

"He was around a few days, said almost nothing to anybody, was what, by civilian standards, would be called rude to many people," according to an army public affairs officer who witnessed LeMay's first weeks at Guam. "He was a big, husky, healthy, rather stocky, full-faced, black-haired man."

LeMay had blunt opinions on military strategy, once declaring, "In a war, you've got to try to keep at least one punch ahead of the other guy all the time. A war is a very tough kind of proposition. If you don't get the enemy, he gets you."

On another occasion, he explained, "I'll tell you what war is about. You've got to kill people, and when you've killed enough they stop fighting."

The worst problem for LeMay and his B-29s was the jet stream, a mysterious natural phenomenon that was almost unknown until November 24, 1944. On that day, a force of 110 Superfortresses took off for Tokyo and collided with a force of nature that essentially killed the American strategy of high-altitude precision bombing. This was the jet stream, and it consisted of multiple layers of unpredictable hurricane blasts of wind up to 500 miles an hour that moved from Siberia to Japan at altitudes around 30,000 feet, close to the stratosphere. Until the B-29s arrived, few planes had ventured that high.

Until then, the Americans had been trying to conduct precision bombing raids on Japanese military and industrial targets from the high altitudes the B-29 was designed for. But only 10 percent of the bombs were hitting their targets due to constant cloud cover and an unexpectedly strong jet stream that scattered the free-falling bombs far from their targets.

"When we got over Japan we found that they had terrific trade winds at 30,000 feet," recalled B-29 crewman James Krantz. "On one mission when we went on the bombing run we were facing a headwind of 150 miles an hour and we were cruising at 200. Which meant we were only going 50 miles per hour ground speed. It took us two to three times as long as it ever did on the average bomb run. We just didn't know about these winds."

Depending on how they approached it, the jet stream could push B-29s into dangerously high speeds or slow them down to zero forward motion over the ground. Regardless of how effective their cutting-edge Norden bombsights were or how skilled the bombardiers were, soon after the bombs were released, the jet stream and weather at lower altitudes would scatter the bombs off target. If any bombs connected with their objective, it was a matter of pure luck from random wind effects. Precision high-altitude bombing, the main strategy of the US Army Air Force, was impossible in these conditions.

General LeMay wrote out countless calculations on paper, pored through bombing manuals, after-action reports, and data charts, and tried to make things work. But he couldn't figure it out. It looked as if the B-29 project were doomed to failure.

―――――

On February 11, 1945, in the midst of LeMay's frustration, Red Erwin and his crew arrived on Guam in the *City of Los Angeles* after a 7,000-mile series of hopscotch flights from Kansas. Soon, most of the rest of the 314th Bombardment Wing arrived. They were commanded by Brig. Gen. Thomas S. Power, who reported to LeMay.

The Bronx-born Power had flown B-24s in Italy before becoming a highly successful troubleshooter in the B-29 training program. Power was a LeMay Mini-Me who, according to one author, was "so cold, hard and demanding that several of his colleagues and subordinates have flatly described him as sadistic." When LeMay was later asked if Power was sadistic, LeMay noted approvingly, "He was. He was sort of an autocratic bastard. He was my best wing commander on Guam. He got things done." Gen. Horace M. Wade, who later worked for Power in the postwar Strategic Air Command, described Power as mean, cruel, and unforgiving. He added, "I used to worry that General Power was not stable." For LeMay, Power was the perfect deputy.

Red soon found out it was rough living for the B-29 crews on Guam. Rats and various exotic jungle critters were frequent guests in the barracks and the mess hall. The food was mediocre at best, but for variety, you could pick coconuts and bananas in the jungle. The weather alternated mostly between constant rain and mind-numbing humidity. They slept on hard bunks either in field tents or a steel-shelled Quonset hut.

Some Japanese troops were still hiding in distant caves, and they occasionally harassed the Americans with small-arms fire and food robberies. The story was told of a quiet Japanese soldier who slipped into the chow line but was busted when he bowed to thank the cooks for his food.

In their downtime, the US airmen had few options other than playing cards, reading, and watching movies at night. The post exchange offered Hershey bars and Pepsodent, and smuggled liquor was available for a price, with Schenley's Black Label being the most popular. In Guam's relaxed, humid climate, many B-29 crewmembers chopped off their long khaki trousers to make shorts.

Ed Shahinian, a B-29 gunner on Saipan, was greeted with a macabre image his first day on the island. When shown his assigned quarters, he saw uniforms hanging in place over freshly made beds. "Hey, we can't go there," he protested, "this place is occupied." The response was, "Don't worry about it. They're all dead." Shahinian recalled, "That's our first day. And I really got a little bit discouraged, you know. What the hell am I doing here? Mommy, I want to go home. The whole crew was 18 or 19. We had an old guy of 26, and we called him Pops."

As the radio operator aboard the *City of Los Angeles*, Red's job was critical, just like that of every other crewman. He had to orchestrate coded radio communications back to the base at Guam, manage the intercom communication within the plane, and meticulously maintain the radio equipment. It was a job that demanded intense concentration, technical skill, keen judgment, and the ability to keep cool under fire, all of which Red had in spades. More than one B-29er called Red the best radio operator in the squadron. He was also the designated first-aid man for the front compartment of the plane; gunner Herb Schnipper was the first-aid man for the rear compartment.

Red intensely studied the first-aid manuals and medical gear so he would be ready to act as a field medic in any emergency likely to happen on the plane, such as bullet and shrapnel wounds, burn wounds, blood loss, and shock. He learned to bandage gaping wounds, inject morphine, and administer plasma—whatever it took to keep his crewmates alive until the plane returned to Guam.

When Lt. Col. Eugene Strouse, the squadron commander, sometimes rode aboard the *City of Los Angeles*, he observed Red, squeezed into the small radio compartment during long hours of inactivity, and noticed something unusual. He couldn't explain it precisely, but somehow, Strouse recalled, it seemed the young airman was "in companionship with the Lord."

One time, when Strouse's superior, Col. Carl Storrie, was aboard the *City of Los Angeles*, the notoriously profane Storrie was heard loosing a string of colorful phrases. And then Red said through the plane's internal interphone circuit, "Lord, please don't pay any attention to the colonel. He talks this way all the time."

Soon after the 314th Bombardment Wing unpacked their bags, they were ordered to prepare for their first mission: an attack on Tokyo. The raid was to be led by General Power, and it was scheduled for February 25, 1945.

Strategists in Washington had been urging General LeMay and his predecessor, General Hansell, to use incendiary bombs in addition to conventional explosive demolition bombs in the hope of igniting fires that would destroy military targets, especially the aviation industry, and expand the firebombing into civilian areas of the cities, which housed smaller feeder factories and workshops among civilian housing.

But Hansell and LeMay resisted, clinging to the hope they could somehow make conventional high-altitude precision attacks with demolition bombs successful. Gradually, however, LeMay became receptive to the idea of using incendiaries, because he realized high-altitude bombing just wasn't working. He also knew if he didn't produce better results, his days in command were numbered. In the meantime, hundreds of thousands of civilians and Allied servicemen were being killed across the Asian and Pacific theaters, and those who had been taken prisoner were suffering horrific tortures and abuses at the hands of their Japanese captors.

"I had to do something," recalled LeMay, "and I had to do something fast." He made a momentous decision: it was time to firebomb civilian areas in Japan.

The idea of attacking civilian areas of Japan with incendiaries was not altogether new. In a 1937 analysis for the Air Corps Tactical School titled "Japan as an Objective for Air Attack," Capt. Thomas D. White observed, "Large sections of Japanese cities are built of flimsy and highly flammable materials. The earthquake disaster of 1924 bears witness to the fearful destruction that may be inflicted by incendiary bombs." In 1939, legendary Japanese Adm. Isoroku Yamamoto, architect of the Pearl Harbor and Midway attacks, admitted as much: "Cities made of wood and paper would burn easily. The army talks big, but if war comes and there were large-scale air raids, there is no telling what would happen."

LeMay was far from the first warrior to bomb cities. The aerial bombing of urban and civilian areas on a mass scale first occurred during World War I, when German Zeppelins, lighter-than-air dirigibles, bombed London and other targets in England and killed more than 500 people and injured more than 1,300. In the 1920s, British aircraft bombed and strafed military and civilian targets while battling a colonial rebellion in Iraq. The Spanish city of Guernica in 1937 was incinerated by German and Italian bombs, killing at least 250 people and inspiring Pablo Picasso's famous painting of the city's agony. In 1940, after German bombs accidentally hit British civilian areas, British Bomber Command began targeting German cities in retaliation.

The Japanese military pioneered the grim concept of area bombing on an industrial scale. From 1938 to 1941, they initiated indiscriminate bombings of urban civilian areas from the air with 200 devastating raids on Chongqing, China, that killed more than 10,000 people, mostly civilians. Japanese aircraft expanded the carnage on the largely defenseless Chinese cities of Shanghai, Beijing, Tianjin, Nanking, and Canton. There were few industrial or military targets in China, so the bombings were solely designed to cause panic, chaos, and mass civilian casualties.

A concentrated bombing assault on Hamburg, Germany, by British and American aircraft in late July 1943 killed some 25,000 people, and gave birth to a gruesome new spectacle: the man-made firestorm capable of devouring entire cities. In February 1945, a wave of Anglo-American air strikes on military targets around the city of Dresden ignited a firestorm that killed as many as 25,000, and ten days later British bombers killed as many as 20,000 people in attacks on the city of Pforzheim.

Until now, the Americans had avoided large-scale bombing of civilian areas in Japan. But in early 1945 any official qualms about civilian casualties were evaporating quickly. In fact, three weeks before the Pearl Harbor attack in 1941, Gen. George C. Marshall had predicted, off the record, "If war with the Japanese does come, we'll fight mercilessly. Flying Fortresses will be dispatched immediately to set the paper cities of Japan on fire. There won't be any hesitation about bombing civilians—it will be all-out." After three years of war, Marshall's prediction was coming true. But B-17s were not to be the agent of destruction; B-29s would fill that role.

LeMay knew he was on the verge of ordering a civilian bloodbath the likes of which the world had never seen, but he saw no other path to victory. He was not a bloodthirsty man, but he was resigned to the tragic inevitability of what seemed necessary to make an intractable foe surrender.

"No matter how you slice it," he told himself, "you're going to kill an awful lot of civilians. Thousands and thousands. But if you don't destroy Japanese industry, we're going to have to invade Japan. And how many Americans will be killed in an invasion? Five hundred thousand seems to be the lowest estimate. We're at war with Japan. Would you rather have Americans killed?"

The chief fire-starting weapon in the US arsenal was the M-69 incendiary bomblet, which was filled with the highly flammable gasoline jelly called napalm, which had been developed by Harvard chemists and produced by Dow Chemical. The bombs had one purpose: to start uncontrollable fires.

"Dropped in loose clusters of 14, or 'amiable' clusters of 38, the finless oil-bombs are exploded by a time fuse four or five seconds after landing," *Time* magazine reported in 1945. "Thereupon M-69s become miniature flamethrowers that hurl cheesecloth socks full of furiously flaming goo for 100 yards. Anything these socks hit is enveloped by clinging, fiery pancakes, each spreading to more than a yard in diameter. Individually, these can be extinguished as easily as a magnesium bomb. But a single oil-bomb cluster produces so many fiery pancakes that the problem for fire fighters, like that of a mother whose child has got loose in the jam pot, is where to begin."

Napalm was a devastating weapon against wooden targets, such as much of Japan's houses and buildings. And it caused severe burn wounds on human beings. Using incendiary bombs meant that fires would spread into civilian areas near military targets, and until now, the Allies had largely avoided bombing civilian areas in the Asian and Pacific theaters.

On February 25, 1945, as an experiment, LeMay sent 230 B-29s, including the *City of Los Angeles*, on the first massive firebombing raid against a Japanese target. It was a daylight attack from an altitude of 25,000 feet, releasing 400 tons of incendiary bombs on the Kanda and Shitaya Wards of Tokyo, where many small- and medium-sized factories were believed to be. Some planes turned back due to mechanical trouble, severe winds, and heavy clouds, but 172 bombers made it to their targets and completed the mission.

It was a disappointing first mission for Red Erwin and the *City of Los Angeles*. Their bomb bay doors froze shut, forcing them to abort the mission and jettison their payload over the ocean while returning to Guam.

But the poststrike reconnaissance photographs revealed the large-scale firebombing raid had been successful. More than twenty thousand buildings were destroyed, and one square mile of the snow-covered city had been wiped out, despite the fact that heavy cloud cover had obscured the target and the planes were forced to bomb by radar guesstimates rather than the more accurate Norden bombsighting system. Tens of thousands of Tokyo residents were now homeless, and an unknown number died as a result of the raid.

B-29s in formation during a daylight raid in 1945 near Mount Fuji, Japan.
(US Air Force)

These results gave General Power and his officers an audacious idea. When they presented the concept to General LeMay, he was spellbound. He knew it was an unusual, incredibly risky idea, but it might change the course of the war in Asia and the Pacific. And it would involve killing multitudes of civilians.

LeMay laid down his pipe, and through weary eyes he uttered aloud the hideous calculation. "I wish there were some other way to bring Japan's leaders to their senses. But an invasion of ground troops would cost at least a million Allied casualties, plus untold hundreds of thousands of Japanese civilians. An invasion should be ordered as a last resort, but only if we fail to create a hell on earth in Japan. That's the only circumstance that their fanatical leaders will understand."

He ordered his staff to put together a detailed plan within twenty-four hours. The operation would send Red Erwin and some three thousand other American airmen into an apocalypse.

Chapter Three

JOURNEY TO THE APOCALYPSE

ON MARCH 9, 1945, A MUTINY WAS ABOUT TO
break out at the Twentieth Air Force's bases on Guam, Saipan, and Tinian
when the airmen learned that General LeMay wanted them to remove
the guns from their 325 planes and then conduct a ferocious *low-level*
bombing raid on the capital of Japan. The attack would be from 5,000 to
8,000 feet rather than 25,000 to 30,000 feet.

The airmen were stunned, and furious.

LeMay tried to give the crew leaders a pep talk, telling them, "You're
going to deliver the biggest firecracker the Japanese have ever seen."

But his plan to radically alter their attack procedure seemed like the
stupidest, most dangerous idea many of the B-29ers had ever heard.

"When that epic order came down, I, like 90 percent of the other
people, was ready to mutiny," reported Ray Clanton, who was then a second lieutenant and pilot. "It was crazy. It was absolutely insane. Because
the airplanes even at 30,000 feet were being shot out of the sky. We were
[already] taking initial hits and losses somewhere in the area of 50 percent
and 60 percent on every mission. When this order came down, we were
ready to revolt, and I do mean that. We thought LeMay was sending us
to our death."

According to Clanton, a mass "combat refusal" broke out during the mission briefing. "Some people actually just went to the back of the room, took their wings off and dropped them in a hat," he said decades later. "You're not going to kill me, baby," Clanton thought.

Orville Blackburn confirmed Clanton's account. "We balked on it and we almost did not fly because we thought 'Iron Pants' LeMay was crazy. He had flown fire raids in Europe and there were some big losses, and we had that in our mind."

Generals LeMay and Power had dubbed the plan Operation Meetinghouse. It was to be a massive strike that would become the single most destructive bombing raid in human history. The target was Tokyo, the military, political, media, business, and education capital of Japan and home of the emperor and the imperial court.

Instead of a high-altitude bombing raid on carefully selected military and industrial targets, this would be a low-altitude "area bombing" raid designed to incinerate an entire district of downtown Tokyo and all the people, buildings, and small to medium feeder factories within it. Incendiary napalm was to be the weapon, and tens of thousands of civilians would surely die. But instead of staging the raid during the day, this mission would happen at night.

The plan called for 325 B-29s to be stripped of everything except their turret guns, stuffed with incendiary bombs, and approach the target area in single file at one-minute intervals rather than as a group formation. All these were significant departures from standard procedure, but LeMay and Power thought these steps could sharply increase the accuracy of the bombing attack, improve fuel efficiency, and increase the odds that the force would survive attacks by Japanese fighters and antiaircraft guns. LeMay speculated that Japanese night fighters were ineffective, and he also guessed there was a possible blind spot that worked in favor of the low-altitude approach, namely, Japanese searchlights and antiaircraft guns would not perform well against the low-flying bombers. "And we could be wrong as hell," he worried.

Red Erwin's plane, the *City of Los Angeles*, had a unique role on this mission. The strong reputation of the crew had caused General Power to select it as his aerial command post and observer plane, which would lead the armada into Tokyo, and then circle above it to witness and analyze the bombing. Power would sit a few feet away from Red, take notes, and command the attack. The plane's three gunners would be replaced by the 314th Wing intelligence officer and two other observers.

"Our preflight briefing was contentious," remembered Red. "They pulled the map curtain back and said, 'We're going to hit Tokyo tonight. We're going to burn it down. If we can burn it down then we can burn any city in Japan. And by the way, we're going to go in at 5,000 feet.' I remember how everybody gasped, 'We're going to get shot down!' We all sat dumbfounded."

Another B-29er described the crew briefing: "All speculation ended as cover sheets were ripped off briefing boards. Mouths dropped open with what they revealed. Colonel [Carl] Storrie began by saying that General LeMay had enough airplanes, bombs, and gasoline and had decided that it was time to finish the Japanese. There would be no more bucking of severe high-altitude winds and trying to knock out individual factories. Tonight, we were going in, in-trail at 5,000 to 9,000 feet with incendiary bombs. We would spread fire over the industrial and working class parts of the city. This type of raid, if it succeeded, would disrupt industry, displace workers, and drive the seat of their government into hiding."

Red recalled that Colonel Storrie, the group commander and a pilot himself, declared, "I'll lead it." Red marveled, "Colonel Storrie was the bravest man I ever knew." The colonel was a tough, lean Texan who had already seen a great deal of action as a bomber pilot in the skies over Europe. He was widely respected and trusted by the airmen.

Storrie's statement of courage and leadership helped stop the revolt-in-progress in its tracks. All the airmen on Guam, Saipan, and Tinian immediately committed themselves to the high-risk operation.

The raid would be a fifteen-hour, 1,500-mile trip across black, empty ocean from Guam to Tokyo and back, and the B-29s' average airspeed would be 225 miles an hour. They would have no fighter escort, and most of their defensive armament would be removed.

Red Erwin described the experience as "hours of boredom mixed with moments of sheer terror."

Their target area was Shitimachi, a 12-square-mile rectangular-shaped district in downtown Tokyo. It was home to as many as a million people, one of the most densely populated places on earth. Most of the houses and buildings were made of wood, paper, and bamboo, often closely packed together and highly vulnerable to fire. There were no big industrial facilities in the area, but scattered throughout the dense residential housing were thought to be many small-scale factories and mom-and-pop feeder workshops that flowed into the overall Japanese war effort. The district also was home to factory workers who commuted to jobs elsewhere in Tokyo. Killing or displacing them would cripple the nation's industry.

The weather forecast for Tokyo predicted three conditions that would be perfect for starting a massive fire from the sky: dry air, clear skies, and high winds with gusts of over 50 to 60 miles per hour.

B-29er Robert Bigelow recalled the moment of takeoff late on the tropical afternoon of March 9, 1945: "Looking down the long line of silver airplanes, we checked our watches. Though the glint of the afternoon sun somewhat distorted our vision, we could see propellers turn in measured precision. Just as precisely, each plane, with its four engines giving a short burst of power, came slowly out of its revetment. Resting squat and heavy on its wheels, it would slowly turn in line and join the armada of B-29s flowing toward the takeoff end of the runway. Although the fears and concerns from the earlier mission briefing lingered with each crew member, confidence was building. The Bombardier in his nose position and the Central Fire Control Gunner in his top dome gave a running account of the progress of the gathering force. As it neared our turn to start engines and join the awesome 'stream,' we knew that we were part of something big and important. We were taking the war to Japan."

As the sun set on the evening of March 9, LeMay watched the long procession of planes take off into the western sky and mused, "If I am sending these men to die, they will string me up for it." Since LeMay had been briefed on the biggest secret of the war effort, the development of an atomic bomb, he had been ordered by Gen. Henry H. "Hap" Arnold, chief of the army air force, not to fly on this or any other missions, because the risk of capture was too high.

Takeoffs began at 5:35 p.m., and it took a full three hours to launch all 334 B-29s into the sky from the six runways on Guam, Tinian, and Saipan. Fifty-five aircraft aborted the mission for technical reasons, but 279 approached Tokyo.

Red Erwin squeezed into the cramped and claustrophobic fuselage of the *City of Los Angeles* and settled into his tiny battle station. The aircraft was not designed for creature comfort but to deliver the maximum tonnage of bombs to its target. Other crewmen crawled into the tiny workspaces that left them very little room to move around, though on homeward journeys some could stretch out in the pressurized tunnel connecting the fore and aft sections to grab a nap. The captain and copilot sat on parachute packs that doubled as seat cushions. The other crewmen, including Red, wore chest packs with clips, and in an emergency, they were supposed to grab a parachute pack, clip it on, and bail out.

"I sat in the front compartment on the right side up against the fuselage," Red remembered. "I didn't have a window and was wedged in by equipment and the .50-caliber gun turret. It was a lonely post. I couldn't see anything outside. All I had to sit on was a little fabric chair for a fifteen-hour mission. Some other radio operators griped that it was the worst job on the plane—absolutely boring! It was twelve hours of boredom mixed with an hour of pure terror. I wore a flight suit on every mission, plus a skull cap, parachute, life preserver, and boots. I sat on my parachute for a cushion, but I wore my Mae West life preserver at all times. I couldn't swim."

When you added in the painstaking preflight preparations, check-lists, and briefings, a single mission from the Marianas could last as long as twenty-four hours, all of which required intense concentration and little if any sleep.

Red's space was packed with cables, codebooks, technical papers, and radio equipment. His head was practically flush against the upper turret, which created a constant rattle. Much of his world consisted of the wires and dials of his four-channel high-frequency SCR-522 command radio set. He wore earphones and had a microphone handy. Near his feet was a small hole in the floor that contained a chute for dropping smoke and phosphorus signal flares from the aircraft. The crew communicated with each other on throat microphones hooked into an interphone intercom system, which Red maintained fastidiously, as he did all the radio equipment.

The plane featured electric food warmers, but the standard in-flight meal was fruit, candy, and sandwiches. There were "honey pots" the crew used to relieve themselves. The pilot and copilot had floor-to-ceiling sheets of armor plating at their backs, and bullet-resistant glass was mounted around their instrument panels. The senior gunner was positioned in an observation dome that protruded from the top of the aircraft. He sat in a kind of swivel-action barber chair under the dome.

Takeoffs from Guam were especially frightening moments for the aircrews since the end of the runway dropped off to a three-hundred-foot cliff, and the planes were weighed down with thousands of gallons of flammable fuel, tons of bombs, and four notoriously temperamental, problem-plagued engines.

The split-second complexity of the B-29's controls could quickly lead to disaster if anyone made a wrong move during a crisis.

"We were rolling down the runway for takeoff on one mission and the number-four engine began to run away," Red recalled. "Captain Simeral yelled to the copilot, Roy Stables, to feather it [shut it down]. But Roy accidentally feathered the wrong engine. So there we are, going down the runway headed toward the cliff with two engines out on the same side of the plane. We were too far down the runway to abort, so Captain Simeral yelled for the tail gunner and crew to prepare to bail out as he lifted the plane off the ground."

To Red, it felt like the aircraft was about to rip itself apart. Captain Simeral struggled to keep the two dead engines elevated as he swung the plane around to reverse course for an emergency landing just as they ran out of runway.

"It was the longest ride of my life!" Red said. "Captain Simeral brought the plane around and made a magnificent landing with two dead engines. After he had taxied to a stop and shut down the engines, the only words he said about the episode were to the young copilot Stables: 'Roy, what are you trying to do? Get us killed?'"

On the night of March 9, however, the takeoff was smooth, and the crewmen of the *City of Los Angeles* settled into their routines. Captain Simeral engaged the autopilot, setting the plane to fly at a fixed speed and course, which he and the copilot would adjust every half hour. As usual, Red monitored the radio and stayed alert for any incoming messages from the base about changes to the mission, but to avoid interception by enemy listening posts, he sent no radio messages during the approach to Japan. When the time was right, Red would transmit a strike report to the base at Guam, detailing the mission highlights, including any visible damage to the target and any enemy response.

The long flight to Japan over the vast, empty Pacific held moments of beauty as well as terror. The round trips almost always featured a sunrise and a sunset. B-29 crews could tune into Japanese radio that played lush orchestral music and romantic ballads from America, and the combination of music and scenery could create a surreal, hallucinatory experience.

One pilot remembered, "We appeared to be floating above a pure white carpet stretching as far as the eye could see, ultimately blending away into a grayish haze." He added, "The reflection of the bright sun created the illusion of being studded with 10 million diamonds. I could not escape the feeling of being in a fairy tale world of castles and fantasy."

Another pilot recalled, "The variations in light and color in the Pacific were fantastically beautiful. They softened our own strain and our anxieties."

Historian Barrett Tillman summarized the airmen's experience: "Amid the hours of tedious routine, and the languorous time spent listening to the pulsing drone of four powerful engines, there were moments of sublime compensation. The glory of a Pacific sunrise, when sea and sky turned from gray-black to vivid golden hues, or the vertical grandeur of a backlit thunderhead cresting 30,000 feet was worth the entire fifteen-hour trip."

At midnight, back on Guam, General LeMay could not sleep. "A lot could go wrong," he mused to one of his officers. "If this raid works the way I think it will, we can shorten the war. We've figured out a punch [the enemy's] not expecting this time. I don't think he's got the right kind of flak to combat this kind of raid, and I don't think he can keep his cities from being burned down—wiped right off the map." LeMay drank from a six-ounce bottle of Coca-Cola and stared into the jungle, thinking of the three thousand young airmen who were about to fly over the heart of the Japanese Empire.

The *City of Los Angeles* arrived over Tokyo around midnight and flew a wide, circular observational pattern at 11,000 feet, eventually climbing to 20,000 feet, while the long B-29 armada followed at 5,000 to 8,000 feet below, maintaining 200-foot intervals in altitude separations to avoid collisions.

The first group carved giant blazing X patterns onto the city with roof-penetrating incendiary bombs to mark the target areas for the following aircraft to focus on. Within an hour, a series of massive fires congealed into an apocalyptic conflagration never before seen on earth. The first of 1,665 tons of bombs struck Tokyo at 12:08 a.m. on March 10. The emergency sirens went off at 12:15 a.m. Most of the bombs were 500-pound, finned E-46 cluster bombs, which burst at 2,000 feet and scattered thirty-eight individual M-69 fused napalm canisters that ignited on impact with whatever they struck.

A French journalist named Robert Guillain witnessed the B-29 assault from a hill on the edge of Tokyo and described the scene: "Their long, glinting wings, sharp as blades, could be seen through the oblique columns of smoke rising from the city, suddenly reflecting the fire from the furnace below, black silhouettes gliding through the fiery sky to reappear further on, shining golden against the dark roof of heaven or glittering blue, like meteors, in the searchlight beams spraying the vault from horizon to horizon."

Brig. Gen. Thomas Power, the 314th Bomb Wing commander and overall commander of the raid, climbed into the Plexiglas nose of the *City of Los Angeles* and stared down at the apocalypse. He squeezed next to the bombardier and began marking a set of maps with a red pencil to record bomb impacts and spreading fires, muttering his approval at the swelling conflagration. At times, he rubbed his eyes and muttered, "Poor bastards." He added, "What a horrible sight! God knows how many thousands are dying below us."

Power turned to Captain Simeral to tell him how the attack was progressing. Simeral was pleased but nervous as the attack continued, especially after seeing a plane hit by antiaircraft fire plunge to the ground.

Even at 20,000 feet, Red recalled, it felt as if they were "flying in a blast furnace," and the sickening smells of a city on fire reached them even at that height. Thermal updrafts were also making it harder and harder for Captain Simeral to control the plane.

Red grew increasingly concerned. "Power wasn't content to fly over the target just once," he recalled. "He wanted to go over Tokyo a second time and a third to see how it was going. You could feel the heat even at that altitude. It did a number on the trailing planes in the formation. They would come in and hit those thermals, and some would flip and crash or soar out of control like a leaf in a chimney."

Red saw some B-29s get trapped in intense thermal updrafts and then be blasted vertically, as much as 10,000 feet, within a matter of seconds. Others were flipped upside down by the raging heat and turbulence.

"We lost fourteen brave crews that night," he remembered.

Thousands of feet above the conflagration, pilot Chester Marshall observed, "We looked upon a ghastly scene spread out before us. Flames and debris were climbing several thousand feet, and a dark cloud of smoke hurled upward to more than 20,000 feet. It was a great relief for us to exit the smoke because the odor of burning flesh and debris was very nauseating."

The aircrews entering the target area after the first wave witnessed surreal, hallucinatory scenes. The firestorm was visible from 150 miles away. One pilot reported that, from 50 miles, it looked like the dawn of a new sun being born on the earth's surface. Robert Rodenhouse, the pilot of *Lucky Strike*, recalled, "When we got over the target it was like a thousand Christmas trees lit up all over."

Some of the aircrews that had tuned into Japanese radio broadcasts swore they overheard love songs whose titles had a macabre relevance to the night's events: "Smoke Gets in Your Eyes," "My Old Flame," and "I Don't Want to Set the World on Fire."

Above the American warplanes was a quarter moon, and below them was enemy airspace with a few intermittent clouds dotting the sky above the titanic, raging megafires.

Bombardier Carl Manone's B-29 approached the mainland at 1:00 a.m. "From my front-row seat in the nose, I noted a red glare in the sky," he reported. "It was becoming apparent that the red sky was a reflection of Tokyo ablaze—fires ignited by the first B-29s to reach the target area. As we headed on a northwest bearing, Mount Fujiyama was clearly visible on our left. We proceeded over Shikoku [Island] and the Inland Sea. We then turned right to head for our target, which had an aiming point between the mouth of Tokyo harbor and the Emperor's Palace—a distance of 5 to 6 miles."

This was the most heavily defended area of Tokyo. Manone recalled, "Suddenly, as we proceeded into the heart of Tokyo, we saw a huge column of smoke, pitch black, right in front of us. We flew directly into the almost stationary smoke column, and as we did, our plane was completely blacked out."

The plane shook and twisted violently, and it felt like the craft was vibrating all over the sky.

Manone remembered, "I activated the two buttons to open both the front and rear bomb bay doors. Immediately, you could smell Tokyo burning. Odors and smoke from the devastating fires below had entered the plane. A minute or two later, the navigator and I determined we had reached the point for 'bombs away.' When the bombs began to drop, the plane lurched from the weight release. As they left our bomb bays, a surprisingly new world suddenly appeared. Our lone B-29 pierced the north side of the cloud column at 5,500 to 6,000 feet. I looked down and Tokyo, stretched out below, was as bright as in daylight. We were smack in the middle of our flight path—north of Tokyo Bay on our right and the Emperor's Palace to our left. In a few minutes, this still untouched part of Tokyo would be flooded with flames. We were right on target."

Manone added, "As soon as we emerged from the towering smoke column, the ground searchlights pounced on our plane. The lights were so bright, I had to partially shield my eyes. I suspect that as many as ten to twelve searchlights flooded our plane at the same time as we continued our flight across the Tokyo landscape. From my firsthand view of the terrain ahead, all I could see was a succession of searchlights, and I knew the flak batteries were coordinated with the lights. Our plane was proceeding straight ahead despite the flak bumps and tracking lights."

The roughly three thousand airmen attacking Tokyo this night had a host of things to worry about, any one of which could get them killed. Beyond the technical demands of flying their enormous aircraft, they were nervous about the possibility of collision in the chaotic sky. Their exterior red and green running lights were off.

Pilot Charles Phillips recalled, "Hundreds of B-29s were all in the same general area, all headed in the same direction at approximately the same speed." He prayed they wouldn't collide with each other.

The B-29ers also worried about antiaircraft fire, being rammed or shot up by fighters, the massive fire on the ground, and the potential structural damage, power loss, or fuel loss that would result if any of these affected them. They always worried about engine fires, which were very hard to extinguish in flight. Some Japanese fighters were equipped with two cannons that fired upward, enabling a pilot to approach the bombers from below, fire at the blind spot of the bomb bays, and destroy the bombers.

Like other Allied personnel in Asia and the Pacific, the crews were terrified at the prospect of being taken captive and the barbaric mistreatment that would follow. Some airmen feared that, if they were hit by enemy fire at low altitude, they wouldn't have sufficient time to get out of the plane. So they decided to unfasten their seat belts as a precautionary measure.

Airmen who couldn't swim (like Red) had reason to worry about ditching in the Pacific. Of the forty-eight B-29s that were known to have ditched in the ocean, only 30 percent of the crewmen had been rescued.

They also had reason to be fearful of a wrong move by a bombardier, who could send an errant bomb on the off-limits imperial palace at the center of Tokyo, with potentially history-changing consequences if the emperor were killed. If such an accident were to happen, the Allies had every reason to expect the Japanese military, already fighting with what was widely seen to be fanatical intensity, would be enraged to an unimaginable magnitude. The civilian population would react similarly, and the prospects of an Allied victory and successful postwar occupation would be made exponentially more difficult.

The bomber nicknamed *T-Square 9* made landfall at 2:00 a.m. Tokyo time and entered a giant cloud created by the raging firestorm. "As our B-29 entered the dirty-gray cloud," Charles Phillips remembered, "it was tossed about by the wildly turbulent air. We were pinned to our seats, and I used all my skill as an instrument pilot to bring us back to a wings-level condition, over and over again."

Approaching the center of the cloud mass, the Superfortress was pushed upward at 2,000 feet per minute in a tremendous shear created by the boiling hot air. "Those of us in the forward compartment saw pieces of window and door frames flying by the airplane. The odor was overpowering. It was the smell of a great fire, but it was also the smell of death. The sharp increase in our airspeed was most alarming. Because of the powerful updraft, our B-29 was approaching the red-line, or placard, airspeed of 300 miles per hour, above which it was too unsafe to fly. I had to pull the power back, using the throttles, until I had all four engines operating at idle. We were still climbing at 2,000 feet per minute, with the air speed exceeding 350 miles per hour, well above the placard speed. We could do nothing but allow the airplane to climb, for fear of breaking up the airplane. And climb we did, popping out at about 14,000 feet. To have held the B-29 down to our briefed altitude would have resulted in increases in airspeed to extremely dangerous proportions. Operating in turbulence well above the placard speed eventually would have led to structural failure and breakup [of the aircraft]. Meanwhile, we were bouncing around like a leaf in a windstorm."

When the B-29 released its 7-ton bombload, the plane abruptly lurched upward several hundred feet. "Suddenly we zoomed out of the big firestorm cloud into clear air," Phillips recalled. "Just then we were caught in a severely violent downdraft. Our shoulders were pinned to the top of the cabin while the airplane dropped out from under us. We hung on to the control columns for dear life. This situation lasted for several seconds. Then we sank back into our seats and regained control of the airplane. For me and my crew, it was the wildest flight with the most severe turbulence I have ever experienced in over seven thousand hours of flying."

Even under ideal conditions, B-29s are hard to fly, and Phillips and his copilot had to fight hard on the half-steering-wheel mechanism to control the plane and keep it steady.

Some planes were slammed straight up in the sky about 5,000 feet or more in a matter of seconds by the thermal updrafts. Aboard *Sentimental*

Journey, pilot Philip Webster was stunned to look out the window and see the giant wings of the aircraft whipping up and down 16 feet in the turbulence, flapping like a bird's wings. The planes were built to allow for this, but the shaking was so severe that Webster wondered when the wings would snap off. The light from the firestorm was so bright, he said he could have read a newspaper in the cockpit.

He recalled, "As we approached, the conflagration was such that it didn't really make any difference where we dropped our bombs, so I tried to pick out a place that was not burning and drop our bombs there. Then we hit the thermals. It flipped me on my back. One of my gunners looked down and he saw nothing but clouds and smoke, and he looked up and all he saw was fire, and he realized we were on our back."

To recover from the inverted position, Webster executed a split-S maneuver with the enormous aircraft, plunging it down in a half roll and pulling away right-side-up in the opposite direction from which he started.

In other late-arriving B-29s, crewmen who didn't have their seat belts buckled were violently thrown around the cabin when they hit the updrafts. Orville Blackburn recalled, "It almost cost us our life [when] we went from 5,000 feet out of control to 13,000 feet." He looked down at the city and saw a maelstrom of fire and swirling debris that reminded him of "a bonfire where everything goes in different directions."

Years later, pilot Ray Clanton explained the experience as "absolutely unreal," adding, "You're being buffeted all over the sky because of these thermals. At 7,500 feet we hit a downdraft, and we dropped 1,000 feet before you could bat an eye. And stuff is flying all over the cabin, all over the aircraft."

For reasons unknown to this day, three bombers from different groups dropped their bombs onto Tokyo and then crashed into 5,657-foot Mount Fubo in the Zao Mountains at nearly the same time, killing all aboard.

Antiaircraft scored a direct hit on *Tall in the Saddle* just after it released its bombs, causing it to plummet straight down into the target area and crash.

Zero Auer, piloted by Robert Auer of the Nineteenth Bombardment Group out of Guam, was hit dead center by antiaircraft, flew several miles north of Tokyo, and then broke apart. All the crewmen died except one, who bailed out.

While the *City of Los Angeles* flew circles over Tokyo, Red climbed up into the astrodome above the bomb bay and on top of the plane, his earphones hooked into an extension so he could monitor the radio. Awestruck, he gazed on a sight never before seen on earth on such a scale: an urban metropolis being devoured by a cataclysmic fire. The crystal-clear night was filled with oceans of fire and smoke and debris. He saw huge sections of the city on fire, flanked by blacked-out sections in total darkness. He saw scores of B-29s illuminated in orange, glistening in the light as they passed over the dark areas. He saw fires erupt in the center of Tokyo near the imperial palace and the railroad station and then spread over the districts on the east side of the Sumida River.

To pilot Tony Simeral, the earth appeared to be alive with colossal Fourth of July sparklers, flickering white and orange, the product of searchlights highlighting thousands of M-69 bomb clusters as they detonated in midair, their long, white tail stabilizers-streamers guiding their fall to the ground.

Twenty thousand feet below Red's observation post in the sky, the gates of Hades opened under Tokyo, and the planet's molten core seemed to flood to the surface and feed upon the city.

French journalist Robert Guillain described the scene: "Bright flashes illuminate the sky's shadows, Christmas trees blossoming with flame in the depths of the night, then hurtling downward in zigzagging bouquets of flame, whistling as they fall. Barely fifteen minutes after the beginning of the attack, the fire whipped up by the wind started to rake through the depths of the wooden city."

Author John Dower reported, "The heat from the conflagration was so intense that in some places canals boiled, metal melted, and buildings and human beings burst spontaneously into flames."

Tokyo's defenses were pathetically weak in the face of such an attack. The Tenth Air Division sortied many of its ninety available night fighters, and the First Antiaircraft Division's searchlight and antiaircraft batteries swept the sky. But they had relatively little effect on the relentless onslaught. The entire Japanese defense system was surprised and saturated by the massive low-level night attack, just as LeMay had hoped.

The severely undermanned, underequipped, and poorly trained Tokyo fire department and civil defense squads lost control of the fires as soon as they started. Only 8,000 firemen were available to cover a city of 213 square miles, with primitive equipment such as towed water carts and hand pumps. Only one fire truck had a working aerial extension ladder. It was an inexplicably poor defense against fire in a highly combustible city, especially since the Great Kanto earthquake of 1923 had triggered fires that destroyed more than half of Tokyo and killed up to 140,000 people.

Those fire trucks that were mobilized on the night of March 9–10, 1945, were often stuck in waves of human congestion. As the Tokyo fire chief raced helplessly from blaze to blaze, his car twice caught fire. Around one hundred fire trucks were incinerated, along with hundreds of firefighters and auxiliaries. In one station, all the firemen were burned to death while attempting to start their equipment.

Pilot Robert Morgan described the scene when his craft entered Tokyo airspace: "Other B-29s around us were outlined in orange from the great groundfires. Hundreds of searchlights swept madly across the skies, the beams mostly eaten up by smoke, like some hellish Hollywood premiere night down there. Debris, great jagged shapes of burning things, floated upward toward us along with the smoke. The smoke must have reached 5 miles into the stratosphere before it thinned out."

The enemy's capital city was almost defenseless: "Most of the Japanese Zeroes and Ginga fighters still sat, some of them melted, on their airstrips. Of those that had managed to get into the air, the thermal windstorms whipped up by the fires tossed them about the skies like helpless kites. As for the ground artillery fire, it was mostly inconsequential—the guns were calibrated for the wrong altitudes."

Morgan added, "We were bombing with damn near impunity."

———

There were few air raid shelters in the city other than the crude so-called *bokugo*, little holes dug in backyards and cellars. One properly hardened shelter was provided on the grounds of the imperial palace for the emperor and his family, who spent the night belowground, listening to the pounding of the bombs while trying to ignore the unpleasant acrid smells drifting through the vents of the air filtration system.

Public parks and large buildings offered no refuge from the flames—waves of fire rolled over multitudes of civilians. Thousands died on the open grounds of the mammoth Sensō-ji temple in Asakusa. A thousand people who sought shelter inside the Meijiza Theater, an imposing five-story ferroconcrete building in the Nihonbashi District, were killed when the roof collapsed and the whole building was incinerated.

Some victims, realizing they were trapped in a collapsing labyrinth of fire with no way out, simply stopped running, surrendered to the spirit of *shikada ga nai* ("it is hopeless to try to do more"), turned toward the imperial palace, and knelt down in the street to pray as the fire overwhelmed them.

Saotome Katsumoto, a twelve-year-old boy, found himself running through the streets with his family, desperately searching for shelter from the rain of fire. "The wind fanned the fires and the fires fed the wind," he recalled. "Countless sparks and embers bore down on us, humming like a swarm of bees." He was stunned by the bizarre apparitions of fleeing people. "It seems that folks completely lose their heads in such situations. While escaping we had seen people carrying tatami mats on their backs, with stone weights used for radish pickling loaded on their bicycles, or with blankets draped over their shoulders like the comic book superhero *Golden Bat*. But Mrs. Torii and her son were even more unforgettable. She had a futon wrapped around her, fastened with thick straw rope, and several pairs of wooden clogs tied to her waist with silk. Her son was wearing an adult's steel helmet with two floor cushions tied around his waist at the front and back and wooden clogs hanging from the silk thread. I looked at him in open-mouthed amazement."

A B-29 emerged from the reddish-purple flames and came straight toward the boy's family, flying so low it seemed to be scraping the top of telegraph poles.

"Reflected in the flames, its wings gleamed bright red like dripping blood," recalled Saotome. Bombs fell and "in an instant the whole area around me was a picture of hell" as blood and body parts littered the landscape.

"We carried on running as the bombs fell from all directions, dodging sputtering incendiaries lodged in the ground and jumping over dead bodies on the road as if we were running an obstacle race."

When he got to the Sumida River in the late morning, Saotome was frozen in horror at the sight of a team of civil defense corpsmen at work. "Looking down, I saw that the river was full of burned and drowned corpses. The men were reeling in the bodies with hooked poles. They bound the stiff corpses with ropes, hauled them up onto the quay, and laid them down in rows like tuna at a fish market. Then I noticed that my father was standing behind me. 'Take a good look, Katsumoto,' he said. 'Look and never forget. This is what war is.' I clearly remember the way he spoke, muttering the words under his breath."

After the bombing started, police photographer Ishikawa Koyo managed to commandeer a police vehicle and searched for a way to help people evacuate. "As I was driving at full speed along Showa Road, fire trucks and police security patrol vehicles overtook me, their sirens wailing," he recounted decades later. "When I got to the Asakusabashi crossroads, I was confronted with a gruesome spectacle—a conflagration of raging flames swirling in the wind. At Ryogoku Bridge, I saw an endless stream of escaping people coming toward me over the bridge from the other side. The congestion and confusion defy description. A policeman was shouting in a shrill voice as he tried to guide the crowds, women were screaming, and civil defense corpsmen were barking instructions. In the sky above, as if they were mocking us, the B-29s were still flying serenely through the black smoke at such low altitude that it seemed you could hold out your hand and touch them. As they descended to drop their bombs again and again, the fires on the ground were reflected on their bodies. With the bright-red flames flickering on their huge fuselages and four engines, they looked like winged demons from Hell."

From a hill overlooking downtown Tokyo, German Catholic priest Gustav Bitter gazed completely spellbound at the infernal spectacle. "They came in majesty," he wrote of the American bombers, "like kings of the Earth. The flak from the ground poured up toward them, but they held their course, proud and regal and haughty, as if they said, 'I am too great for any man to do me harm.' I watched them as if I were in a trance." Father Bitter described "the red and yellow flames reflected from below on the silvery undersides [of the planes] so that they were like giant dragon flies with jeweled wings against the upper darkness."

Hashimoto Yoshiko, a twenty-four-year-old mother, found herself on a raft in a river, clinging to her thirteen-month-old son, Hiroshi, whose eyes were wide open in shock. "As the raft floated along, I looked up at Sanno Bridge. The flames were leaping like living creatures among the terrified crowds with a tremendous roaring sound. In the water underneath the bridge, people huddled together under a sheet of burned tinplate were frantically chanting sutras [Buddhist scriptures]."

When nineteen-year-old Kokubo Takako heard a roar of hooves, she thought she saw phantoms, and then realized it was a pack of snorting horses, some of their manes on fire, running straight toward her. "Scared out of my wits, I couldn't breathe and my legs went stiff. It was on a narrow street with the canal on the left and burning houses on the right.

There was no place to hide. As I pressed myself close to the side of a garbage box, I thought 'I'm not even married and I'm about to be trampled to death by wild horses.' I just cowered there and begged them to spare me."

Kokubo made it to the edge of a canal, where a mob was panicking at the entrance to a bridge whose wooden girders were aflame. "I said a prayer to the memorial tablets in my bag, jumped onto the flaming bridge and dashed across it," she remembered. "Behind me I heard someone shout 'It's all right, we can make it across!' and everyone followed me. When I got to the other side and turned around to look, the bridge was no longer there. It had collapsed and fallen into the canal together with the people on it. The moaning, screaming, and desperate cries of children calling out for their mothers were unbearable. The burning bridge had crumbled and fallen into the water over them with a terrible crackling and hissing. It was like a scene from Hell. Red flames were swelling above the water and twisting over it like huge snakes. Trying desperately to find something to cling on to above the surface, people were throwing up their hands and shaking their heads from side to side as they squirmed for dear life."

Koyo Ishikawa, a Tokyo policeman, spent the night amid the ruins of a house, lying still in a sunken bathtub, soaked in water. "I could hear the sound of houses burning, houses collapsing, B-29s overhead and firebombs exploding," he said. At one point he peered out and saw a woman running for shelter. "All of her clothes suddenly caught fire at once," he remembered. "The wind blew her down and she rolled, burning and screaming."

There were many accounts of babies being carried on their mothers' backs and catching fire. On the banks of the Sumida River, hundreds of people sought refuge only to be pushed into the water by newcomers and drowned.

Seizo Hashimoto, a thirteen-year-old boy, saw a woman dressed in a red kimono "seized by the firestorm, whipped and twisted in the air, and ignited: a human torch."

A Dutch diplomat, watching the scene from a few kilometers away, described the cylinders of incendiary napalm jelly floating down "like a cascade of silvery water."

Kikujima Koji, a thirteen-year-old boy, was swept with his family into a mob trying to escape over the Kototoi Bridge that spanned the Sumida River. "We were caught between the people pushing us forward from behind and the wave of people and their luggage bearing down on us from the front. Unable to move forward or backward, the six of us became nailed against the railings on the right of the bridge. Two fire trucks had also been brought to a standstill next to us and a fireman was yelling in a hoarse voice. The night sky was scorched red with fire. From the direction of Asakusa, a blizzard of sparks and embers was blowing over the bridge and our heads. In no time people's belongings caught fire and there was no way of putting them out."

Pilot Robert Morgan witnessed the same scene from a few thousand feet above: "On a bridge spanning the Kototoi River, a mob fleeing in one direction collided with a mob headed toward them. Seven tons of fresh firebombs incinerated the whole vast horde."

Several thousand people perished at this one spot of Tokyo. According to Morgan, "It was claimed, in later years, that screams could be heard aboard some of the B-29s trailing in at 7,000 feet."

The fires in various Tokyo neighborhoods connected and created a conflagration consisting of waves of fire preceded by a wall of super-heated vapors that ignited everything flammable in their path.

"A fully developed firestorm is a horrifically mesmerizing sight," wrote Barrett Tillman. "It seems a living, malicious creature that feeds upon itself, generating ever higher winds that whirl cyclonically, breeding updrafts that suck the oxygen out of the atmosphere even while the flames consume the fuel—buildings—that feed the monster's ravenous appetite. Most firestorm victims do not burn to death. Rather, as carbon monoxide quickly reaches lethal levels, people suffocate from lack of oxygen and excessive smoke inhalation. In those frightful hours humans watched things happen on a scale that probably had never been seen. The super-heated ambient air boiled the water out of ponds and canals while rains of liquid glass flew, propelled by cyclonic winds. Temperatures reached 1,800 degrees Fahrenheit, melting the frames of emergency vehicles and causing some people to erupt in spontaneous combustion."

Hideo Tsuchikura, a factory worker, peered out of his makeshift shelter inside a water tank atop a school building and looked out at the city. He recalled seeing "fire-winds filled with burning particles rushing up and down the streets. I watched people—adults and children—running for their lives, dashing madly about like rats. The flames raced after them like living things, striking them down. They died by the hundreds right in front of me. Wherever I turned my eyes, I saw people running away from the school grounds seeking air to breathe. They raced away from the school in a devils' cauldron of twisting, seething fire. The whole spectacle with its blinding lights and thundering noise reminded me of the paintings of purgatory—a real inferno out of the depths of Hell itself."

———

In a prison cell inside a filthy horse stable on the outer edge of the imperial palace grounds in the center of Tokyo, Raymond F. "Hap" Halloran, a captured American navigator, experienced the horror of the firebombing at ground level. He was twenty-three years old and enduring his sixth week of torture, starvation, and solitary confinement in enemy captivity.

Every day his captors beat him with rifle butts. They beat all parts of his body. Every day he feared execution as a war criminal or dying of his wounds, lost and forgotten in a black hole of despair. Every day, for much of the day, he cried uncontrollably. It was an involuntary reflex to the horrors he was enduring, but somehow he felt it gave him an outlet of relief. And every day, throughout the day, he uttered short prayers and dialogues with God, repeating them over and over. They were variations on a central thought, a single phrase he repeated over and over: *God, I need Your help now, please.*

Hap Halloran and Red Erwin did not know each other. Their crews had been based on different islands; Halloran on Saipan and Erwin on Guam. But they shared an unshakable faith in God and the power of prayer.

Sixty years later, several years after my grandfather died, I met Hap Halloran at a reunion of B-29 veterans. He was a tall, powerfully built man who exuded confidence, vitality, and humor. At first he punctuated our rapid-fire conversation with reassuring, infectious bursts of booming laughter.

On January 27, 1945, the day Hap Halloran was shot down over Japan, he was aboard a plane that had two nicknames—*V-Square 27* and *Rover Boys Express*—assigned to the 878th Bomb Squadron, 499th Bomb Group, 73rd Bomb Wing. They were on their fourth combat mission. As they neared the target, the squadron was intercepted by swarms of fighters in a fierce, running air battle.

Hap told me, "Our target was the Nakajima Aircraft Engine Plant west of the Tokyo outskirts. It was heavily defended with fighters and antiaircraft fire. We had lost planes previously over that target and our apprehension was strong. On that particular day, January 27, we only had sixty-seven planes. I've heard it described as the toughest mission over the toughest target. At the preflight briefing, they told us, you'll experience light flak and antiaircraft fire over the target today, and there will be very few, if any, fighter planes at your altitude. You know, 'Good luck!' They were wrong. It turned out there were over three hundred fighters up to meet us that day."

When they began their bomb run, at about 30,000 feet and just after passing Mount Fuji, as the bomb bay doors were opening, a twin-engine interceptor, a Kawasaki Ki-45 *Toryu* ("Dragonslayer"), flying at the edge of its operational altitude, made a single catastrophic pass at Halloran's B-29. The enemy plane shredded the American plane with 37-mm cannon fire that killed one gunner, wounded two crewmen, blew out the nose of the plane, and disabled the instruments, electrical system, and three of the four engines. The bomber was unflyable.

The crew began abandoning the aircraft at 27,000 feet over a northeast suburb of Tokyo, plunging into a blast of –58 degrees Fahrenheit, a sudden 128-degree drop from the cabin temperature of 70 degrees. Before jumping out, Halloran, not sure when he would eat again, wolfed down a turkey sandwich and chocolate pudding he'd brought along. He snapped on his parachute and hurled himself into the thin air.

Halloran knew that Japanese pilots often killed parachutists in midair, so he dropped 23,000 feet in free fall before pulling the rip cord at about 3,500 feet. Drifting under his parachute, his heart sank when he saw three Japanese planes closing in on him, so close that their propeller wash sent his parachute into a violent swinging motion. Two peeled off, but the third came to within 200 feet of the helpless airman, seemingly for the kill.

There was nothing he could do, so for some reason, Halloran decided to wave at the Japanese pilot. "He throttled back and was just below me slightly and I was hanging in the chute. I could look right down onto him, and I thought he was going to shoot me. But he stayed below me. And he raised his hand in a salute. I thought, *What's going on here?* I couldn't even conceptualize what just happened. Then he pulled away."

For some reason, the pilot spared Halloran's life and offered him the salute of a chivalrous brother airman. But looking down, Halloran could see throngs of people, as many as two thousand, following his parachute. He braced himself and made an extremely hard landing.

At this point in the story, Halloran's voice wavered and tears formed in his eyes. "I was laying there, and they moved in," he said. "I was beaten severely with clubs and metal bars. And rocks."

He paused. "You know, it was pretty tough—"

Halloran began to cry, burying his face in his hands and trembling severely. Just a few minutes before, he was an avuncular, room-filling presence whose laughter boomed off the walls. Now he was a huddled, sobbing figure, transported in time into the body of a twenty-three-year-old who was being beaten to death.

His head sank low as he sobbed uncontrollably. He appeared to feel once again the waves of pain he absorbed over and over on that day sixty years ago.

Slowly Halloran composed himself. "I had no control," he explained, regaining the narrative. "There was nothing I could do. I faded in and out. Then I looked up and saw these strange faces and thought it was just like a bad dream. I was helpless. Then, after a while, some soldiers came in and I was loaded onto a truck. Another minute or two and I would have been dead."

Halloran was in critical condition with blunt-force injuries all over his body, but he was denied medical care. Instead, he was taken to the downtown Tokyo headquarters and torture chambers of the dreaded Japanese military police, the *Kempeitai*, an organization described by POW Fiske Hanley as a group of "sadistic goons, especially picked for their brutality."

Guns were placed to Halloran's head, and he was ordered to sign both a confession that he had intentionally bombed civilians and a waiver of Geneva Convention rules requiring humane treatment for prisoners of war. He was then placed in a cage and tortured and interrogated for weeks. When he was given any food, it was infested with bugs. He soon lost 100 pounds in weight. Chained up in a horse stable beside the moat surrounding the imperial palace, Halloran and other imprisoned airmen spent the night of the March 9–10 firebombing in a state of terror as they sensed all of Tokyo was on fire.

Several weeks later, Halloran was subjected to an especially fiendish humiliation. He was stripped naked and placed on public display as an attraction at the Ueno Zoo in Tokyo, the oldest zoo in Japan. In 1943 the zoo had closed after all the animals had been poisoned, strangled, or starved to death by city officials who were afraid the beasts would run loose in the streets in the event of an air raid. Now the zoo was reopened, with Hap Halloran as the sole exhibition.

"I was in a tiger cage," he said. "It reminded me of the Cincinnati Zoo with the bars in the front. I was all alone. I couldn't stand. My hands were tied to the bars, and I had running sores from the fleas and bedbugs. I was trying to look like an air force guy and give it my best and look as good as I could—but I probably didn't look very good."

For two days, Tokyo citizens filed by to gawk at Halloran in the tiger cage. "Most of the people who walked by were elderly ladies," he recalled. "A few of them had babies. But somehow, either truthfully or by desire, I saw compassion in the eyes of some of those ladies as they turned sideways and looked up at me. Maybe I saw it. Maybe I was just hoping for it. Maybe they had a son somewhere who also was going through pain."

Through all his ordeal as a prisoner, Hap Halloran prayed a short, simple prayer over and over, as he did on the night of March 9–10, 1945, when Tokyo fell into the fires of hell: *God, I need Your help now, please.*

———

At 1:21 a.m., inside Red's B-29, some 20,000 feet over Halloran's prison cell, so much smoke was rising from Tokyo that it was hard to observe details on the ground anymore, and updrafts were buffeting the aircraft. Gen. Tommy Power decided it was time to break radio silence and flash the first strike report back to General LeMay and prepare to turn back for Guam.

Power passed the message to Red, who tapped the report in code over the radio: "Bombs away—General conflagration—Flak moderate to heavy—Fighters none." This would be music to General LeMay's ears. Things seemed to be going well and a colossal firestorm had been ignited. Power and the crew estimated the fire-damaged area at 15 square miles, which wound up being very close to the actual figure: 15.8 square miles. Once they were clear of the Tokyo area, Power told Red to relay their expected arrival time to Guam so LeMay could meet them on the runway.

The receding glow of the Tokyo firestorm remained visible from the tail gunner's window of the *City of Los Angeles* for 150 miles before it slipped below the horizon. For the last two hours of the return flight, General Power took the controls from Captain Simeral. When the B-29 landed at Guam's North Field at 9:00 a.m., after a mission lasting fifteen hours and four minutes, General LeMay was on the tarmac to meet it. General Power shouted down to LeMay from an open cockpit window, "It was a hell of a good mission." He rushed out of the aircraft and unfurled his marked maps beside the runway to point out the highlights to the commander. LeMay wore the faintest grimace of a smile. American casualties turned out to be relatively low.

An exhausted Red and his crewmates quickly left the airfield and retreated to their quarters to sleep.

Gens. Lauris Norstad, Curtis LeMay (with pipe), and Thomas Power review Power's battle notes, taken aboard Red Erwin's B-29, on the tarmac at Guam immediately after the most destructive air raid in human history, March 9–10, 1945. (US Air Force)

At the Pentagon, when Gen. Hap Arnold received the first reports of the raid, he was elated. He sent a cable to LeMay: "Congratulations. This mission shows your crews have the guts for anything."

General Power noted, "That fire raid was the most destructive single military action in the history of the world. In fact, that raid caused more casualties than the atom-bomb attacks on Hiroshima and Nagasaki. If you had sat up there as I did and watched the fire develop, you would understand that. The best way to describe what it looks like when these fire bombs come out of the bomb bay of an airplane is to compare it to a giant pouring a big shovelful of white-hot coals all over the ground, covering an area about 2,500 feet in length and some 500 feet wide—that's what each single B-29 was doing! . . . They started fires everywhere. Of course, Tokyo was a highly inflammable city, and as the fire swathes widened and came together, they built up into one vast fire."

The human and material damage to Tokyo was staggering to consider. As a result of the three-hour attack, at least 80,000 people had been killed, with some estimates at close to 100,000. One million people were left homeless. And more than 250,000 buildings were destroyed, consisting of nearly 16 square miles of the Japanese capital. A Tokyo police official wrote that his department could not issue a complete report "because of the horrifying conditions beyond imagination."

A US Army publication soon announced, "The great city of Tokyo— third largest in the world—is dead. The heart, guts, core—whatever you want to call everything that makes a modern metropolis a living, functioning organism—is a waste of white ash, endless fields of ashes, blowing in the wind. Not even the shells of walls stand in large areas of the Japanese capital. The streets are desolate, the people are dead or departed, the city lies broken and prostrate and destroyed. The men who accomplished the job study the photographs brought back by their recon pilots and stand speechless and awed. They shake their heads at each other and bend over the photos again, and then shake their heads again, and no one says a word."

Eight days after the raid, on March 18, Emperor Hirohito overruled his staff and insisted on seeing the most damaged areas near the Sumida River for himself, since information from his officials seemed confused.

The emperor put on his riding boots, general's uniform, and ceremonial sword and slipped out of the imperial palace grounds in his armored Mercedes-Benz 770 maroon limousine, which was appointed with a red-and-gold chrysanthemum pennant. The motorcade proceeded at 20 miles per hour with only a small motorcycle escort so as to not attract potential fire from American aircraft.

The emperor did not have to go far to see the ruins of his capital city, as the maelstrom had stopped barely a mile from his palace. He absorbed the devastation of rubble, wreckage, ashes, and streams of sewage from the car windows and briefly stopped to talk with some stunned survivors and local officials, some of whom were so dazed and in shock from the bombing that they neglected to bow to the royal figure. Then he went back home.

In a rational universe, Emperor Hirohito would have stopped the war then and there. The Americans obviously now had the power and the will to pulverize his empire into oblivion. Incredibly, Hirohito already knew this. It was clear to anyone capable of reading a map that Japan had lost all forward momentum since the Battle of Midway in June 1942, barely six months after the Pearl Harbor attack. Japan had been retreating ever since.

Even as far back as June 1943, in fact, Hirohito had directed Prime Minister Hideki Tojo to ask the military leadership where the Allies would be stopped. The blunt reply from Tojo's advisor was, "Neither the Army nor the Navy can possibly draw up a plan to stop them."

But whether Hirohito was blinded by arrogance, cowardice, cluelessness, or helplessness in the face of his fanatical military advisors, he permitted the bloodbath to continue after the devastating March 9–10, 1945, raid for another five months, as countless human beings suffered and died.

Many Americans, including Red Erwin, thought the US military had no alternative to the firebombing assault on Japan, since the Japanese government and military showed little intent to surrender unconditionally and vowed to defend the island nation from invasion down to the last man, woman, and child.

"We would have been forced to just mow down literally millions of civilians to take Japan," recalled Don Thurow, an intelligence officer. "The bombing we did, horrendous as it was, saved Japan, saved Japanese culture and saved millions of Japanese lives, plus a few of our own, probably including my own."

After the war, some American servicemen said they had no qualms about the firebombing. Gunner Ed Shahinian explained that he "never considered as to whether I was killing babies or dogs or animals. We were doing a job and that's all we cared about."

Others had spiritual doubts and questions about the things they witnessed and took part in, such as B-29 veteran Robert Rodenhouse. "I'm sort of a religious person," he said. "I was brought up with a strong faith. And I couldn't understand why there was a God that would permit that to happen, and use me to see that it was being done, you know. And it bothered me a lot. It bothered me a lot. And I never forget I wrote home to my pastor about that, and he says, 'You know, that's a secret that's known only to God. He did what He wanted to have done.'"

This was the beginning of a five-month firebombing campaign against the Japanese mainland that an aide to Gen. Douglas MacArthur described as "one of the most ruthless and barbaric killings of noncombatants in all history."

The victims were "scorched and boiled and baked to death," Curtis LeMay later said. "Killing Japanese didn't bother me very much at that time," he added. "I suppose if I had lost the war, I would have been tried as a war criminal. Luckily, I was on the winning side." LeMay admitted to occasionally thinking of flashing, horrific images like "a child lying in bed with a whole ton of masonry tumbling down on top of him," but he observed that, in order to do your job and keep your sanity, you had to banish such thoughts from your brain.

For Red Erwin's part, the horrors he witnessed seemed like the only way to end the war as fast as possible and thereby stop the world's suffering.

Emboldened by the results of the Tokyo raid, over the next eight days, General LeMay launched hundreds of B-29s on fire raids against the cities of Nagoya, Osaka, and Kobe. On the night of March 13, 274 B-29s appeared over Osaka, Japan's third-largest city. When their bombs detonated on the 150-acre military arsenal there, the colossal multiple detonations shook 70-ton Superfortresses in the air one mile overhead.

One bomber, *Topsy-Turvy*, was suddenly pushed 7,000 feet up to 12,000 feet, flipped over, and fell 10,000 feet before the pilot stabilized it.

In another plane, the bombardier was hurled into the copilot's lap and then slammed into the controls, and the captain was thrown out of his seat as the plane flipped on its side. They all survived.

After eight such raids, the B-29 force ran out of incendiary bombs, and LeMay ordered a pause for the exhausted air and ground crews.

While these follow-up raids were not as destructive as the Tokyo raid of March 9–10, the Americans decided they had discovered a potentially war-winning formula: low-level area bombing of military and civilian targets with incendiaries, including urban areas, which could fatally grind down Japan's war capacity and morale. Mass civilian casualties were an inevitable by-product. The apparent success of LeMay's strategy salvaged the reputation of the US Army Air Force in the Asia–Pacific theater and set the Allies on a new and presumably faster course to victory over Japan.

For Japan, this was the beginning of a wave of fire that would rage through the spring and summer of 1945.

For Staff Sgt. Henry "Red" Erwin, his personal day of reckoning would come less than five weeks later, on April 12, 1945.

Meanwhile, in Alabama, Red's wife, Betty, waited for her man to come home. The newlyweds had dreams of finding a nice house and starting a family together, and they couldn't wait to enjoy married life. But they'd only been married for three months before Red was off to war.

During this time, when Red was in combat over the Pacific, Betty continued to exchange letters with him, but no one has ever found those letters. Maybe they were just too personal and painful for her to hold on to.

"Once the war started like that, you didn't know where they were, you didn't know if they were alive or dead," explained Dolores Silva, one of the millions of American women who were left behind. "You didn't know if you were going to get a letter from them and then find out that they had died right after they had written the letter. So, it just kept building up inside of you."

While the war ground on and casualties kept rising, many wives and families were understandably horrified by the steady flow of news headlines, letters, telegrams, and rumors. Some mothers spent hours in their houses of worship and prayed for their sons.

In Louisiana, Jackie Greer used a map to trace the path of her boyfriend across Europe. "Following that war was the best history lesson I ever had," she recalled decades later. "I got a big map, and every day I'd get crayons out. Every day. Certain colors meant this group is here. Certain colors meant they'd moved there. And I kept up with that war. I learned more about Europe than I had ever learned at school."

Jeroline Green of Kansas explained, "There was a sense of urgency because you didn't know what or when or how. The war might be over in another day or it might last for another hundred years."

Some six million women joined the workforce by 1943, and almost half of them were working in military industries, like the mythical Rosie the Riveter, whose government-created slogan was "We Can Do It." Many women volunteered for war-related organizations like the Red Cross and for military support jobs, such as driving trucks, flying cargo

JOURNEY TO THE APOCALYPSE

planes, rigging parachutes, and serving as radio operators. About 350,000 American women served in uniform around the world as volunteers for the Women's Army Auxiliary Corps (WAAC, later called the Women's Army Corps), the navy's Women's Reserve (WAVES [Women Accepted for Volunteer Emergency Service]), the Marine Corps Women's Reserve, the Coast Guard Women's Reserve (SPARS), the Women Airforce Service Pilots (WASPS), the Navy Nurse Corps, and the Army Nurse Corps.

At home, wrote historian Stephen Ambrose, women "became proficient cooks and housekeepers, managed the finances, learned to fix the car, worked in a defense plant, and wrote letters to their soldier husbands that were consistently upbeat."

Nancy Potter from Connecticut, who was, like Betty Erwin, a teenager, reflected on how the war affected her and her peers: "I think for girls and women, and perhaps boys and men, of my generation the war forced them to grow up prematurely. It made them far more serious about the bare realities of life: life, death, values. It robbed them, in a sense, of some childhood."

In Alabama, women made up one-fourth of the labor force in defense industries, and many women volunteered for the Red Cross, the Army-Navy USO Club, or one of the military auxiliaries. Women who had been public schoolteachers found jobs as welders at the Mobile shipyards at four times the salary. Civilians helped the war effort with war bond drives, clothing drives, and scrap drives for metals and rubber. Rationing was widespread, especially for daily staples such as sugar, gasoline, meat, and coffee.

For her part, in the desperate months that her brand-new husband was off to war, Betty Erwin kept her little piece of the home front secure for Red's eventual return by spending time with his and her families and by sending him letters of love and encouragement.

All the while, she prayed and yearned for him to come home safe—and soon.

65

Chapter Four

DAY OF DESTINY

ON APRIL 12, 1945, RED ERWIN'S LIFE CHANGED forever.

At 2:00 a.m., Erwin and his crewmates assembled at their aircraft on Guam's North Field for takeoff on their tenth combat mission. It would be one of the longest distance missions ever attempted against Japan from Guam, a round trip of 3,041 miles.

Their target was the Hodogaya Chemical Plant at Koriyama, in Japan's Fukushima Prefecture, 120 miles north of Tokyo. The target was of great strategic importance, as it produced one-third of Japan's tetraethyl lead, a main component of high-octane aviation fuel used in combat aircraft.

The *City of Los Angeles* was designated as the lead plane, or pathfinder, in a stream of eighty-five bombers from the 314th Bombardment Wing assigned to take part in the mission, in addition to a parallel mission against the same target on the same day by eighty-two B-29s of the 313th Bombardment Wing.

As usual, Capt. George "Tony" Simeral piloted the *City of Los Angeles*, and on this day, his superior officer, the Fifty-Second Squadron's commander, Lt. Col. Eugene Strouse, originally from Muscoda, Wisconsin, would ride along as an observer, making a total of twelve men on the mission. They planned to be over the target at 12:35 p.m., bombing from altitudes of 7,000 to 9,000 feet. Clear visibility was expected. Their bombload was a mix of demolition and incendiary bombs.

On earlier missions, the thing Red hated most was the helpless, exposed feeling of exploding antiaircraft shells peppering the sky around the *City of Los Angeles*, creating concussions that rocked the giant aircraft. Sometimes Red felt as if the pilot was about to lose control of the plane, and the enemy shells were so thick you could walk across the sky on them.

When the B-29s neared the coast of Japan, radio-linked spotters in picket boats alerted the rudimentary but sometimes lethal enemy military defense network. Antiaircraft batteries peppered the sky with exploding shells, and fighter planes scrambled to attack them. But once the B-29s committed to their flight path, there was little they could do in the way of evasive maneuvers—they were under ironclad orders to continue straight to the target, no matter what.

Beyond the myriad dangers and unknowns that bombing missions to Japan held, Red was grappling with an intensely personal, private event on this day. His wife, Betty, had recently told him in a letter that she had suffered a miscarriage of a pregnancy that would have resulted in their first child. The experience of miscarriage can produce significant feelings of grief, anxiety, depression, and isolation in women, and it can also damage men's psychological and social well-being. Both Betty and Red were resilient, but the miscarriage was a devastating blow to both of them, and the impact was magnified by the thousands of miles of separation and by their knowledge that Red was regularly embarking on combat missions that could easily get him killed.

To save fuel, B-29s typically flew individually to an assembly point off the Japanese coast; then the squadron regrouped into a tight formation for the attack. On this day the assembly point was the small volcanic island of Aogashima, 223 miles south of Tokyo.

As the *City of Los Angeles* approached Aogashima, it was 9:30 a.m.

and the morning sun illuminated the horizon. Following standard attack procedure, Captain Simeral moved his lead plane into a circular arc and signaled radioman Red Erwin to prepare to drop a series of three multi-colored smoke grenades and one white-phosphorus bomb through a three-and-a-half-foot chute in the plane deck. These flares would tumble from the bottom of the plane to mark the assembly point for the other planes, which were spread out over dozens of miles. The planes would rally on the flares and form into a broad formation. This was an extra duty for Red, and he'd done it many times before in training and in combat. The opening for the chute was near his feet in the radio operator's compartment.

First, Red dropped the smoke grenades through the chute. Then he picked up the 20-pound, 16-inch-long steel canister containing the explosive white phosphorus, carefully pulled the arming pin to set the six-second delayed-action fuse, and dropped it into the chute. Red was barearmed and bareheaded and wore a life preserver flotation device over his shirt.

The phosphorus bomb was supposed to fall several hundred feet, and then detonate into a huge, highly visible midair shower of fire and yellow-and-white smoke trails to mark the rally point. The phosphorus burned at over 1,000 degrees Fahrenheit and produced a spectacular explosion visible for dozens of miles.

But something went terribly wrong. Instead of falling out of the plane, the phosphorus bomb backfired and ricocheted up the chute, possibly after slamming into a stuck valve.

"It may have had a defective firing pin, or the wind velocity may have been so high it blew it back into the plane," Red said. "I sensed it too. I had a premonition. I knew that sucker was coming back. I thought, *Oh, this sucker is going to come back in here*, and that's when I tried to put my foot over the tube. I knew it was coming back, and I tried to put my foot on it and kick it out, but it shot back into the plane and exploded at my feet. All at once it exploded. It took my hair off my head. It took my right ear off. It blinded me. Phosphorus was all over me and burning."

The phosphorus bomb struck the right side of Red's face and blanketed his upper body with a sticky coating of white phosphorus burning at over 1,300 degrees Fahrenheit. According to the notes compiled by journalist Robert St. John during interviews in 1946 with Red, "The inside of the B-29 was lit up as though by glaring arc lights."

In an instant, much of Red's right ear and nose were seared away. His face, hair, and arms were on fire and his eyes were blinded. The bomb canister flipped around on the floor, churning out billows of fire and thick, noxious white and yellow smoke that quickly filled the aircraft's forward compartment.

Suddenly Captain Simeral could not see the instrument panel in front of him. The plane began a steep, out-of-control dive toward the ocean at a sixty-degree angle.

Through a tidal wave of pain, Red's mind focused on two imminent, split-second catastrophes. The plane was on a path to slam into the Pacific, break apart, and sink, but before that could happen, the detonating phosphorus canister would easily burn through the plane's metal deck and tumble into the bomb bay and ignite the bombload, setting off a spectacular series of explosions that could even detonate the assembling bomber formation. Either way, everyone on the *City of Los Angeles* was doomed.

Red, now blind and on fire, fell to his knees and swept his arms around the deck frantically, trying to feel his way to the bomb. Ten seconds elapsed. There was, theoretically, one way out of this predicament, but it would require superhuman strength and miraculous courage.

Red had been a Christian for as long as he could remember, and he had led prayer services as a Methodist youth group leader. He could feel death approaching both him and his brother airmen with the speed of a bullet, and his body was registering the mind-boggling pain of being incinerated by white phosphorus.

What he did next came naturally to him.

He prayed.

Lord, I need Your help now!

Red remembered the cardinal rules that had been hammered over and over into him in flight training: *expect the unexpected* and *don't panic.*

"If you panic, you'll make the wrong move," Red recalled. "If you panic, you cannot think of what to do. You cannot find it. Don't get emotional. Keep your presence of mind, figure out what's going on, and work the problem through. If you don't panic, there's always a way out. That way you always have an escape possibility."

He said, "I didn't panic. I asked the good Lord to help me. And I've thought about this a million times over the years. I didn't pray *God have mercy on my soul* as if death was inevitable. I prayed for God's help." He asked for God's help to conquer death in that moment and show him a way through the crisis.

Red's prayer wasn't just an invocation for God to help him figure out what to do next; it was a reaction to the nearly infinite severity of the pain his body was registering as it was being consumed by fire. This was an entirely new universe of pain, the likes of which Red never dreamed possible. He recalled what went through his mind as he registered the impact of second- and third-degree burns all over his body.

"I was in a sense praying to die. I was in such desperate pain that death would actually have been a blessing."

As soon as he uttered his prayer, Red felt the presence and the guidance of God. According to Red, in that moment, the Supreme Being became the central player in the drama.

Instantly, Red recalled, three things happened simultaneously. First, he felt no pain. It was canceled out, perhaps by adrenaline and divine intercession.

Second, his mind locked onto the one microscopic chance he had to save everyone's life—to somehow get the bomb to the nearest window that could be opened, which was thirty feet forward in the pilot's compartment, and get it out of the plane.

He explained, "I knew that somehow I had to hit that window. *Hit that window!*"

Third, and this is where his story becomes truly cosmic, he sensed the presence of angels or some other unearthly presence very near him, and they were giving him a loud-and-clear message: *Go! Go! Go! You can make it!*

With those words in his mind, he recalled, "I was blinded but managed to grope around until I found the grenade. It took me ten seconds to find that sucker with my feet and hands, but I could tell the plane was going down."

Red found the fireball, scooped it up with his bare hands, cradled it against his right side like a football, and somehow struggled to his feet. His torso and the internal organs around his chest were partially shielded by the Mae West flotation vest he always wore on missions because he couldn't swim, but he was sustaining severe third-degree burns to his head, face, neck, hands, forearms, and legs.

A first-degree burn resembles a sunburn and usually heals on its own within a few days. A second-degree burn triggers blistering, but the skin heals, and skin grafts are needed only for very deep burns. But third-degree burns, the kind Red was suffering, penetrate all five layers of skin, unleashing prolonged, agonizing pain. And if the victim lives through the injury and survives the high risk of infection, skin grafting is always required. Such burns are among the hardest injuries to survive and treat successfully, because they unleash toxins that attack so many different body systems, including the heart, blood, kidneys, pancreas, and hormonal and immune systems. "There's no other injury that has such a devastating effect on the body—no disease process, no cancer, nothing," noted Canadian burn specialist Walter Peters.

Through the thick smoke, Red's stunned crewmates beheld an apparition from Dante's *Inferno*—a blind man, enveloped in flames, crawling and stumbling through the aircraft toward the cockpit. As Red passed by with much of his body on fire, his crewmates heard the unfailingly polite southerner say, "Excuse me."

Red's thirty-foot path to the cockpit was blocked by the gun turret, various stacked supplies, and the locked-down navigator's table. There was no way around it.

Still clutching the flaming phosphorus bomb against his right side, Red forced his burning right hand to fumble beneath the table, unlatch the hinge, and flip it up. The raging phosphorus actually melted layers of his skin so that it was fused into the table, but Red managed to pull off what was left of his hand and continue toward the cockpit.

"Those thirty feet felt like an eternity," he remembered. "I was crawling by instinct."

Red stumbled toward the pilot and copilot, who were frantically trying to stabilize the smoke-choked aircraft as it plummeted to 700 feet, then 600 feet, then 500 feet.

As a boy growing up during the Great Depression, Red Erwin had seen his family experience several close calls with hardship, tough times, and even a few brushes with financial disaster, as so many families did. When this happened, his mother conducted a kind of prayer chant that she repeated over and over: *The Lord will help us. He will get us through . . . The Lord will help us. He will get us through . . .*"

If there was ever a moment that Red needed the Lord's help, it was now. And the voice—either of God or of angels—was by his side, encouraging him, *Go! Go! Go! You can do it!*

Red called out, "Open the window, sir! Open the window!" He crawled into the cockpit.

Captain Simeral screamed, "Get it out the window!"

"Pardon me, sir," Red said to Colonel Strouse as he maneuvered around him. "Is the window open, sir?"

Someone pushed the window open. Red leaned over and forced his burning body toward it. The rushing air started to suck the smoke out of the cockpit.

Red manhandled the bomb, still showering fire and smoke in all directions, through the open window, and flipped it into the open air. He collapsed on the copilot's throttle stick, and then onto the floor.

As the smoke was sucked out of the plane, Captain Simeral could again see his instrument panel. The altitude gauge plummeted from 380 to 350 to 320 feet as he and the copilot frantically tried to regain control of the aircraft. Finally, at 300 feet above the desolate ocean surface, at the last moment, they were able to stabilize the aircraft, level off, pull up, and gain altitude.

The crew turned a fire extinguisher on the prostrate, burning body of Red Erwin. But Red's skin was still sizzling and smoldering. The fiendish chemistry of a phosphorus burn on human skin is such that it can smolder for weeks, as long as it has contact with oxygen. He completed the 30-foot journey in 12 seconds, and he had been on fire for about 22 seconds total. But his skin continued to burn and smolder for months.

Navigator Pershing Youngkin described what happened next. "I saw Red lying on the flight deck, and I just don't know how to describe it. It was horrible. He was in tremendous pain. [Bombardier] Bill Loesch tried to inject some plasma and had a hard time. He couldn't find a vein. Then [gunner] Herb Schnipper came up to help and they were able to find a vein and gave him a shot of plasma. I heard later a medic said that if they hadn't given him that shot of plasma he would have died of shock. It kept him alive. They also gave him morphine."

Red recalled the desperate scene: "I was laying on the deck, and I was in sheer agony. Bill Loesch and Herb Schnipper got the first aid kit down, and I told Herb to give me a syrette of morphine. But they wanted to keep giving me morphine, and as the plane's first aid man, I knew that was dangerous. I was mortally afraid they were going to give me too much morphine." He told his crewmates, "You're going to kill me if you give me more morphine. Don't give me too much of that stuff, you'll kill me!"

Red remained conscious, so he was feeling the severe pain of his wounds again, but he was able to supervise his treatment. If he had passed out, he probably would have died. Nevertheless, he said, "I was in such pain and agony that I was actually wishing to die. I was so badly burned it would have been a blessing if I had been unconscious."

Despite the pain, Red managed to whisper to his crewmates, "Don't worry about me. Go on with the mission." He was coughing, crying, and spraying blood as his crewmates gently cradled him on the deck of the aircraft. According to Schnipper, "He was praying to God and to his mother."

The crew of the *City of Los Angeles* faced a dilemma.

They were carrying a mortally wounded man with severe burn wounds, and he was in excruciating pain, dying before their eyes. They had to get him to a hospital. But they had standing orders to never, under any circumstances, deviate from their mission as long as the plane was airworthy. As always, by this point in the flight, they were totally committed to the mission. They had to get to the target and drop their bombload, no matter what, before they turned back. This edict by their commander, General LeMay, was unalterable.

But there was a senior officer aboard the *City of Los Angeles* that day: Lt. Col. Eugene Strouse. He was their squadron commander, and he was only one level below LeMay. If anyone had the authority to override LeMay's directive, it was Strouse. He saw the hideously burned form of Red Erwin and decided to divert the aircraft to the nearest US medical facility, which was on the recently captured island of Iwo Jima. He knew this decision could result in a court-martial, but he knew what he had to do.

"My God, abort this mission!" Strouse yelled. "Turn this plane around! Abort the mission. Emergency run to Iwo. Let's get him to Iwo quick!"

The crew jettisoned the bombload, radioed the following B-29s of their decision, pulled the craft up to a fast-cruising altitude of 26,000 feet, swung around to a southbound flight plan, and began a desperate dash to Iwo Jima, which was 600 air miles and three hours away. The strike force proceeded to the target and completed the mission, inflicting significant damage on the enemy chemical factory.

Through a coincidence of timing and geography, Iwo Jima offered a slender but potentially miraculous possibility of saving Red's life. The clock was quickly ticking down toward death for him through blood loss and shock, and the hospital at Guam was at least a six-hour flight away. Although the facilities on Iwo Jima were smaller, they were just three hours away by air. It had been open for only a few weeks.

The epic, incredibly bloody Battle of Iwo Jima had officially ended on March 26, 1945, five weeks after US Marines landed on the volcanic island to vanquish the twenty-one thousand entrenched Japanese defenders and less than three weeks before Red Erwin's injury. The Americans sustained 26,040 casualties in taking the island, including 6,821 killed. The hope was that Iwo Jima's three airfields (one of them unfinished at the time of the American invasion) could be used to attack the Japanese mainland, some 750 miles away. In the meantime, navy construction battalions quickly built bases and a rudimentary military hospital on the island and adapted the airfields to serve as emergency landing strips for B-29s in distress. That achievement eventually spelled salvation for many airmen, and it now offered Red Erwin a chance at survival.

As the crew of the *City of Los Angeles* made their desperate dash to Iwo Jima, they had no way of knowing this act would spark a race against time that would involve a series of medical miracles, the Pentagon, and the president of the United States.

Chapter Five

RACE AGAINST TIME

AS THE *CITY OF LOS ANGELES* HURTLED SOUTH over the ocean, Red Erwin barely clung to life. The moment he was wounded, a countdown clock started ticking down to his death. He could die within minutes or hours, but it was a clock that could only be slowed or stopped through a series of miracles, big and small.

A white phosphorus burn over a large area of the body has two devastating effects: an immediate thermal injury and a lingering, embedded chemical burn that can continue for weeks. Burns from white phosphorus are intensely painful, as painful as hydrofluoric acid and more painful than caustic soda and sulfuric acid.

Sudden death can occur soon after burns to 10 to 15 percent of the total body surface area, and Red had sustained burns well over 20 percent of his body. Without immediate medical treatment, he could die from a wide spectrum of crises that threatened to overwhelm his body, including kidney failure, shock caused by fluid loss, and infection.

As soon as Red's body processed the effect of the wounds, he experienced severe, instantaneous physiological changes, including effects on his heart, lungs, liver, and nervous system. As surgeon Larry Jones of Ohio State University and his colleagues explained in a 2015 research paper, "When skin, an organ about as thick as a sheet of paper toweling, is severely damaged, nearly every system in the body reacts. The metabolic system goes haywire and accelerates; the immune system changes, and the cardiovascular system falters. A first-degree burn has slight impact, but a second-degree burn destroys all of the epidermis (the top layer of skin) and part of the dermis (the underlying layer), and a third-degree burn consumes both. Serious burns cause a catastrophic loss of fluid through the burned area by evaporation and through leakage from damaged capillaries."

The amount of calcium in Red's blood plasma plunged in reaction to the white phosphorus his body was absorbing. This threatened to kill him in as little as sixty minutes, either by shutting down his nervous system or by flooding his body with phosphate, which pushes down calcium levels in the bloodstream. This creates the risk of kidney failure or cardiac arrest. White phosphorus particles spontaneously oxidize and ignite when in contact with oxygen in the atmosphere, forming phosphorus pentoxide, a strong dehydrating agent, which can push fluid levels even further down to dangerous lows.

Red was sustaining tissue damage from the corrosive effects of the phosphorus, and if his body fat absorbed too much of it, hepatic necrosis or renal damage would occur. As minutes and hours ticked by, his risk of fatal immune deficiency spiked, as the availability of his helper-T defensive white blood cells decreased in reaction to the injury.

As long as he was medically untreated, Red's risk of death from multiple organ failure due to infection increased. He had lost the protective barrier of his skin, which keeps blood and fluids in the body and keeps bacteria and viruses out. An invasive infection could easily occur. Roughly 90 percent of burn victims who succumb to the injury are killed by infection. Red needed antibiotics, both locally on the skin and system-wide to his body, but there were none in the B-29 and no one qualified to administer them; and there were very few types of antibiotics available at the time to begin with.

Examining details and photos of Red Erwin's wounds in 2019, leading Israeli reconstructive plastic surgeon and burn specialist Uri Aviv explained, "White phosphorus absorbed through a burn can produce serious electrolyte disturbances, including hyperphosphatemia and hypocalcemia with calcium-phosphate shifts, as soon as one hour after the burn is sustained. This change is responsible for cardiac arrhythmias (heart rate and rhythm abnormalities) post-burn, including prolonged QT intervals, ST-T wave changes, and progressive bradycardia, all of which can lead to cardiac arrest and immediate death. The absorption of a large amount of phosphorus can cause also liver and kidney failure. Furthermore, a relatively small surface area of 10 to 15 percent TBSA [total body surface area] can evoke a sudden and often unexpected death."

According to David Barillo, who served as chief of the US Army's Burn Flight Team from 2005 to 2009 and who reviewed Red's case in 2019, "Once you hit a 20 percent body surface area burn, basically everything in the body does not work correctly. Your heart goes into overdrive, your heart rate goes up from 60 to 80 to about 120 beats per minute, and your blood pressure drops to compensate. Pretty much every organ system is screwed up. Your endocrine system gets very strange, hormones are secreted, cortisol is secreted, your immune system kicks into overdrive. All of that continues until you close the burn. Getting the burn closed fast is really, really important. The reason for the high fatality risk is that your body can't withstand that kind of stress."

As he lay on the deck of the B-29, Red's crewmates saw smoke coming out of his mouth, indicating a possible smoke inhalation injury, which also increases the risk of death. The ignition of white phosphorus creates phosphorus pentoxide, a severe pulmonary irritant. When concentrated in an enclosed space such as the B-29 cabin, it can inflame the respiratory system and interfere with breathing.

Crew members kneeled next to Red, opened the first aid kit, and pulled out needles and medical packs. Through his pain, Red guided Bill Loesch through the process of giving him a shot of morphine and a shot of plasma to try to replenish the copious volume of blood and essential body fluids he was hemorrhaging. But the massive extent of Red's wounds meant these efforts were like drops in the ocean.

In 1945, the standard practice was to inject morphine straight into a muscle rather than a blood vessel. It was not understood that this resulted in most of the morphine simply sitting in the muscle rather than circulating through the bloodstream. So after Loesch injected the morphine shot, Red would have experienced little, if any, immediate pain relief. But this held an advantage. If too much morphine was absorbed into Red's bloodstream too quickly as it hemorrhaged fluids, his blood pressure, which had already plunged, could drop and render him unconscious. Another factor working to Red's advantage was that he was healthy when he was injured, which increased the odds of his withstanding his injuries.

White phosphorus is fat soluble, meaning it can be absorbed through a burn. Contemporary burn doctors understand the best intervention possible is to surgically debride the burns, or remove all the affected tissue, in less than an hour, which is rarely feasible but definitely necessary within the first twenty-four hours. But in 1945, this was not known.

Burn injuries have plagued mankind throughout history. Most of the ancient remedies for burns consisted of topical treatments. An Egyptian papyrus from 1600 BC suggested using salves of honey; Chinese records from 600 BC proposed tea leaves; and Hippocrates in 400 BC proposed pig fat, warm vinegar soaks, and oak bark lotions. In the first century AD, the Roman medical writer Celsus reported the use of wine as a burn solution, and the Arabian physician Muhammad ibn Zakariya al-Razi (also known as Rhases) advocated cold water for pain relief. Few of these methods helped burn victims, though vinegar has antibacterial properties that can prevent infections, one of the major causes of death.

In the sixteenth and seventeenth centuries, some European doctors sensed the importance of early burn removal by surgical excision, but poor hygiene and the lack of antiseptic surgical techniques doomed what was a profound insight.

As for the now-common practice of skin grafting, the first record of it dates from India in the fifth century AD, when a surgeon named Sushrutha used skin strips from the forehead and buttocks and grafted them over the wounds of noses that had been amputated as punishment for crimes. In the 1800s, experiments in skin grafting took place across Europe, and grafting for burns was used by some surgeons into World War II.

But according to contemporary burn surgeon James Holmes, "They got poor results, and surgeons didn't understand what they were doing. From World War I until the 1970s, we went back in time in terms of burn care. The standard treatment for a big burn was to just literally let the burn rot off, as it got picked at and cleaned every day."

There were, however, two fire disasters that led to research breakthroughs in burn care and insights that would help to save Red Erwin's life. The first was the 1921 fire at the Rialto Theatre in New Haven, Connecticut. In studying the cases of the seven fatalities and eighty injured survivors, pharmacologist Frank Underhill suggested that burn deaths may be due to the rapid loss of fluids from the body and that early fluid resuscitation was critical. His conclusion was widely published and adopted into practice.

The second disaster was the 1942 Coconut Grove nightclub fire in Boston that killed 492 people, injured more than 150, and triggered several critical burn care innovations. Intravenous drips of penicillin, which was only then entering mass production, were used successfully to combat staphylococcus bacteria and prevent infection in a number of the victims. This was the first time penicillin was used on non-test subjects.

Doctors confirmed the fluid shift theory of early fluid resuscitation first observed from the Rialto fire victims, and they improved on it by developing precise formulas for giving patients certain amounts of plasma and saline, based on the percentage of body surface area that was burned.

At Massachusetts General Hospital, according to the *British Medical Journal*, plastic surgeon Bradford Cannon developed a new way to treat the burn victims of the Coconut Grove fire. "He discarded the accepted approach of using dyes and tannic acid as the primary treatment for burned tissues, having shown it to be harmful," the article related. "Instead, he and colleagues used gauze containing boric acid and coated with petroleum jelly." The doctors also removed the most severely damaged flesh and used skin grafts.

These innovations were circulated throughout the civilian medical community and widely practiced by military doctors and surgeons, for whom burn injuries became a top priority during World War II.

Two months earlier, on February 19, 1945, seventy thousand US Marines had hit the volcanic black-sand beaches of Iwo Jima (which in Japanese means Sulfur Island). According to one journalist, the extraterrestrially rocky, barren island projected "a sullen sense of evil." Now, Red's hopes for survival lay with a small team of military doctors on Iwo Jima, where so many had died so that others, like Red, could live.

The island was just 650 nautical miles south of Tokyo, directly on the B-29 flight path to Japan, and was used by Japanese fighters to attack the bombers. As a precaution, B-29s flying from the Marianas zigzagged hundreds of miles away from Iwo Jima to minimize the threat. Japanese small and medium bombers also used the island's two operational airfields as a base to stage harassment raids on the B-29 bases themselves, especially on Saipan.

If the Americans could capture the island, they would eliminate these threats, provide a closer base for B-29 raids on Japan, enable fighter escorts to protect the bombers, and provide an emergency landing strip for crippled or low-on-fuel B-29s.

On February 19, D-day of Operation Detachment, marines of the veteran Third, Fourth, and Fifth Divisions stormed ashore against light opposition, which led to a false sense of an easy victory. They were accompanied by shiploads of ammunition and supplies, including a year's supply of toilet paper, one hundred million cigarettes for the Fourth Division alone, and enough food to feed the city of Columbus, Ohio, for a month.

Waiting for them were more than twenty-one thousand Japanese troops commanded by Lt. Gen. Tadamichi Kuribayashi, a brilliant strategist who, before the war, had traveled extensively in the United States and believed it was "the last country in the world that Japan should fight." They had spent months creating an ingenious network of above-ground concrete blockhouses and pillboxes, subterranean bunkers, tunnels, and spider holes, and roll-out guns hidden in cliffside caves to inflict maximum carnage on the invasion force.

At 10:00 a.m., Kuribayashi sprang his trap. "Mortars fell in cascade from hundreds of concealed pits," wrote Sgt. Bill Ross. "Heavy artillery and rapid-firing antiaircraft guns, barrels lowered to rake the beaches, slammed shells into oncoming landing craft and support vessels." Marines were pinned down on the beach, crawling on their bellies and praying.

"The worst was that first night," recalled Col. Frank Caldwell. "We were packed in so tight there was no room to move. They knew right where we were, and of course we were all so concentrated we made a perfect target. They used to fire something we called a 'burping betty,' which looked like a 55-gallon oil drum coming through the air at you. They shot it with rockets off railroad tracks coming out of a cave. It wasn't accurate, but it made enormous craters and was a terrifying weapon until you got used to it."

On February 23, the fourth day of combat, the first marine patrol reached the 556-foot summit of Mount Suribachi and raised the American flag. An image captured by Associated Press photographer Joe Rosenthal of a second marine detachment raising a larger flag became one of the most iconic photographs in American history.

But weeks of brutal fighting would follow. "There were no trees left or brush, really, no cover of any kind," Colonel Caldwell recalled. "It was just throwing flesh against concrete, yard by yard: frontal assault the whole time."

A lone Japanese officer ran out of a cave and charged a flame-throwing tank armed only with his samurai sword. Caldwell marveled, "All by himself. Against a tank. I don't know what the hell he thought he was doing, but the tank just moved that stream right up his body and burned him to a crisp."

Caldwell's troops dropped a phosphorus grenade into a suspicious hole in the rocks, "and in a minute the rocks came all apart and out came this Japanese soldier with a hand grenade, smoking from the phosphorus burns, right at us. We all turned and shot him, just another dirty Jap, you know. Except his helmet came off, and there in the top, inside was a picture of him and his family. He had six kids. There he was with his wife and kids, all dressed up, looking proud. Like one of us. I still remember that."

It took six weeks of savage combat to take the island from the Japanese. In one engagement dubbed "the Meat Grinder," more than eight hundred marines perished while trying to overrun a Japanese position.

Robert Sherrod, a *Time* and *Life* journalist, reported, "Iwo Jima can only be described as a nightmare in hell."

On March 4, 1945, the first emergency landing by a B-29 on Iwo Jima was made when the *Dinah Might*, low on fuel, touched down. On March 26 the Americans declared the island secure, but skirmishes with Japanese holdouts continued for weeks.

Twenty-seven marines and sailors were awarded the Medal of Honor for their actions during the fighting for Iwo Jima, and more than half were posthumous. It was the highest number of Medals of Honor given in any World War II battle. Adm. Chester W. Nimitz, commander of the US Pacific Fleet, declared that "uncommon valor was a common virtue" on Iwo Jima.

But the cost of victory was horrific. The battle caused 26,040 US casualties, including 6,821 fatalities, with another 2,600 Americans incapacitated due to combat fatigue. It was the deadliest battle of the war for the marines, and one general dubbed it "the most savage and the most costly battle in the history of the Marine Corps." Most of the twenty-one thousand Japanese troops on the island were killed.

Was it worth it? Unfortunately, one of the main justifications for Operation Detachment—to provide fighter escorts for B-29 raids—was achieved only minimally, as only ten such escort missions ever occurred. Even the newest American fighter, the P-51D Mustang, didn't have adequate navigational equipment and range for the 1,500-mile round trip necessary to reach most Japanese targets.

The victory, however, did provide an emergency landing strip for crippled B-29s, but less so than has often been reported. After the war, many accounts noted that 2,251 B-29s landed on the island through the rest of the war, and because each plane carried eleven crewmen, the lives of a total of 24,761 airmen were saved. But military historian Capt. Robert Burrell analyzed the evidence and concluded that most of the landings were not major emergencies but minor repairs, reloading bombs, training, or refueling. "Of the 2,251 touchdowns popularized in most history texts, the vast majority did not result from crucial or unavoidable crises," he wrote. "Most landings were for the purpose of refueling, planned or otherwise." He concluded that capturing Iwo Jima was helpful to the B-29 effort but not worth the cost in American lives.

Yet, for Red Erwin, the sacrifice of those marines created a possibility for his salvation.

––––––

When the *City of Los Angeles* landed at Iwo Jima, Red was lowered by a crane, using the B-29's side hatch adjacent to the flight engineer's position, and rushed to a field hospital complex consisting of wooden shacks and tents dug into the volcanic soil and a medical station that had originally been dug into a cave by the Japanese defenders.

Red heard the panicked voice of a doctor. "We've got to get this phosphorus out of his eyes. Otherwise he's going to be blind!"

The doctors and nurses went to work on his horrible wounds, and he drifted in and out of consciousness.

Several things happened quickly, almost simultaneously. The doctors and nurses monitored his heartbeat and conducted an airway and breathing evaluation to check for obstructions. They asked Red's crewmates for all the details of the injury. They administered morphine. They hooked Red up to an intravenous plasma drip and injected him with Ringer's lactate solution, a water-based solution of sodium chloride, sodium lactate, potassium chloride, and calcium chloride. These steps were intended to offset the loss of blood, water, and electrolytes and to keep his blood pressure up and reduce the very high risk of sudden heart failure.

The medical team removed Red's phosphorus-embedded shirt, pants, and flotation device. They focused on removing pieces of phosphorus from his head, face, hands, right arm, and right torso. They irrigated his wounds with water, spread anti-infection boric acid cream on them, and closed them with saline-soaked gauze to stop oxygen from reigniting the phosphorus particles.

Regardless of how heroic and skilled the doctors and nurses were, given the severity of his wounds and the relatively primitive state of burn care in 1945, it would be a miracle if Red survived the first day. His crewmates visited him at the medical station, and then they flew the *City of Los Angeles* back to Guam to resume their duties.

At one point, Red heard sad, dirge-like music, the kind you hear at funerals. *Oh no, angels!* he thought, speculating that the angels who accompanied him during his encounter with the phosphorus bomb were returning to escort him to another world. He addressed his thoughts directly to the Creator: *God, You saved me. Surely You're not going to come get me now. I want to go home!*

But the music turned out to be from a radio announcement of the death of President Franklin D. Roosevelt. When much of America was praying for the soul of the late president, Red Erwin was praying for the strength to conquer death.

Four months before Red Erwin made his desperate plea for divine inter-vention in the sky over the Pacific Ocean, another soldier's prayer may have shaped the course of World War II in Europe.

On the morning of December 8, 1944, at Third Army headquar-ters in an old barracks in France, Lt. Gen. George S. Patton Jr. placed a call to chaplain James O'Neill, a Roman Catholic priest, stationed in a nearby building. Weeks of heavy rains had stalled the Allied advance across Western Europe. The legendary Patton, a churchgoing Episcopalian, was furious and desperate. He decided it was time to ask for God's help.

"This is General Patton," he announced to the priest. "Do you have a good prayer for weather? We must do something about those rains if we are to win the war."

The chaplain noted, "It usually isn't a customary thing among men of my profession to pray for clear weather to kill fellow men."

Patton ignored the comment and insisted, "We've got to get not only the chaplains but every man in the Third Army to pray. We must ask God to stop these rains."

The chaplain went off to check his prayer books but couldn't find any weather prayers. So he composed one and typed it on an index card, writing in the grandiloquent style he figured Patton would like.

Almighty and most merciful Father, we humbly beseech Thee, of Thy great goodness, to restrain these immoderate rains with which we have had to contend. Grant us fair weather for Battle. Graciously hearken to us as soldiers who call upon Thee that, armed with Thy power, we may advance from victory to victory, and crush the oppression and wickedness of our enemies and establish Thy justice among men and nations.

O'Neill strode across the rainy courtyard in a heavy trench coat and deliv-ered the draft to the general.

Patton loved the prayer. He told the chaplain, "Have 250,000 copies printed and see to it that every man in the Third Army gets one."

The surprised chaplain replied, "Very well, sir!"

"Chaplain, sit down for a moment," said Patton. "I want to talk to you about this business of prayer."

Years later, O'Neill described the scene: "He rubbed his face in his hands, was silent for a moment, then rose and walked over to the high window, and stood there with his back toward me as he looked out on the falling rain. As usual, he was dressed stunningly, and his six-foot-two powerfully built physique made an unforgettable silhouette against the great window. The General Patton I saw there was the Army Commander to whom the welfare of the men under him was a matter of personal responsibility."

Patton asked, "Chaplain, how much praying is being done in the Third Army?"

"Does the General mean by chaplains or by the men?"

"By everybody," Patton replied.

O'Neill said, "I am afraid to admit it, but I do not believe that much praying is going on. When there is fighting, everyone prays, but now with this constant rain—when things are quiet, dangerously quiet—men just sit and wait for things to happen. Prayer out here is difficult. Both chaplains and men are removed from a special building with a steeple. Prayer to most of them is a formal, ritualized affair, involving special posture and a liturgical setting. I do not believe that much praying is being done."

Patton sat down at his desk and leaned back in his chair, fiddling with a pencil. "Chaplain," he explained, "I am a strong believer in prayer. There are three ways that men get what they want: by planning, by working, and by praying. Any great military operation takes careful planning or thinking. Then you must have well-trained troops to carry it out: that's working. But between the plan and the operation there is always an unknown. That unknown spells defeat or victory, success or failure. It is the reaction of the actors to the ordeal when it actually comes. Some people call that getting the breaks; I call it God. God has His part or margin in everything. That's where prayer comes in."

The general continued, "Up to now, in the Third Army, God has been very good to us. We have never retreated; we have suffered no defeats, no famine, no epidemics. This is because a lot of people back home are praying for us. We were lucky in Africa, in Sicily, and in Italy. Simply because people prayed. But we have to pray for ourselves, too." If all his soldiers prayed, Patton suggested, "It will be like plugging in on a current whose source is in Heaven."

To reinforce the power of the 250,000 prayer cards, Patton ordered the chaplain to issue 3,200 copies of a training letter to be sent out to chaplains and officers in every unit of the Third Army, directing them to exhort their men to "Pray alone. Pray with others. Pray by night and pray by day. Pray for the cessation of immoderate rains, for good weather for Battle. Pray for the defeat of our wicked enemy whose banner is injustice and whose good is oppression. Pray for victory. Pray for our Army, and Pray for Peace." The letter concluded, "With prayer, we cannot fail."

Mass distribution of both the prayer cards and the letter was completed by December 12. Patton and his men, tens of thousands of them, began to pray.

Four days later, on December 16, Adolf Hitler launched what became known as the Battle of the Bulge, a massive counteroffensive that buzz-sawed through the Allied lines and threw Patton's troops into disarray. "The Germans crept out of the Schnee Eifel Forest in the midst of heavy rains, thick fogs, and swirling ground mists that muffled sound, blotted out the sun, and reduced visibility to a few yards," wrote Chaplain O'Neill. A ferocious battle ensued, and American troops in some areas had to pull back. The Germans were on the verge of gaining the strategic initiative and stopping the Allied liberation of Europe for an unknown period of time.

The rains continued, and Patton's men kept fighting—and praying. Then, on December 20, the rains stopped and a bright sun appeared.

A full week of clear skies and ideal flying weather opened up, enabling Allied planes to bomb and strafe the German positions with impunity and throw Hitler's army back on its heels. "Our planes came over by tens, hundreds, and thousands," remembered O'Neill. "They knocked out hundreds of tanks, killed thousands of enemy troops in the Bastogne salient, and harried the enemy as he valiantly tried to bring up reinforcements. The 101st Airborne, with the Fourth, Ninth, and Tenth Armored Divisions, which saved Bastogne, and other divisions which assisted so valiantly in driving the Germans home, will testify to the great support rendered by our air forces. General Patton prayed for fair weather for battle. He got it."

The Allies regained momentum on the western front and resumed their grinding and ultimately victorious march into Germany.

"That man did some potent praying," Patton marveled about Chaplain O'Neill.

He awarded the priest a Bronze Star.

———

At 9:30 a.m. on April 12, 1945, at a point 225 miles south of Tokyo and 1,500 feet over the Pacific Ocean, Sgt. Henry "Red" Erwin had held the lives of twelve Americans in his hands, including his own. He also held in his hands the existence and potential of the hundreds of descendants those airmen were destined to have if God were to bless them with children, grandchildren, and great-grandchildren. The officers and crew were like brothers to him, and now their lives depended on what he did. In those few seconds, Red Erwin prayed to God for a miracle—and it happened. That night, as Red lay in a hospital bed with severe, life-threatening burn wounds, another series of miracles would be needed if he were to survive.

While Red lay on the edge of survival, his superiors, stunned by the magnitude of what he had done and endured, hastily typed up a Medal of Honor recommendation. Early the next morning they relayed it to

General LeMay on Guam, who signed it immediately and relayed it to his superior, Brig. Gen. Lauris Norstad, chief of staff of the Twentieth Air Force in Washington, DC, stressing that time was of the essence to get final approval before Erwin died of his wounds.

At the Pentagon, General Norstad rushed through approvals by General Arnold, the chief of US Army Air Forces, and Gen. George C. Marshall, chief of staff of the US Army, in record time—six and a half hours. It is believed to be the fastest approval in modern history for the Medal of Honor. The paperwork was then rushed to the White House for final approval and signature by President Harry S. Truman.

———

The Medal of Honor is the highest award the United States can bestow on a member of the military services. It is a distinction reserved for only the most extraordinary displays of "conspicuous gallantry and intrepidity at the risk of life above and beyond the call of duty," and it is approved and awarded by the president on behalf of the US Congress.

Since the Civil War, more than forty million men and women have served in the US Army, Navy, Air Force, Marine Corps, and Coast Guard. Thus far, only 3,505 of them have been awarded the Medal of Honor.

The origins of the medal trace back to 1782, when Gen. George Washington began the tradition of recognizing acts of courage on the battlefield with a purple heart made of cloth for those soldiers who had been wounded. During the war with Mexico, in 1847, a certificate of merit was instituted to recognize soldiers who showed distinction in action.

The system of military awards as a formal process began during the Civil War, when Abraham Lincoln approved a navy medal of valor "to be bestowed upon such petty officers, seamen, landsmen, and Marines as shall most distinguish themselves by their gallantry and other seaman-like qualities during the present war," and an army medal of honor "to such noncommissioned officers and privates as shall most distinguish themselves by their gallantry in action, and other soldier-like qualities, during the present insurrection." In 1863, Congress made the Medal of Honor a permanent decoration.

The first action to be recognized with a Medal of Honor was performed on February 13–14, 1861, just before the beginning of the Civil War, when Irish-born US Army assistant surgeon Bernard J. D. Irwin rescued sixty soldiers of the Seventh Infantry from Apache warriors in Arizona by bluffing them into believing he had an arriving rescue force much larger than the mere fourteen troops he commanded. But the Medal of Honor had not yet been created by Congress and wouldn't be presented in Irwin's honor until 1894.

The first Medals of Honor ever presented were given on March 25, 1863, to six soldiers known as Andrew's Raiders by Secretary of War Edwin Stanton in his office in the War Department. The six men had volunteered for a raiding-and-sabotage operation later dubbed the Great Locomotive Chase and led by spymaster James J. Andrews. They stole a train 200 miles behind Confederate lines at Big Shanty (now known as Kennesaw), Georgia, on April 12, 1862, in an attempt to knock out a vital railroad running from Atlanta to Chattanooga, Tennessee. After the award ceremony, the first Medal of Honor recipients had a private audience with President Lincoln at the White House.

Four days of combat at Gettysburg, Pennsylvania, in 1863 resulted in fifty-eight Medals of Honor being awarded, including the first Hispanic awardee, Corp. Joseph De Castro.

During the climactic Pickett's Charge on the third day at Gettysburg, Lt. Alonzo H. Cushing was killed as he stood and fought while ten thousand Confederate troops rushed his artillery battery. His Medal of Honor story wasn't fully appreciated until 150 years later, when President Barack Obama finalized the honor and presented the medal to a distant relative.

The first black awardee was former slave William Harvey Carney for his actions on July 18, 1863, at Fort Wagner, South Carolina, with the Fifty-Fourth Massachusetts Infantry.

One epic story is that of Union flag–bearer Pvt. Thomas J. Higgins at the siege of Vicksburg, Mississippi, in May 1863. Prior to an assault on the Confederate position around the besieged city, Higgins was told not to stop until he planted the regimental colors inside the Confederate lines. Most of his company of the Ninety-Ninth Illinois was wiped out in the attack, but Higgins continued to run forward, tripping over bodies and holding his banner high. Amazed Texas troops decided to hold their fire and cheered him on. They waved their hats at him and pulled him over as he tumbled into their fieldworks. He planted his flag—and was taken prisoner. In the 1890s, those same Confederate troops testified on his behalf before Congress and helped Higgins receive the Medal of Honor.

To date, there have been eighty-eight African American recipients, fifty-nine Hispanic American recipients, thirty-three Asian American recipients, and thirty-two Native American recipients. Many of these recipients received the award decades after the action for which they were honored, when it was evident that racist sentiments prevented or delayed their awards. Today there are only seventy-one living recipients of the Medal of Honor.

In 1917, a Medal of Honor review board struck the names of 911 medal recipients from the honor roll, ruling that during and after the Civil War, the medal was distributed too liberally and even frivolously. In one case, 864 members of the Twenty-Seventh Maine were awarded the nation's highest honor just for reenlisting.

For actions during the Pearl Harbor attack on December 7, 1941, fifteen sailors were awarded the medal, but only five survived the battle. About half of all Medals of Honor have been awarded posthumously. Of the 238 men who earned Medals of Honor for actions during the Vietnam War, 63 gave up their own lives by falling on land mines or grenades to save their brothers in arms.

Several times Congress waived the combat requirement so peacetime achievements could be honored with the medal, including Col. Charles Lindbergh's historic 1927 transatlantic flight, the 1933 daring and dangerous deep-sea rescue by an experimental diving bell of thirty-three men trapped aboard the sunken submarine USS *Squalus* off the coast of New Hampshire, Comdr. Richard E. Byrd's polar explorations, and even the valiant rescue of a hotel guest during an earthquake in Japan.

Medals of Honor were posthumously awarded to twenty-four soldiers for their actions at the Battle of the Little Bighorn. The Indian Wars of the nineteenth century produced 423 Medals of Honor, just ten fewer than World War II. Almost sixty military personnel received the award for actions during the 1900 Boxer Rebellion in China, an episode long forgotten by many Americans.

Some Medal of Honor awardees died in combat and never knew their sacrifices would be recognized. Others lived long lives that were defined at least in part by the medal they wore on special occasions. The army, navy, and air force each has its own Medal of Honor design, and the marines and coast guard use the navy version. The army version is described by the Army's Institute of Heraldry as:

A gold five-pointed star, each point tipped with trefoils, 1–1/2 inches [3.8 cm] wide, surrounded by a green laurel wreath and suspended from a gold bar inscribed VALOR, surmounted by an eagle. In the center of the star, Minerva's head surrounded by the words UNITED STATES OF AMERICA. On each ray of the star is a green oak leaf. On the reverse is a bar engraved THE CONGRESS TO with a space for engraving the name of the recipient. [The pendant and suspension bar are made of gilding metal, with the eye, jump rings, and suspension ring made of red brass.] The finish on the pendant and suspension bar is hard enameled, gold plated, and rose-gold plated, with polished highlights.

One awardee, World War II veteran Bob Maxwell, kept his Medal of Honor for nearly seventy-five years after the event that triggered it: grabbing a blanket and throwing himself on a German hand grenade in

France to save his squad mates. Maxwell died on May 11, 2019, in Bend, Oregon, at the age of ninety-eight. At the time of his death, he was the nation's oldest Medal of Honor recipient.

The Medal of Honor was issued to one president, Theodore Roosevelt, for his actions in the Spanish-American War. It was awarded to one woman, Civil War surgeon and POW Mary Edwards Walker, for her civilian service during the First Battle of Bull Run and other actions. And the highest military award was presented to one coast guardsman, Signalman First Class Douglas Munro, a Canadian-born serviceman who was killed while evacuating five hundred marines under fire on September 27, 1942, during the Battle of Guadalcanal.

Medal of Honor awardees have included teenagers and late-career soldiers. Recipients have hailed from every state and every branch of the service and have included pilots, seamen, chaplains, truck drivers, and medics.

Why did the Medal of Honor recipients risk their lives the way they did? "Some talked of entering a zone of slow-motion invulnerability, where they were spectators at their own heroism," noted Nick Del Calzo, who has studied the accounts of scores of Medal of Honor recipients. "But for most, the answer was simpler and more straightforward: They couldn't let their buddies down."

According to Col. Jack Jacobs, who earned a Medal of Honor for rescuing thirteen Allied soldiers under fire while advising a South Vietnamese infantry battalion in 1968 and being severely wounded himself, "When you're in a combat situation, you're surrounded by your comrades and your buddies, many of whom were killed or wounded and you have an impulse to not abandon them and do what you can to make sure the mission gets completed and the rest of the force gets saved."

Many recipients have explained their actions as reflex actions to save their brother warriors or said they were just doing their jobs. Many have said they do not consider themselves to be heroes, but they accepted and wear the Medal of Honor as a tribute to the real heroes: the men and women they served with and the many who did not return from combat. After battle, some Medal of Honor recipients sought out a church or a quiet spot to pray both for their comrades and for the enemy troops who fell in battle.

Some Medal of Honor stories seem too incredible to be true. During the Battle of Okinawa in April and May 1945, PFC Desmond Doss, a religious conscientious objector who served as a medic and refused to carry a weapon, saved seventy-five wounded Americans on the battlefield by singlehandedly roping them one by one down a 400-foot-cliff. Like Red Erwin, he was sustained by prayer in his moment of destiny, repeatedly declaring, *Dear God, please let me get just one more man.*

Many Medal of Honor recipients have gone on to live lives of great distinction and fulfillment, but others have been burdened by the recognition. "For those who earn it, the medal is a loaded gift," wrote the *Wall Street Journal*'s Michael Phillips in 2019. "It's a source of instant celebrity, and an entree into a world of opportunity and adulation. It's also a reminder of what is often the worst day of their lives. And it is a summons to a lifetime of service from those who did something so courageous as young men—so at odds with their own chances of survival—that it was beyond what duty demands. Some embrace the role of Medal of Honor recipient, spending their lives speaking to civic groups, raising money for charities, and hobnobbing with movie stars, politicians and professional athletes. Others resent having their private grief turned into a public display."

Some recipients have battled depression, post-traumatic stress disorder (PTSD), and periods of great despair and failure in civilian life. Pvt. Thomas C. Neibaur of Idaho was the first Mormon to receive the Medal of Honor, which recognized his actions in France on October 16, 1918. In 1939, discouraged by misfortune and unable to feed his family, Neibaur mailed his Medal of Honor and other decorations to Congress, stating, "I cannot eat them." Within three years, both he and his wife died, and their four sons were sent to an orphanage in Michigan.

An equally tragic story was that of Vietnam-era Medal of Honor recipient Kenneth M. Kays, who originally fled to Canada to avoid the draft as a conscientious objector, and then joined the 101st Airborne as a medic. Despite having his leg blown off on May 7, 1970, during a firefight in Hue, he crawled around the battlefield to administer first aid to other soldiers. Back home in Illinois after receiving the Medal of Honor, Kays suffered from mental health and drug problems. He was committed to a hospital for the criminally insane, and he committed suicide at age forty-two.

For Sgt. Dakota Meyer, the recognition reminded him of the worst day of his life. As a twenty-one-year-old corporal, he saved several lives during a 2009 ambush in Afghanistan, but he was too late to save three other marines and a navy medical corpsman. The Medal of Honor enabled him to meet the president of the United States, receive free tickets to NASCAR races and the Super Bowl, and collect a monthly stipend of $1,366. But Meyer said, "I look at that medal and I could throw up. I hate it and I resent it."

For Red Erwin, the question wasn't how the Medal of Honor would affect his life, but whether the army could get him the medal before he died.

Chapter Six

THE GATES OF ETERNITY

EARLY ON THE AFTERNOON OF APRIL 12, 1945,
the same day a phosphorus bomb exploded on Red Erwin in the *City of Los Angeles*, the president of the United States announced, "I have a terrific pain in the back of my head."

Franklin D. Roosevelt was at his vacation retreat in Warm Springs, Georgia, sitting for a portrait. With him were two of his most beloved companions: his Yorkshire terrier, Fala, and former mistress, Lucy Mercer. His wife, Eleanor, was in Washington, DC, unaware of Mercer's recent reappearance in the president's life.

The pain the sixty-three-year-old president was feeling was a massive cerebral hemorrhage, and it knocked him unconscious.

He slumped forward and was carried to his bed, where cardiologist Howard Bruenn injected a shot of adrenaline into FDR's heart to revive him. It didn't work.

On the exact same day that Red Erwin fell toward the abyss of death, his commander in chief was struggling for life as well, the victim of wartime stress, exhaustion, timid and incompetent medical treatment, twelve years of notoriously inedible and undernutritious White House meals concocted by housekeeper-turned-chef Henrietta Nesbitt (a friend of

Eleanor's who the first lady insisted on keeping despite FDR's protests), decades of chain-smoking, and a lack of exercise due to the polio that had paralyzed his legs since the age of thirty-nine.

Roosevelt lingered for some two hours but died at 3:35 p.m. He had been the president for more than twelve years, and he led the nation through the Depression and to the edge of victory in the Second World War. Now he was dead. Mercer and the portrait artist quietly departed Warm Springs.

On Capitol Hill in Washington, DC, at 5:00 p.m., Vice President Harry S. Truman was about to enjoy a glass of bourbon in the office of Speaker of the House Samuel T. Rayburn when he was told to call the White House. This was unusual because, so far, Truman had spent his eighty-two days as vice president almost completely ignored by Roosevelt. In cabinet meetings and in two short one-on-one meetings with Roosevelt, Truman could see how sick the president was and how skeletal he appeared.

Truman was told to get to the White House "as fast as you can." He turned to Rayburn and exclaimed, with a premonition of what was about to happen, "Jesus Christ and General Jackson!" Truman raced across the capital city by car and arrived at 1600 Pennsylvania Avenue at 5:25 p.m.

"Harry, the president is dead," said Eleanor Roosevelt. Technically, Truman had been president for about two hours, since Roosevelt's heart stopped beating, but he didn't know it until now.

Hours later, Truman recalled, "I felt like the moon, the stars, and all the planets had fallen on me."

Truman had admired FDR as the titanic figure he was, but he saw his flaws too, and he was bitter about Roosevelt inexplicably shutting him out of Oval Office affairs at a time when FDR must have known how sick he was. "I was handicapped by lack of knowledge of both foreign and domestic affairs—due principally to Mr. Roosevelt's inability to pass on responsibility. He was always careful to see that no credit went to anyone else for accomplishment." Truman later privately asserted that FDR's cabinet was a "mudhole," and the people he inherited from FDR were "crackpots and the lunatic fringe," including one longtime Roosevelt crony, Henry Morgenthau Jr., the secretary of the treasury, who Truman thought was a "blockhead" and a "nut."

As Red Erwin battled for life in a hospital bed on Iwo Jima, his new commander in chief took up his post at the top of the Allied war effort in the Oval Office, the cockpit of what would soon become the world's first nuclear superpower.

Despite their age difference—Erwin was twenty-four years old and Truman was sixty-one—they had many things in common. They were both modest, humble, reliable men from the heartland of small-town America. They were both dirt farmers who had known struggle and hardship. They both lacked a college education but knew the value of hard work. Both were God-fearing men who studied the Bible and loved reading history and current events. They were both men of integrity who were madly in love with their wives. And they had both experienced the horrors of combat.

Truman and Erwin had something else in common: they generated great affection from the people who knew them, the product of their warm, modest, reliable, and humble personalities. In Truman's case, the effect was remarkable in light of his exalted position and how it continued even when he was president and had the pressures of the world on his shoulders.

Longtime White House clerk William Hopkins explained, "Truman probably had the human touch to the greatest extent of any president I've worked for."

Presidential assistant David Stowe recalled, "Each and every one of us had a close personal relationship with him. In my case, I felt he was like a second father to me; he was kind, he was decisive, he never bawled anybody out in public; if he had anything to say to them, he always said it in private. A guy like that you just have to love."

When Secretary of State Dean Acheson had to leave the country when his wife was gravely ill, Truman called the hospital each day to check on her status and then relayed the news to Acheson by transoceanic telephone. Acheson confessed, "Well, this is the kind of person that one can adore."

The love for Truman went deep, even to the lowliest White House employees. A White House messenger explained: "The first thing you find out is that he calls you by name. You don't feel like some kind of a servant, but like a real human being. One day he was walking along with General George Marshall, and I tried to slip by quickly, but he stopped and introduced me to General Marshall in a way that seemed like I was somebody who was real important."

A White House usher agreed, saying, "When a butler or doorman or usher would enter the room, the Trumans would introduce him to whoever happened to be sitting in the room, even if it were a king or a prime minister."

Truman assistant Ken Hechler explained, "He always made everybody feel they were a part of a great team. This extended not only to the staff members but also to the cooks and ushers and carpenters and electricians, all of whom just revered Truman because he knew about them as individuals and knew about their families."

On his first full day as president, April 13, Truman entered the Oval Office at 9:00 a.m., sat in FDR's chair, squirmed, rolled it back and forth, leaned back, let out a sigh, pulled up to the desk, and plunged into his work. Adm. William D. Leahy, the military chief of staff, brought in a pile of urgent papers and thought the pile looked taller than Truman in the chair. Another aide looked in and saw Truman swiveling in the chair, peering anxiously through his thick spectacles. "I'm not big enough," he muttered. "I'm not big enough for this job."

Truman had no grand vision, no master plan, only an in-box that was soon overflowing with the colossal challenges of finishing the war, postwar economic conversion, demobilization of hundreds of thousands of American troops, and the emergency needs of entire nations of refugees wandering across the ruins of Europe. Above all, he grappled with the inevitable clash between the two ideological empires of democracy and communism. Ahead lay Hiroshima, the Marshall Plan, the Cold War, the nuclear age, and Korea.

The man at the desk wore a double-breasted suit adorned with a World War I discharge button. He was a compact five-eight and 175 pounds, with warm hazel eyes and thick glasses that the chief White House usher said "magnified his eyes enormously, giving him a peering, owlish gaze." At sixty-one, he was the flesh-and-blood incarnation of the disappointments and promise of middle America in the early twentieth century. He had grown up in small-town Missouri at the convergence of the West, the South, and the Midwest. He had swept floors and bussed tables at the malt shop on the town square. He had wooed and won the hand of a local girl from a well-to-do family. And he spent ten years plowing fields as a dirt farmer before going to war at the age of thirty-two.

In 1918, as a captain of an artillery battery charging into the slaughterhouse of the Meuse-Argonne forest, a single battle that killed twenty-six thousand American troops, Truman quickly discovered two talents that later defined his style as president: a skill for fast, instinctive decision-making and the ability to inspire fierce loyalty among his men.

Nearly eighty years after the battle, Truman's chief mechanic, McKinley Wooden, reflected on his boss: "He was the best in the world. For the simple reason that he was a gentleman from the word *go*. If you soldiered, he got along with you. If you didn't, he gave you some trouble."

Earlier that summer, in fact, Truman's men had panicked, broken, and run under a nighttime barrage, and Truman chased, screamed, and swore at them until they stood their ground.

"In combat, he was pretty cool," the 103-year-old Wooden recalled in 1996. "He gave you credit, and he backed you up all the way."

Truman said that combat had taught him a crucial lesson: "There are a great many different factors that go into the making of a command decision, but in the end there has to be just one decision—or there is no command."

In his first few days in office, as Red Erwin hovered between life and death in the Pacific, Truman delivered a radio address to the country's armed forces: "As a veteran of the First World War, I have seen death on the battlefield," he said. "When I fought in France with the Thirty-fifth Division, I saw good officers and men fall and be replaced. . . . I know the strain, the mud, the misery, the utter weariness of the soldier in the field. And I know too his courage, his stamina, his faith in his comrades, his country and himself."

Truman's postwar career was a mixture of failure and comebacks: near bankruptcy from the collapse of his haberdashery business, election as a county commissioner, defeat for reelection, two years in a career wilderness as a membership salesman for the Kansas City Automobile Association, seven years as presiding judge of Jackson County, and ten years as a New Deal US senator, when he gained national attention for investigating defense industry waste and fraud.

"His personal and professional experience, like that of many men, had been an ambiguous blend of success and failure," observed Alonzo Hamby. "The security and confidence he had achieved were fragile."

"I get up at five-thirty every morning," Truman told reporter John Hersey. "Most people don't know when the best part of the day is: it's the early morning."

Many mornings he would charge through the streets and parks of Washington on a vigorous power walk for a mile or two at the military regulation pace of 120 steps per minute, swinging a rubber-tipped walking cane and accompanied by ten Secret Service agents, some wielding machine guns.

"I've been taking these walks for thirty years now. I got in the habit of getting up and moving around smart in the early mornings on the farm, and then when I got into politics, I couldn't stop," he explained as Hersey trotted alongside. "A man in my position has a public duty to keep himself in good condition. You can't be mentally fit unless you're physically fit. A walk like this keeps your circulation up to where you can think clearly. That old pump has to keep squirting the juice into your brain, you know."

After his morning walk, Truman worked out in the small gym and then ate a light breakfast with a shot of bourbon. He fit into suits he wore fifteen years earlier. As early as 7:00 a.m., he would enter the Oval Office, park his briefcase on the walnut desk, and dump out the papers he had worked on the night before.

Truman's Oval Office executive style was relentlessly decisive. He tackled most every decision quickly and clearly, and he worked through his in-box at machine-gun speed. In his memoirs, he wrote, "I discovered that being a president is like riding a tiger. A man has to keep on riding or be swallowed. The fantastically crowded nine months of 1945 taught me that a president either is constantly on top of events or, if he hesitates, events will soon be on top of him. I never felt that I could let up for a single moment."

"You could go into his office with a question and come out with a decision more swiftly than any man I have ever known," Averell Harriman observed.

In sharp contrast to the roundabout decision-making style of patrician FDR, "Truman was a dirt farmer," said assistant Kenneth Hechler. "He plowed a straight furrow when it came to issuing directions and making decisions."

Truman aide David Bell recalled, "We hadn't expected very much, but as time went on, we realized, here was a guy with a backbone of iron! Here was a guy came from the middle of the United States and was not well educated, who was thoroughly up on the world, and was doing his damnedest."

———

On one of his first days as president, Harry S. Truman approved the recommendation for Red Erwin's Medal of Honor. Truman had epic decisions ahead of him, on monumental issues affecting America and the world, but Red's medal was one of the easiest decisions he ever had to make.

Truman was to personally present Medals of Honor to many American servicemen during his seven years in office, often in Rose Garden ceremonies, and his awe and respect for their deeds of courage was so great that he often told the recipients, "I'd rather wear that medal than be president of the United States."

Red Erwin had no way of knowing this, but Truman would also soon be responsible for showing Red what he would do with the rest of his life, what his destiny would be, and what he was put on earth for.

Word quickly arrived from the Pentagon that Red's Medal of Honor was signed off on by the president. In the meantime, General LeMay's staff had canvassed the Pacific, trying to find a Medal of Honor to present to Red before he died. None were available except for one in a display case in the office of Maj. Gen. Robert C. Richardson, commander of the US Army, Pacific (Hawaiian Department), at Hickam Field in Hawaii, nearly four thousand miles away.

LeMay dispatched a B-29 to Hawaii with orders for the crew to get their hands on the medal. When they arrived at Hickam, the glass case was locked and the general and the key were nowhere to be found. So they smashed open the case, seized the medal, and bolted back to Guam.

Red lingered at the Iwo Jima field hospital for three days while doctors frantically labored to stabilize his grave condition. Sections of his scorched skin were removed, multiple units of plasma were administered, and he was wrapped from head to toe in sterile gauze. He resembled an Egyptian mummy.

The job of informing Red's family of his injuries fell to a Roman Catholic chaplain on Iwo Jima, Capt. George Lehman. On April 16, just after Red was evacuated to the larger hospital at Guam, Lehman wrote to Betty: "It is my duty to inform you that your husband, Henry E. Erwin, was admitted into our hospital for the treatment of third degree burns of his head, face, neck, hands, forearms, and legs." After some reassuring words on Red's progress, he added, "He was a remarkable patient. In spite of his intense discomfort, he was unusually considerate, concerned less about himself, really, than about you. His first request when I came to his side was that I write you."

On April 19, at a brief bedside ceremony in Fleet Hospital 103 on Guam, with the officers and crew of the *City of Los Angeles* looking on, General LeMay and Maj. Gen. Willis H. Hale, the commanding general, Army Air Forces, Pacific Ocean Areas, and deputy commander of the Twentieth Air Force, presented the Medal of Honor to Sgt. Henry E. Erwin.

General LeMay told Red, "Your effort to save the lives of your fellow airmen is the most extraordinary kind of heroism I know."

When they told Red he was going to receive a Medal of Honor, he was too wracked with pain to care. "I was not in any condition to appreciate anything," he said later.

Red was the only Superfortress crewman to receive the Medal of Honor for service aboard a B-29. One of LeMay's pilots, however, Michael J. Novosel, would be awarded the medal twenty-four years later for his actions as a helicopter pilot in Vietnam at the age of forty-seven.

General Hale gently laid the medal on the bedsheet covering Red, who was swathed in gauze, his body almost completely hidden except for a small area of his face. Hale said, "Today is the first time I have ever had the honor of presenting the Congressional Medal of Honor. I've never known of one being more deserved. It is an example of sheer guts and will power in overcoming physical agony. I think the event as expressed in the citation is outstanding in military history."

Two photographs were taken of the bedside ceremony, and in them, the expressions on the faces of Red's crewmates are funereal, reflecting sadness at his wounds and sadness at their impending farewell. LeMay does not appear in the photos, perhaps not wanting to intrude on the solemnity and fragility of the moment.

The Medal of Honor was presented to Henry E. Erwin on April 19, 1945, at his Guam hospital bedside. (US Air Force)

Usually, it takes months or even years for a Medal of Honor recommendation to be approved and the medal awarded. In the case of Red Erwin, it took seven hours and thirty minutes for approval by the Department of Defense and just six days for the medal to be presented to him. It happened so quickly that the official general order wouldn't be published for seven weeks:

MEDAL OF HONOR

STAFF SERGEANT HENRY EUGENE ERWIN (Air Mission)

Rank and organization: Staff Sergeant, US Army Air Corps, 52d Bombardment Squadron, 29th Bombardment Group, 20th Air Force

Place and date: Koriyama, Japan, 12 April 1945

Entered service at: Bessemer, Ala.

G.O. No.: 44, 6 June 1945

Citation: He was the radio operator of a B-29 airplane leading a group formation to attack Koriyama, Japan. He was charged with the additional duty of dropping phosphorus smoke bombs to aid in assembling the group when the launching point was reached. Upon entering the assembly area, aircraft fire and enemy fighter opposition was encountered. Among the phosphoresce bombs launched by S/Sgt. Erwin, 1 proved faulty, exploding in the launching chute, and shot back into the interior of the aircraft, striking him in the face. The burning phosphorus obliterated his nose and completely blinded him. Smoke filled the plane, obscuring the vision of the pilot. S/Sgt. Erwin realized that the aircraft and crew would be lost if the burning bomb remained in the plane. Without regard for his own safety, he picked it up and feeling his way, instinctively, crawled around the gun turret and headed for the copilot's window. He found the navigator's table obstructing his passage. Grasping the burning bomb between his forearm and body, he unleashed the spring lock and raised the table. Struggling through the narrow passage he stumbled forward into the smoke-filled pilot's compartment. Groping with his burning hands, he located the window and threw the bomb out. Completely aflame, he fell back upon the floor. The smoke cleared, the pilot, at 300 feet, pulled the plane out of its dive. S/Sgt. Erwin's gallantry and heroism above and beyond the call of duty saved the lives of his comrades.

In the days and weeks following Red's Medal of Honor action, army officials rushed to offer praise to him and his family. And slowly, incredibly, and despite constant, indescribable pain, Red Erwin began to recover from his wounds.

On April 20, the day after the bedside presentation, Gen. Thomas Power, commander of the 314th Bombardment Wing, sent a letter to Red's mother: "It is with a deep sense of pride and gratification that I am writing to you of the unselfish and heroic deed performed by your son, Staff Sergeant Henry Eugene Erwin. The courage and bravery which your son displayed in removing a burning smoke-bomb from one of our planes undoubtedly saved the plane and the lives of his fellow crewmen. . . . [Red] is the type of man that makes me humbly proud to be his Commanding General."

He added, "A man of Sergeant Erwin's character and personality is not the product of instinct or accident. His life reflects the training of the home that reared him and the happiness of the home which he himself is now building. All of you who love him, and who have made him what he is, played a vital part in this heroic act, and you too have a share in these tributes of praise."

On April 26, Gen. Lauris Norstad wrote to Red's wife, Betty: "Outstanding amongst all of the heroic acts achieved by members of the Twentieth Air Force in over a year's operation is the glorious self-sacrifice of your husband, Staff Sergeant Henry E. Erwin." He continued, "His transcendent heroism moves me, as a professional soldier, to pay him tribute. His deed lifts him to a place with the bravest men in all history, and as we consider the courage he displayed we gain a new and humbling appreciation of the valor inherent in mankind."

At the hospital on Guam, doctors worked heroically to keep Red alive. His burns were so deep and severe that they feared a fatal infection would soon erupt. The doctors painstakingly scraped phosphorus out of his eyes and off the rest of his body, but it kept reigniting and tormenting the young airman. They performed improvised surgeries and gave him blood transfusions and antibiotics.

Red remembered, "They kept me in all these bandages while I was soaked in a saline solution in a little tub, so what little flesh I had wouldn't come off. I always felt like I'd wet the bed or something."

Gen. Henry H. "Hap" Arnold later wrote to Red, "I regard your act as one of the bravest in the records of the war." On other occasions, Arnold wrote, "The country's highest honor will still be inadequate recognition of the inspiring heroism of this man. . . . Few men, officers or enlisted, in any Army of any service look back upon an act of such stark courage as his."

Capt. Tony Simeral described Erwin's action as "an ordeal with the fires of hell."

One of Red's visitors on Guam on May 7 was General LeMay, who asked, "Is there anything I can do for you, sergeant?"

"Yes, there is, sir," whispered Red through his bandages. "My brother Howard is with the marines over on Saipan. I'd like to see him. Would you see if you can get my brother to come over?"

Red hadn't seen Howard in four years, and he yearned to make a family connection in the midst of his despair.

LeMay replied, "He'll be here tomorrow morning." A special flight was arranged, and the pilot was 1st Lt. Tyrone Power, a swashbuckling Hollywood actor who was doing his wartime service as a marine transport pilot, supporting the just-concluded Battle of Iwo Jima and the upcoming Battle for Okinawa.

The next morning, the two Erwin brothers had a reunion at Red's hospital bedside. Still blind, Red couldn't see Howard, and his burn wounds prevented them from embracing, but Red was thrilled to hear Howard's voice. They exchanged hours of whispered small talk.

"That was a very proud moment," recalled Red. "It made tears come to my eyes because I was in such sad shape, to be very frank with you, but I just enjoyed being there with him. I couldn't see him, but I knew he was there and that was a great comfort."

After checking with Red, Howard touched him on a rare unburned section of his torso, which thrilled Red. Here was the touch of someone he truly loved, a kid brother who he'd grown up with through countless backyard games and rough-and-tumbles on the grass.

Red's burn wounds were so severe that the slightest touch of a bed or a pillow would cause him to scream in searing pain, but Howard brought with him a precious therapeutic agent—hope. "He stayed with me for twenty-four hours," remembered Red. "When he visited me, I knew I was going to live, despite the pain I was in."

The military doctors on Iwo Jima and Guam had saved Red's life, at least for now, but they knew he would need years of intensive medical care, surgical reconstruction, and physical rehabilitation to regain any semblance of a normal life.

On May 7, Red was put on a plane to the States for a series of hopscotch flights that would take him home to Alabama, to be with his family and the woman he loved.

Chapter Seven

HOMECOMING

IN MAY 1945, THE MOMENT RED ERWIN FEARED more than anything else arrived.

His wife, Betty, was coming to see him in the burn ward at Northington Hospital in Tuscaloosa, Alabama. He had arrived there on May 7, after a series of special military flights from Guam, Hawaii, and Sacramento. At Northington, a series of excruciating, complex operations began, with surgeons beginning to scrape most of the unstable, constantly reigniting phosphorus from the area around his eyes. Already some sight had been restored to his right eye. Miraculously, the doctors, aided by Red's prayers and his fierce will to live and come home to his family, were pulling him out of the jaws of death, despite the relatively primitive state of burn rehabilitation and reconstructive surgery. He was alive, but just barely.

"I was in so much misery and pain I was praying to die," he explained. "And then I got so near dying that I was praying to live." He thought, *Why did God save me?*

"I was in the hospital a long, long time," Red remembered. "When you see a lot of boys around you in so much worse shape than I was—arms off, legs off, paralyzed so they can't move at all—you can't waste time feeling sorry for yourself. I'm lucky to be alive."

But for days Red witnessed a series of heartbreaking scenes among his fellow wounded patients. Wives and girlfriends would freeze in shock at the mangled remains of the men who once were their true loves before they went to war. Some of the patients lacked arms and legs. Some were blinded and burned even worse than Red.

"While I was in the hospital, I saw many episodes of badly wounded soldiers being rejected by their wives," Red recalled. "They would come to the hospital, see their wounded mate, then take off their wedding band, lay it on the bed, and walk out."

"I didn't know what to expect," he said of Betty's coming. Would his wife, to whom he had been married only three months before he went overseas, do the same? The last time she saw him, he was a movie-star handsome soldier. And now? She had been told he had sustained third-degree burns over much of his body, but how would she react when she saw him in person? Red lay helpless and flat in the bed. His head was still bandaged and much of his body was immobilized. He was horribly scarred and disfigured but clinging to life. His weight had plummeted to 87 pounds, as his body could only take in liquids for nourishment.

Red's mother waited outside the hospital room. She had been told how badly burned he was, and she couldn't yet bring herself to go inside.

And then Betty walked into the ward.

But instead of giving a look of shock or horror, she smiled—a serene, confident, loving smile. In fact, it seemed as if she hardly noticed Red's injuries at all. She didn't hesitate for a moment. She leaned down, found the one small, undamaged, unburned section of skin on his left cheek, and gently kissed it. In that moment, and for the rest of their lives together, her attitude toward his appearance was like a fairy tale. Where everyone else saw the terrible effects of severe burns, she saw only goodness and beauty. He was still the best-looking man she had ever laid eyes on.

"Welcome home, Gene," she said. "It's good to have you home. I love you. I am here for you."

Red could do nothing but cry.

Betty Erwin committed to stay at Red's side for the rest of her life, just as she'd promised when she married him. Nothing would change that. Red had just celebrated his twenty-fourth birthday, and she was just turning nineteen.

"The thought of leaving him never entered my mind," she told me many years later.

They would stay together, for love and honor, for the next fifty-seven years.

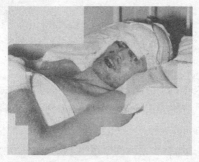

Red Erwin recovering back in the United States, 1945. He would endure forty-one surgical procedures over the next two years. (Erwin Family Collection)

One memorable day in June 1945, the well-known disability rights champion Helen Keller came to visit Red at Northington Hospital. Now sixty-four, the Alabama-born Keller, the victim of a childhood illness that rendered her blind, deaf, and speechless, had become a globe-trotting advocate for the rights and potential of handicapped people.

When Keller met Red at his bedside and heard his story, she was moved to tears and gave Red a memory he cherished for the rest of his life. The next day she dictated a letter to him:

Dear Sergeant Erwin,

This is what I tried to say to you yesterday when I had the touching, unforgettable honor of visiting you. I love you because of what you did for the crew in the plane. That act, so simply wrought, is a life given—a gift which no words can compass. . . . As I stood in your modest, regal presence, I was conscious of something which transcends my own experience. The chronicle of the handicapped is a chapter in the world's history, which I have been proud to interpret for others, but, 'Red' Erwin, you have reached heights of handicap higher than any I know, and I proudly bow before your indomitable spirit as I remember your saying you would do it over again. You have translated sheer deprivation into courage that will fortify an increasing number of soldiers of limitation far down the centuries.

———

On August 6, 1945, the B-29 Superfortress *Enola Gay* detonated an atomic bomb over Hiroshima, Japan. Three days later, the B-29 *Bockscar* detonated another on Nagasaki.

Five days later, Emperor Hirohito held a conference in the air raid shelter at the imperial palace. His cabinet was divided over whether to accept the unconditional surrender demanded by the Allies in the Potsdam Declaration.

The emperor broke the deadlock and said, "I cannot endure the thought of letting my people suffer any longer. A continuation of the war would bring death to tens, perhaps even hundreds, of thousands of people. The whole nation would be reduced to ashes." He concluded, "It is my desire that you, my Ministers of State, accede to my wishes and forthwith accept the Allied reply." The next day, Hirohito publicly ordered the surrender.

By then there were almost no undamaged strategic targets remaining in Japan, as most of the nation's ability to wage war had been destroyed by demolition and incendiary bombs dropped by the B-29 force and the combined power of the Allies. The conventional and atomic attacks, combined with the USSR's last-minute entry into the war on Japan on the side of the Allies, brought the war to an end.

From March to August 1945, American firebombs had killed more than 300,000 civilians in 67 cities, injured 412,000 others, and left close to 10 million people homeless. Half of the capital city of Tokyo had been obliterated. The Hiroshima and Nagasaki bombings killed at least 120,000 people, mostly civilians. During the war, 437 American B-29s were lost, many to malfunctions, and more than 3,000 officers and men were lost forever.

After the war, various Japanese officials argued that conventional B-29 bombing would have ended the war soon enough, even though hard-core militarist factions had, until early August 1945, paralyzed the Japanese government into what seemed like an indefinite war mentality.

"Fundamentally the thing that brought about the determination to make peace," said former Japanese prime minister Fumimaro Konoye, "was the prolonged bombing by the B-29s."

Other Japanese officials agreed. "I, myself, on the basis of the B-29 raids, felt that the case was hopeless," said Adm. Kantaro Suzuki, who was the prime minister from April 7 to August 17, 1945, and a key player in the final surrender negotiations.

Naruhiko Higashikuni, commander in chief of Home Defense Headquarters, argued, "The war was lost when the Marianas were taken away from Japan, and when we heard the B-29s were coming out. We had nothing in Japan that we could use against such a weapon. From the point of view of the Home Defense Command, we felt that the war was lost, and we said so."

Katsumoto Saotome, a writer and antiwar campaigner and survivor of the March 9–10 Tokyo air raid, told a journalist, "The firebombing probably led to an earlier end of the war. But I think killing noncombatants was an unforgivable violation of human morality." After a momentary pause, he added, "But in fact it was Japan that was the first to kill noncombatants, when it bombed cities like Chongqing in China."

On the morning of September 2, 1945, B-29s flew their last mission over Japan. It was unlike any mission they had flown before.

It was the day Red Erwin and millions of other people around the world had prayed for: the official last day of World War II, a war that killed some seventy-five million people.

Emperor Hirohito had broadcast a capitulation speech two weeks earlier, on August 14, but Gen. Douglas MacArthur, supreme commander of the Allied powers, gave the Japanese two weeks to get the word out to seven million far-flung Japanese troops to complete the surrender. MacArthur made a historic landing at Atsugi Airfield near Yokohama on August 30, with a corncob pipe in his mouth, and he was chauffeured by his Japanese hosts in a vintage Lincoln limousine to a steak dinner at the Yokohama Grand Hotel. American army and marine units soon charged ashore from landing craft at spots around Tokyo Bay and elsewhere along the Japanese coast, peacefully occupying strategic strongpoints around the vanquished nation.

Now, on this morning in early September, hundreds of Allied aircraft thundered toward the scene to provide an awesome finale to a solemn surrender ceremony that unfolded aboard the battleship *Missouri*, flagship of Adm. William Halsey Jr.'s Third Fleet, anchored in Tokyo Bay, along with nearly 260 Allied warships. There were no aircraft carriers at the scene—they were on alert farther out, in case there might be a last-minute attack by disaffected Japanese military factions.

The *Missouri* was flying the Stars and Stripes that had flown atop the US Capitol on December 7, 1941, and the warship was near the spot where Cmdre. Matthew C. Perry had arrived in 1853 with his "black ships" when he aimed his guns at Japan and opened the nation to the Western world.

The battleship was packed to overflowing with Allied generals and admirals from the United States, the United Kingdom, China, the Soviet Union, Canada, France, Australia, New Zealand, and the Netherlands and with US Navy personnel and journalists from around the world.

"Brother, I hope those are my discharge papers," joked an American when he saw the surrender documents being assembled.

Shortly before 9:00 a.m., eleven Japanese military and diplomatic representatives, some wearing formal top hats and striped pants, walked onto the deck of the *Missouri*. They represented the emperor and the military and foreign services. The weather was gray and overcast.

Leading the delegation was Foreign Minister Mamoru Shigemitsu, recently a leader of the peace faction in the Japanese government, wearing a black top hat, white gloves, and morning coat and walking with great difficulty (his right leg had been destroyed in a 1932 assassination attempt by a Korean patriot). Shigemitsu had to be helped up the ladder. He smiled at a friendly face in the crowd, a Canadian doctor who had saved his life in the 1932 attack at Shanghai.

Shigemitsu was followed by stone-faced Gen. Yoshijiro Umezu, the Japanese army chief of staff and soon-to-be-imprisoned war criminal, who snapped off a salute to the Americans as he boarded the ship in high leather boots.

In a startling scene that anticipated a new foundation of the postwar world order, American and Japanese military officials exchanged salutes as the delegation boarded the ship.

Gazing at the scene was *Life* magazine photographer Carl Mydans, who had been a prisoner of the Japanese at the brutal Santo Tomas Internment Camp in Manila. "I watched Shigemitsu limp forward," he recalled, "his wooden leg tapping out his progress in the silence. He was helped by two servicemen to a chair. He leaned on his cane, took off his top hat, and stripped off his gloves, and for an instant seemed confused. As I watched this man, at what for him must have been a terrible moment, I suddenly felt all my pent-up wartime anger drain away, and compassion filled my heart."

Once they stood on the veranda deck of the *Missouri*, beneath the colossal number-two gun turret, recalled Toshikazu Kase, one of two foreign service deputies in the delegation, "a million eyes seemed to beat on us with the million shafts of a rattling storm of arrows barbed with fire." All was quiet except for whispers among the thousands of Allied observers and the cranking of newsreel cameras. "I felt their keenness sink into my body with a sharp physical pain. Never had I realized that the glance of staring eyes could hurt so much." The Japanese delegation waited, he said, "like penitent schoolboys awaiting the dreaded schoolmaster." He looked up and spotted a row of painted rising suns on a nearby wall, marking enemy kills by the crew of the *Missouri*. "As I tried to count these markings, tears rose in my throat and quickly gathered to the eyes, flooding them. I could hardly bear the sight now."

Katsuo Okazaki, the other civilian deputy, was a graduate of Amherst and Harvard Universities. He remembered the scene vividly, describing the warships "that so lately belched forth their crashing battle, now holding in their swift thunder and floating like calm sea birds on the subjugated water."

A squeaky phonograph played "The Star-Spangled Banner," and a navy chaplain offered a short prayer.

Shortly after 9:00 a.m., General MacArthur appeared before the microphones to take charge of the ceremony and announce "a solemn agreement whereby peace may be restored." The issues of the war were settled in battle and not for debate, he declared, but they were not meeting "in a spirit of distrust, malice or hatred but rather, it is for us, both victors and vanquished, to rise to that higher dignity which alone befits the sacred purposes we are about to serve." He spoke not of conquest but of freedom, tolerance, and justice.

These words of conciliation by the tall, imperious, sixty-five-year-old MacArthur hit Toshikazu Kase, facing him from a few feet away, with the force of a freight train. "For me, who expected the worst humiliation, this was a complete surprise," he explained. "I was thrilled beyond words, spellbound, thunderstruck."

General MacArthur gestured to Foreign Minister Shigemitsu to sign the instrument of surrender documents. MacArthur supervised the proceedings with the regal confidence of an emperor himself. It was the pinnacle of his life and career. Other Japanese representatives signed, then representatives of eight Allied powers. When MacArthur signed the document, as if on a perfectly timed cue, shafts of sunlight penetrated the heavy overcast and illuminated the scene.

Returning to the microphone, MacArthur grandly intoned, "Let us pray that peace be now restored to the world and that God will preserve it always. These proceedings are closed."

A mechanical buzz that had been building in the distance became a thunderous roar, and more than four hundred B-29s from every squadron of the Twentieth Air Force flew over the *Missouri*, joined by fifteen hundred carrier planes, the biggest overflight thus far in history.

"Was the day beclouded by mists or trailing clouds?" MacArthur later wrote. "I cannot remember, but this I do—the all embracing pride I felt in my country's monumental victory."

At long last, the war was over.

A report of the proceedings by Shunichi Kase was rushed to an anxious Emperor Hirohito. He ended his report with the question of "whether it would have been possible for us, had we been victorious, to embrace the vanquished with a similar magnanimity."

At this, according to an eyewitness, the emperor nodded and sighed.

———

Red's eyes were periodically sewn shut for twelve months in order to save his sight. Doctors periodically opened them to scrape out any lingering smoldering phosphorus. His arm was sewn to his abdomen for several months in order to grow new flesh on his severely damaged right arm. His mouth was sewn shut to prepare him for skin grafts to replace his lips, which had been burned away. So he had to drink and eat through a straw. His skin from his abdomen was grafted to create a new ear to replace the one that had been burned off. He had to have numerous skin grafts to replace the burned right side of his face.

"The pain was so bad that I just wanted to die," Red said. "Then when I came so close to really dying, I began to pray to live. I didn't give up." He surprised everyone, not only by surviving, but by recovering.

Red Erwin was in and out of hospitalizations for the next two and a half years at medical facilities in Alabama, Massachusetts, and Pennsylvania.

Starting in August 1946, Red had an extended stay at Cushing General Hospital in Framingham, Massachusetts, a giant army hospital that specialized in neurosurgery and in pampering wounded personnel. Here, Red underwent a series of critical attempts at reconstructive surgery and rehabilitation of his wounds. Betty came to Framingham with him, and she worked at a ward in the hospital so she could be close to him.

When the special hospital train brought Red and Betty onto the tree-lined, 110-acre hospital grounds, they were astonished and grateful at their new home. It was a city within a city, with the most advanced medical equipment, labs, x-ray machines and operating rooms, swimming pool, post office, fire department, and an ornate interfaith chapel built in 1943 by Italian masons who were prisoners of war. A shuttle bus took ambulatory patients on outings to downtown Framingham to watch movies at the St. George Theater, quaff a beer at the Blue Moon Café, or enjoy a "turkey dinner with all the fixin's" at the Wellworth restaurant for forty cents. The hospital's corridors converged at a spot called Times Square, where an auditorium featured performances by celebrities such as Bing Crosby and Bob Hope, and where patients could relax in a comfortable lounge and have a smoke, a snack, or a card game.

Patients at Cushing, which was also called the City of Mercy, were given the red-carpet treatment. It was a huge hospital, with eighteen hundred beds, and had been specially designed by the War Department to welcome returning wounded personnel and make them feel at home. Patients came from battlefields across the world and had endured brain and spinal cord injuries, shattered limbs and eyes, and severe burns such as Red's, but the atmosphere at the hospital was remarkably happy and peaceful.

One patient who had been wounded at Anzio, Corp. Stanley Smith, recuperated there for two years and said he "couldn't recall anybody grumbling and moaning about the position they were in."

The residents of Framingham showered the patients with love and attention. Members of the Garden Club placed fresh flowers in the mess hall, the Elks Lodge was converted into a mini-USO Club for the wounded troops, and Boy Scout leader Peter Mespelli taught his troop to cook Wednesday night spaghetti dinners that patients loved. At Christmastime, they sang carols to the wounded.

Red needed all the love and comfort he could get, as he was enduring what he described as the worst pain he had ever experienced, like "being skinned alive." The procedure was recently dubbed "incredibly barbaric and heinous" by burn surgeon James Holmes of Wake Forest University.

Military burn specialist David Barillo explained recently that instead of surgically removing the burned area within two weeks as is now standard practice and results in much less pain and fast recovery, "In the 1940s we let the burn separate by itself, which could take months. For weeks on end, Erwin would have been placed in a man-sized tub called a Hubbard tank, the water would run like a whirlpool, and he'd just sit there for endless hours as doctors and nurses picked off pieces of the burn with scissors and tweezers, which was just incredibly painful and incredibly stressful. As much as you tried to treat them for pain, you can't really control that kind of pain. That would go on for weeks and months, day after day. At some point all of the burn would be peeled off and you'd have a nice layer of skin-granulation tissue under it, and at that point you could start skin grafting."

Eventually, flaps of skin were grafted from Red's lower body and shoulder to create the semblance of a right ear. His right eyebrow was cut from a piece of his scalp. Miraculously, his eyesight returned over three years. Doctors wanted to amputate his right arm, but Red begged them not to. So for two years the doctors worked to create something out of nothing. It was never fully completed.

In 1948, journalist Sidney Shalett, who interviewed Red extensively, reported of his arm, "The effort to save it involved one particularly excruciating operation wherein the skin of his abdomen was slit and the arm attached to it. It stayed bound to his body for three months while the skin grew to his wrist. He has flesh on his wrist and forearm now, but it is swollen and unpretty. Then they discovered that his wrist was in a distorted, claw-like position, so they fractured the wrist and braced it with a bone taken from his hip region in another operation. The piece of bone from the hip was held in place with a Steinmann pin—a surgical steel spike driven into Red's hand."

Red spent the rest of his life not being able to move his right arm and with the immobile remains of three fingers on a right hand that resembled a small loaf of bread. Much of his left index finger was missing, but his legs and feet were good and his mind was sharp.

The phosphorus lodged in Red's skin continued to smolder and reignite for months after his injury. He had no less than forty-one surgical procedures until he decided he'd had enough and was ready to reenter civilian life. Surgeons had reassembled Red's face and body into an imperfect but, considering the circumstances, fairly good reflection of what he looked like before he was wounded, though the natural process of skin aging would gradually and increasingly accent the visibility of his wounds and surgeries. His red hair grew back.

Red's right arm remained nearly useless, visibly scarred with major wounds that hadn't healed well. It was locked into a right angle for the rest of his life. In 1945, doctors had managed to save the arm from amputation, but the skin was extremely rigid from scarring, and burn injury rehabilitation practices were primitive. Red didn't have the years of physical therapy that he should have had, so any remaining muscle function in the arm atrophied completely. His right hand, also useless, was also badly distorted from imperfect and unfinished reconstructions. Surgeons gave him a new right ear and rebuilt his nose and lips with skin grafts. The index finger on his left hand was partially amputated because of the burns. He was blind in his right eye, but he regained sight in his left eye. He had the full use of the left side of his body, and eventually much of the right side, other than the arm. Gradually, after spending months as a living skeleton, as his ability to take nourishment returned, his weight went from a low of 87 pounds back toward his normal 165. He regained the full ability to walk and talk.

On October 8, 1947, Red was discharged from the US Army Air Forces as a master sergeant. In addition to the Medal of Honor and two Air Medals received earlier in 1945, he was also awarded the Purple Heart, the

World War II Victory Medal, the American Campaign Medal, three Good Conduct Medals, the Asiatic-Pacific Campaign Medal with two bronze campaign stars (for participation in the Air Offensive Japan and Western Pacific campaigns), and the Distinguished Unit Citation Emblem.

Red's challenge after finally being able to leave the hospital for short periods in late 1945 was to find a place to live and a professional mission that would enable him to provide for Betty and what he hoped would be a good-sized family.

In October 1945, the city of Bessemer, Alabama, staged a Hero's Welcome Home Parade for the still-frail and recovering Red Erwin, complete with brass bands and marching military and Red Cross units, while flag-waving throngs lined the sidewalk. The parade was staged to raise funds to buy a house for the young couple. Three thousand people packed the city hall auditorium and a thousand more gathered outside to get a glimpse of the modest red-haired war hero. The fund drive collected $10,000 from the Kiwanis, Lions, and Rotary Clubs, the Junior Chamber of Commerce, and the American Legion. A group of children in the Fairfield Highlands community raised $54 by collecting dimes, nickels, and pennies. One boy took the money he earned by cutting grass and gave it to the fund.

The fund drive resulted in a white-framed house being given to Red and Betty. It consisted of two bedrooms and a bath, a neat kitchen, a refrigerator, an electric stove, and lots of cabinets, complete with a big fenced-in backyard with two swing sets for future children. Betty and Red loved the house.

Harry Truman then reentered Red Erwin's story, opening a door that shaped the rest of Red's life.

While he was still hospitalized, Red heard in September 1945 that President Truman had issued an executive order decreeing that Medal of Honor recipients were entitled to a job with the Veterans Administration as a contact representative, or benefits counselor, without having to comply with the requirements of civil service rules.

Soon after he was discharged in October 1947, Red applied for the job with the VA, which in classic bureaucratic fashion gave him a job, not as a contact representative at a salary of $3,400 per year, but as a file clerk in the medical department of the VA at the Jefferson County Courthouse in Birmingham at only $1,954 per year, taking care of five thousand case files on sick and wounded veterans. Red was glad to find work and did the file clerk job well, but he was determined to get what had been promised him. He pushed for the correct job until he finally received it on January 4, 1948.

For the next thirty-seven years, until he retired on April 3, 1985, Red Erwin worked as a contact representative and benefits counselor at the Veterans Administration Hospital in Birmingham, acting as a one-man champion and SWAT team to get sick and wounded veterans the help, treatment, benefits, and respect they deserved.

Red Erwin in action, fighting for his fellow wounded veterans, which he would do for thirty-seven years. (Erwin Family Collection)

Red's new mission in life was to deliver comfort, compassion, and critical medical and financial aid to soldiers, sailors, marines, and air force veterans of the Spanish-American War, World War I, World War II, the Korean War, the Vietnam War, and peacetime service. From all accounts, he executed his mission as heroically as he did his Medal of Honor action.

In the hours and months after his accident, as he endured the agony of his injuries, treatments, and surgeries, Red freely admitted he had moments of black despair, when he wished his life was over and prayed for death as a merciful delivery from his pain. Perhaps he suffered from post-traumatic stress disorder (PTSD), an anxiety disorder that is triggered by a psychologically distressing, traumatic event and causes a cluster of symptoms in victims that can include intense terror, fear, helplessness, hypervigilance and hyperarousal, emotional numbing, intrusive nightmares, flashbacks, and hallucinations about the traumatic event.

Many members of the so-called Greatest Generation who emerged from the severe circumstances of both the Depression and World War II seemed both unequipped and highly reluctant to dwell on the severe stresses and anxieties they endured. In fact, the condition known as PTSD was little understood prior to the 1980s. Psychologists Elizabeth Clipp of the Veterans Administration and Glen Elder Jr. of the University of North Carolina reviewed the research on the subject and wrote a quarter-century ago of their findings: "The disorder is widespread among aging veterans of World War II, that symptoms may be quite serious in later life, and that a substantial number of its victims are currently undiagnosed because of an unwillingness to admit war-related problems or misdiagnosed as having anxiety, alcoholism, depression or chronic physical conditions."

It would be perfectly understandable if Red suffered from some form of PTSD, especially early on. But each time he had feelings of ultimate despair, Red's love for God and his love for Betty and his family pulled him through, and he emerged from his epic ordeals as a better, more fulfilled, and more thriving human being. It is pure conjecture, but Red may have experienced a fascinating, little-known condition that can coexist with PTSD but is instead associated with powerful positive effects—a condition called post-traumatic growth (PTG). According to researchers, "In many studies PTG and PTSD are found to stem from similar traumatic events and to be positively correlated."

In the 1990s, psychologists Richard Tedeschi and Lawrence Calhoun first described the concept of PTG as a positive psychological response to trauma that is marked by improvements in relationships, personality, self-efficacy, spiritual development, openness to new possibilities, feelings of personal strength, and a greater appreciation of life. PTG has been observed in survivors of war, severe medical events, terrorism, rape, accidents, and natural disasters. The theory suggests that people who struggle psychologically after adversity can often experience positive growth afterward. Professor Tedeschi explained, "People develop new understandings of themselves, the world they live in, how to relate to other people, the kind of future they might have and a better understanding of how to live life."

The characteristics that researchers positively associate with PTG, in fact, read like a road map to the personality of the Red Erwin that my family and I knew and loved: humor, kindness, leadership, curiosity, honesty, bravery, judgment, forgiveness, modesty, fairness, gratitude, hope, extraversion, effort and perseverance, and strong religious beliefs. According to a recent analysis, 50 percent of all contemporary veterans and 72 percent of veterans with PTSD report at least moderate PTG in connection to their worst traumatic event.

Red may have naturally been highly resilient, but he also may have been a case history in the power of post-traumatic growth to enhance life after terrible adversity.

———

Red Erwin never had the occasion to visit Japan after the war, but several of his B-29 comrades did. One of them was Hap Halloran, the navigator of the *Rover Boys Express* who had been shot down over Japan on January 27, 1945, and put on display in a Tokyo zoo.

After the Japanese surrender on August 14, 1945, Hap and several hundred other prisoners lingered for a time at the Omori prisoner-of-war camp near Tokyo, waiting for repatriation and living on rations air-dropped from B-29s.

"One day there were ships in Tokyo harbor," he told me sixty years later. "They looked like Americans. You can just imagine what we felt. Then some B-29s came over. They were at low altitude and the bomb bay doors were open, and they gently made a dry run past and then came back and disgorged pallets with 55-gallon drums with all kinds of clothing and medication. Those were our guys! Those B-29s never looked better than when they were doing that for us. I understand we lost seven planes on all those relief missions. So here are those guys doing their best for us, and they lost their lives. After that, some US Marines came in on landing craft and picked us up. Can you imagine that? To see the American flag flying? It was August 29, 1945, and it was the happiest day of my life. We were taken aboard the hospital ship *Benevolence*. It was white and clean and perfect. And that was the first chance I had to wash. It took months because of all the sores, and my skin had changed color. You couldn't rub very hard. But I was on the way home."

Hap was lucky to be rescued. Scores of other B-29ers captured by the Japanese were beheaded, burned, starved, beaten, and tortured to death before the war ended.

On September 2, while Hap was still aboard the *Benevolence* in Tokyo Bay, he heard a tremendous commotion. So he dragged himself out of sick bay and made it outside to the rail. "There must have been a total of eight hundred planes coming over Tokyo Bay, and they were our planes! They were fighter planes and medium bombers and everything."

It was the flyover of the USS *Missouri* that marked the final Japanese surrender. He heard a wave of thunder gathering beyond the horizon, growing louder and louder. He knew it could only be one thing. It was an armada of hundreds of B-29s that filled the sky and swooped at low altitude over the ceremony aboard the *Missouri*.

"God, I just screamed," Hap told me. "And if I was proud in Harrington, Kansas, the first time I saw a B-29, I think I was ten times prouder as they came over that day."

Within a year, Hap came home and left the military. "I was not fit to serve," he explained.

Today, we would probably diagnose it as severe post-traumatic stress disorder, but back then there was much less medical knowledge about such things. For nearly forty years, Hap was plagued by nightmares, about falling through space, about fire, and about being beaten. Sometimes he would break windows, run out into the street, or flee into closets to cower from the beatings. People in adjoining hotel rooms would call the management to report their next-door neighbor was being attacked. He covered it up by working hard in a business career and feeling satisfied when his efforts were rewarded, but the nightmares never ended.

Then Hap started thinking about going back to Japan. He wanted to reconnect with people like the good people he met there, people who stepped in to comfort him at crucial points during his six months in hell. "Like the lady who gave me seven beans from out in her garden," he told me. "The lady who gave me a small piece of soap when that was a risk to her. The fellow who talked me out of a problem. The guard who kept smiling and saying 'Ohio' to me. I hated him and accused him of cruelty, because I thought he was taunting me about home. But then I found out that he was just saying the word for 'good morning' in Japanese. He was just trying to be a human being. I was so regretful about that. People like the administrator from our prison camp who tried to help us and gave us a Bible. I thought there must be a lot of people back there like that."

Hap went back to Japan a total of nine times, beginning in 1984. He visited most of the major cities and toured the grounds of the emperor's palace. On one of his visits, he befriended a man in Shizuoka who took him up two hundred stairs to the crest of a mountain. He carried two bouquets of flowers. On top of the mountain were two obelisks. One was to honor some two thousand civilians killed in a B-29 raid on the city on June 19–20, 1945, and the other was to honor the twenty-three deceased B-29 crewmen from the 314th Bomb Wing who crashed that day after a midair collision.

Hap learned that Fukumatsu Itoh, a brave Japanese farmer, town councilman, and devout Buddhist, had come across the bodies and wreckage of the B-29s the day after they crashed, and he insisted on giving the Americans a decent burial beside the graves of the Japanese victims. When the war was over, Itoh built the two monuments to the Japanese and American victims and placed them next to each other on the summit of Mount Shizuhata, not far from Mount Fuji.

Hap also learned that Itoh had found a fire-scarred, partly crushed US Army canteen in the wreckage of one of the bombers, bearing the handprint of what Itoh assumed was the canteen's owner. Every year, on the anniversary of the air raid, Itoh visited the crash site, said a prayer, and poured bourbon whiskey from the canteen on the ground to honor the spirits of the fallen. The ritual of healing and forgiveness earned him scorn from some in his community, but he kept doing it.

After Itoh died, a younger helper named Hiroyo Sugano continued the tradition. In 1991, he began an annual tradition of bringing the so-called Blackened Canteen to the *Arizona* memorial at Pearl Harbor and pouring whiskey from the canteen into the water, along with flower petals. Over time, Japanese and American veterans, military officers, and citizens joined both annual ceremonies, and the tradition continues to this day.

Standing before the two obelisks, the Japanese man told Hap, "If you would put your flowers on the civilians, I'll put mine on the B-29 men. We'd like to honor them." Hap Halloran and his new friend placed their flowers on the monuments. They bowed their heads and said a prayer together.

This was only one of the many surprises Hap experienced in Japan. He learned that a B-29 crewman who perished in the March 9–10 air raid was found the next day in a wheat field near a small town east of Tokyo. The townspeople, Halloran learned, "brought him to the temple and he was treated with dignity and honor, and eventually cremated and put into a box with silk lining and placed in a place of prominence in that temple." Working from information on the fallen airman's dog tags, Halloran was able to bring the news back to the man's family, who never knew what happened to him.

On another occasion, Hap tracked down and befriended Kaneyuki Kobayashi, one of his captors at the Omori camp, where he had spent seven months in captivity. Kobayashi was a guard who had befriended him and had shared a few bites of chocolate and words of encouragement with him.

Incredibly, with the help of Japanese researchers and historians, Hap Halloran managed to track down two former enemy pilots who played a huge role in his life's journey: Isamu Kashiide, the ace who shot down the *Rover Boys Express*, and Hideichi Kaiho, the pilot who saluted and held his fire as Halloran descended by parachute to earth.

Hap spent two days with Kashiide, who had shot down the most B-29s during the war, a total of seven. His approach was to attack from the front and target the Plexiglas nose of the aircraft. The two veterans discussed golf, family, and other things that older men think of, and they drank a toast to peace and friendship.

In 2002 and 2003, Hap visited Kaiho, who explained that his squadron followed the traditional bushido code of warrior chivalry rather than the brutal interpretation of the code that pervaded the Japanese military. Hap recalled the scene: "He was bedridden, but our reunion was a wonderful occasion. I was scheduled for a third visit on June 24, 2004; however he died one day before. I was invited to his pre-funeral in Tokyo. His son opened the casket for my final viewing of this gentleman flyer— the one who saluted me when I was helpless in my chute fifty-nine years earlier. I prayed as I stood at his casket and recalled those long-ago days. I saluted him as I walked away from his casket."

Once he began visiting Japan, Hap Halloran experienced something wonderful. His nightmares stopped. He was a free man again, at peace and happy to be alive with his family and new Japanese friends.

Chapter Eight

GUARDIAN ANGEL

ON JUNE 5, 1945, WHILE RED ERWIN WAS IN THE burn ward at Northington Hospital in Alabama, the *City of Los Angeles* was damaged by antiaircraft fire and enemy fighters during a bombing mission over Kobe, Japan, and was forced to make an emergency landing on Iwo Jima with the fuel gauges at near zero, one dead engine, and a damaged wing and flaps. The wreckage of another B-29 blocked the main airstrip, and the *City of Los Angeles* had to land on the shorter fighter runway. Pilot Maj. Tony Simeral was awarded the Distinguished Service Cross (the predecessor of the Air Force Cross), the highest award for valor next to the Medal of Honor.

All the crew of the *City of Los Angeles* survived the war. When the fighting ended, they went their separate ways and entered the anonymity of postwar life, along with millions of other returning veterans.

Some of the crew adjusted easily and achieved swift personal and career success, but others struggled to gain their footing in the vast demobilization. Red stayed in touch with most of them. Many of the crew got married and had children, meaning that the probable grand total of people whose lives Red saved—and made possible—could number in the hundreds.

Tony Simeral, the *City of Los Angeles* air commander, retired from the

Air Force as a full colonel in 1968, became a stockbroker and real estate investor, and died in 2000. In 1989, he joined Red for an oral history interview with an air force historian, passages from which are quoted in this book.

Pilot LeRoy Stables earned graduate degrees in physics and engineering, had two children, and retired in Florida. After the war, he became one of Red's closest friends, and the two stayed in touch for the rest of their lives. Over the years, the one thing Stables declined to talk about with Red and Red's family was April 12, 1945, the day Red was injured. All he would say was, "It was the darkest day of my life."

Navigator Pershing Youngkin became a petroleum engineer for Standard Oil of California, had five children and three grandchildren, and retired in Texas. Bombardier William Loesch started a successful business in Houston and retired there, and then moved to Florida. He had two children and five grandchildren. Leo D. Connors, the radar observer, became a postman in Madison, Wisconsin, and died around 1954. Flight engineer Vern W. Schiller stayed in the aviation business for the rest of his life. He was an engineer for Eastern Airlines, Pan Am, and Boeing Aircraft. He retired in Seattle.

Gunner Kenneth E. Young moved back to Norwood, Ohio, after the war. Gunner Howard Stubstad moved back to his native St. Paul, Minnesota, and had three children and a bunch of grandchildren. He became a carpenter, managed a building materials store, and spent eight years as the mayor of Buffalo, Minnesota. His free time was spent between golf, hunting, and fishing. Gunner Vernon G. Widemeyer returned to North Dakota and got into the television and electronics business. He lived on a small farm where he enjoyed camping, fishing, and hunting.

By far the most tragic fate befell Lt. Col. Eugene Strouse, the squadron commander who had ridden along on the mission that saw Red earn the Medal of Honor. After Red saved the lives of Strouse and the crew, Strouse saved Red's life by breaking protocol and ordering the plane to Iwo Jima so he could receive emergency medical treatment.

After the war, Strouse became the head pilot for Reeve Aleutian Airways, a civilian airline company based in Alaska. On September 24, 1959, while piloting a C-54 aircraft in good flying condition and in normal weather, Strouse flew the plane into the side of a mountain on Great Sitkin Island. The crash killed Strouse, five crew, and eleven passengers, consisting of two civilians and nine servicemen: seven from the air force and one each from the army and navy.

According to author Gregory Liefer, an investigation revealed that Strouse was overdue on a flight evaluation, a clear violation of regulations, and he had apparently falsified his flight record to show he had received the required semiannual medical exams, when he hadn't had one for three and a half years. When the doctor who had last examined Strouse was interviewed, he reported that Strouse had been diagnosed not only with glaucoma but with cerebrovascular disease, which can impair judgment and cause memory loss. If the Federal Aviation Administration had known this, Strouse would have been grounded.

Gen. Curtis E. LeMay remembered Red Erwin fondly and appeared with him at a war bonds event in Alabama after the war. LeMay went on to run the Berlin Airlift in 1948 and became commander of the Cold War–era Strategic Air Command (SAC) that same year. During the 1962 Cuban Missile Crisis, as Air Force chief of staff, LeMay made an astonishing outburst to President John F. Kennedy at a White House meeting. LeMay advocated an immediate bombing and invasion of Cuba to destroy the Soviet nuclear missile sites and was disgusted by what he saw as JFK's weak plan of a naval quarantine, or blockade, of the island and negotiations for a solution.

As JFK's secret tape recorder captured LeMay's words, the general told Kennedy that his plan "is almost as bad as the appeasement at Munich." Comparing JFK to British prime minister Neville Chamberlain was the most shocking insult a general could hurl at a postwar president. Luckily, Kennedy ignored LeMay's demand for "direct military intervention, right now" and navigated the world to a peaceful solution of the crisis. If JFK had taken LeMay's advice, there is a good chance that nuclear war would have erupted, as neither man knew that Soviet officers stationed in Cuba had been given the authority to launch short- and intermediate-range nuclear missiles at US targets in the event of an American first strike or invasion, which likely would have ignited wider barrages of nuclear weapons. Roughly one hundred million people worldwide would have died in such a conflagration. At the time, JFK thought the chances of nuclear war were "fifty/fifty."

Some Japanese were appalled in late 1964 when LeMay was awarded the First-Class Order of Merit of the Grand Cordon of the Rising Sun by the Japanese government, its highest decoration for a foreigner, for his work in establishing Japan's postwar air self-defense force.

Announcement of the award triggered a vigorous debate in the Japanese Parliament, where socialist member Hiroichi Tsujihara charged that "the government had disregarded the feelings of the people" in decorating a general involved in the atomic bombings of Hiroshima and Nagasaki. Curiously, the debate focused on the atomic bombings, in which LeMay's role was only to give the go signal when the takeoff weather was clear, rather than on the increasingly forgotten firebombings of Tokyo and other Japanese cites, of which LeMay was the hands-on mastermind.

The award was defended in Parliament by Japanese prime minister Eisaku Sato and Jun'ya Koizumi, director general of Japan's Defense Agency. "Bygones are bygones," said Prime Minister Sato, who in 1974 received the Nobel Peace Prize for bringing Japan into the Nuclear Non-Proliferation Treaty. Sato added, "It should be but natural that we reward the general with a decoration for his great contribution to our Air Self-Defense Units." Koizumi declared that "as far as the Defense Agency knows, General LeMay was not responsible for the dropping of the atomic bombs."

LeMay was presented the award by Japanese Air Self-Defense Force chief of staff Gen. Shigeru Ura at the Iruma Air Base. It was a striking illustration of the world-shaping military and economic embrace of the United States and Japan in the postwar age.

General Shigeru Ura, Japan's Self-Defense Forces chief of staff, bestows the First Order of Merit of the Grand Cordon of the Rising Sun upon General Curtis E. LeMay, US Air Force chief of staff. (AP, https://outlet.historicimages.com /products/rsn05449)

In 1968, Curtis LeMay, now retired from the air force and a fierce Vietnam War hawk, ran as the vice presidential candidate on the third-party ticket of former Alabama governor and notorious segregationist George Wallace. By then, a quote from his 1965 book *Mission with LeMay*, about the Vietnam War, had gained wide attention and would largely define his image in popular culture as an unhinged warmonger: "My solution to the problem would be to tell them [the North Vietnamese] frankly that they've got to draw in their horns and stop their aggression, or we're going to bomb them back into the Stone Age."

Gen. Thomas S. Power, Red's wing commander in 1945 and LeMay's deputy, was LeMay's successor as head at SAC, and during the Cuban Missile Crisis, he took actions that some thought highly dangerous. One of Power's subordinates, Gen. Horace M. Wade, said, "I used to worry about the fact that he had control over so many [nuclear] weapons and weapons systems and could, under certain conditions, launch the force." During one discussion of nuclear risks with a government contractor, Power exploded at the idea of not attacking Soviet cities. He said, "Restraint? Why are you so concerned with saving their lives? The whole idea is to kill the bastards. At the end of the war if there are two Americans and one Russian left alive, we win!"

During the Cuban Missile Crisis, both of Red's former bosses, Curtis LeMay and Thomas Power, took actions that could have been extremely dangerous and risked hundreds of thousands, if not millions, of lives. Both Power and LeMay reportedly tried to rush the thermonuclear 9-megaton B53 gravity bomb into service at the Bunker Hill Air Force Base in Indiana. A civilian Pentagon official ruled it unsafe and blocked the request.

At the time, as SAC commander, General Power had both the ability to launch airborne nuclear forces and, under contingency plans approved by President Dwight Eisenhower and still in effect under President Kennedy, the legal authority to order a nuclear launch if the president couldn't be reached. Some three thousand nuclear warheads were under the command of Power, a man who was, in the eyes of some who knew him, "certifiably off the deep end" and "not the sort of person who could be counted on to follow strict orders of the political leadership during a nuclear crisis," according to nuclear historian Bruce Blair.

On October 23, 1962, the day after President Kennedy announced the existence of Soviet offensive missiles in Cuba in a nationwide television address, the stock market plunged, and in Florida there was a run on rifles and shotguns in sporting-goods stores.

In Los Angeles, civil defense officials announced that stores would be closed for five days if a war occurred, sparking a stampede on supermarkets. In one store, hand-to-hand fighting erupted over the last can of pork and beans.

Kennedy asked a civil defense official, "Can we, maybe before we invade, evacuate these cities?"

The air force dispersed hundreds of B-47 Sratojet bombers to scattered civilian airfields to escape the first Soviet missile detonations, and one thousand combat aircraft swarmed into Florida air bases to join more than a hundred thousand troops poised to invade Cuba.

The risks of human or mechanical errors introduced the horrific possibility of an accidental nuclear launch. On the night of October 26, an American U-2 reconnaissance aircraft strayed into Soviet airspace over the Chukchi Peninsula when its navigation system failed. The pilot radioed his base in a panic, "Hey, I think I'm lost. I may be over Siberia. For Christ's sake, tell me how to get home!" MiG interceptors scrambled to chase and shoot down the plane. Responding to the U-2's SOS, several American F-102A Delta Dagger interceptors, fully armed with Falcon air-to-air nuclear missiles, were launched from Galena Air Force Base in western Alaska. While still over Siberia, the U-2 exhausted its fuel, flamed out, and began to glide back toward Alaska, steadily losing altitude. Over the Bering Strait, one of the F-102As spotted the U-2 and escorted it to a landing site on the Alaska coast.

On October 27, technicians at a New Jersey radar post signaled the national command headquarters that a missile had been fired from Cuba and was about to land on Tampa, Florida. Other US commands were informed that a nuclear assault seemed to have begun. It was soon recognized as a false alarm, triggered by test software accidentally inserted into the radar screen.

At the height of the thirteen-day nuclear crisis, without the president's knowledge and against procedure, General Power broadcast a DEFCON 2 nuclear alert of SAC (approved by Secretary of Defense Robert McNamara) on an open frequency so Soviet forces could pick it up, urging his pilots to be cautious and double-check all orders.

In response, according to former Soviet military officers interviewed by Bruce Blair, the Soviet Strategic Rocket Forces received orders to go on maximum combat alert, warheads were loaded onto ICBMs for a two-hour launch capability, and strategic bombers went on runway alert.

On top of this, the commander in chief of the United Kingdom's Bomber Command, on his own initiative, ordered a full combat alert of all British nuclear weapons, including 140 bombers, plus 60 PGM-17 Thor nuclear missiles poised to strike 230 Soviet Bloc targets in fifteen minutes or less.

With his DEFCON broadcast, General Power may have made an incredibly dangerous moment even more hazardous.

After retiring from the air force, Thomas Power became chairman of the board of Schick Inc., a razor blade company. He died of a heart attack in Palm Springs, California, in 1970, at the age of sixty-five.

After the war, he said he had "absolutely no regrets" about the firebombing of Tokyo.

Curtis LeMay died in 1990, at the age of eighty-three, also with no regrets.

———

Henry E. "Red" Erwin died on January 16, 2002, at eighty years of age, fifty-seven years after he was expected to die of his severe burns in the Pacific War. He was buried at Elmwood Cemetery in Birmingham, Alabama.

After Red died, Betty told me, "I wouldn't have been anything without him. I wonder what would have happened to me if he hadn't come home from the war."

Reflecting on the wounds he sustained on April 12, 1945, wounds that were highly visible for the world to see for the rest of his life, Betty said, "The only thing that bothered me about it, much more than it did him, was when people looked at him and stared at him. I just didn't like it. Little children would ask, 'Mister, what's wrong with your eyes? What happened to you?' I just didn't want people to do that. It bothered me, but it didn't bother him."

Betty Erwin died in 2018.

Red and Betty had four children—Nancy, Karen, Bette, and Hank Jr.— and eight grandchildren and fourteen great-grandchildren.

After Red's funeral, my father, Hank Jr., gave our honor flag to representatives of the Air Force Enlisted Heritage Hall at Gunter Air Force Base in Montgomery, Alabama. Today, it resides in a special display case built in Red's memory to inspire coming generations of air force enlisted personnel.

In the decades that followed, the Medal of Honor story of Red Erwin continued to inspire. In 1951, it was recreated as a sequence in a movie about the B-29s, *The Wild Blue Yonder*.

In 1997, the air force created the Henry E. Erwin Outstanding Enlisted Aircrew Member of the Year Award. It is presented annually to an airman, noncommissioned officer, and senior noncommissioned officer in the flight engineering, air surveillance, loadmaster, and related career fields.

In 2002, the Erwin Professional Military Education Center at Kadena Air Base, Japan, was dedicated to Red's memory and rededicated in 2011 after a major expansion.

At Anderson Air Force Base in Guam, the Thirty-sixth Contingency Response Group headquarters bears the name of Red Erwin.

In 2004, the Gunter Air Force Base library was named the Henry E. "Red" Erwin Library in Red's honor. A large mural of Red and his B-29 by artist John Witt is on display, and a bust of Red's upper body is on a nearby stand to greet arriving students. In earlier years, Red often spoke there at dedication ceremonies and addressed graduating classes.

Betty Erwin with one of her eight grandchildren in front of the painting of Red Erwin at Maxwell Air Force Base, Alabama. (US Air Force)

One notable admirer of Red Erwin is pilot Chesley "Sully" Sullenberger, who performed his own split-second, lifesaving aviation rescue achievement on January 15, 2009, when he safely crash-landed US Airways Flight 1549 in the Hudson River, off Manhattan Island, after a bird strike disabled both of the jet's engines. He evacuated all 155 passengers and crew on the aircraft. In his autobiography, Sullenberger cited Red as a personal inspiration.

One year when the veterans of the Twenty-ninth Bombardment Group held their biennial reunion in Kansas City, Missouri, Red Erwin and his comrades traveled to nearby Independence, Missouri. There, they each placed a rose on the grave of their scrappy former commander in chief, Harry S. Truman, the man who approved Red's Medal of Honor and created a professional mission that Red followed the rest of his working life.

When the veterans of the crew of the *City of Los Angeles* got together for their first reunion, navigator Pershing Youngkin said to Red, "I never had a chance to thank you for what you did for us."

Red said, "Well, any one of the crew would have done the same thing."

Decades later Youngkin told me, "You know, looking back on that, I think, no, that took an extraordinary amount of willpower to do that, and I don't know whether I would have been able to do it." He added, "He didn't just save twelve people, he saved generations of people. Our family wouldn't be here today. Our grandchildren wouldn't be here today. You wouldn't be here today. And the same thing with the rest of the crew. What he did was extraordinary. He had a real faith in God, and I think that faith is what carried him through."

All of Red Erwin's fellow crewmen are gone now except for Herbert Schnipper, one of the three gunners on the *City of Los Angeles*. When the war ended, he studied forestry at Syracuse University and worked in the lumber business in New York for fifty-three years. Today, he lives in an independent living community for retired people on Long Island, New York, and he helped with the research for this book.

Beginning in the 1950s, the crew of the *City of Los Angeles* got together for reunions every two years or so, and Red attended whenever he could. The first time Schnipper saw Red at a reunion, he was startled at his appearance. "When I knew him, he was a pretty good-looking guy," he recalled, but after his injury, "the doctors didn't do a good job on him. I thought they did a lousy job."

In 1995, Schnipper couldn't make it to the fiftieth anniversary of the incident, so he sent a note to Red: "I'm trying to remember our first meeting in Pratt, Kansas, when we formed as a crew under Tony Simeral. At that time you impressed me to the extent that I knew we had the best radio operator in B-29s. I knew then that you could be counted on to do whatever was necessary to complete our mission. We trained together, we lived together, and we flew together for about eight months. I only remember you as kind, considerate, and completely honorable in every act and deed. For almost fifty years you have been a part of my life. Though we have been a thousand miles apart I often think of you and all that you have accomplished."

Schnipper credited Red for giving him many extra decades of life on earth. "If Red didn't do what he did," he told a reporter, "we all would have been killed."

Recently, Schnipper, now ninety-four years old, reflected on where life had brought him, some seventy-five years after the day Red was injured and saved his life. "I'm doing really good," he reported. "I went to the gym today, walked a half a mile, and I'm still driving. I go to the gym almost every day. Tomorrow is Thanksgiving Day, and we're going to have a big family dinner. I have three boys and one girl, and four great-grandchildren now. The oldest is going to be six in January. I have another great-grandchild on the way. Everybody's healthy and everybody's doing well. They all worry about me, and I wish they wouldn't, but they do. My wife died a while ago. Now I have a girlfriend who I've had for about nine years. She's a younger woman. She just had her birthday. She's eighty-eight."

Schnipper said he still thinks about Red Erwin often. "He saved our lives in two ways—he threw the bomb out and he aborted our mission over Koriyama, which was a long mission over land in Japan. We could easily have been shot down."

———

After the war, the firebomb attacks on Japan and the cataclysmic Tokyo raid of March 9–10, 1945, were largely forgotten in Japan's rush to modernize and rebuild. "For some reason the story of the Tokyo air raid was not talked about after the war," said Kayoko Ebina, who lost most of her family in the raid. "It was as if somebody had locked the story up and hidden it somewhere."

According to historian Toshihiro Itaya, "I think Japanese just wanted to forget about it. Japan lost the war and people just wanted to get on rebuilding their lives, not dwelling on the past."

In Tokyo today there are a few small monuments and markers here and there about the firebombing, and some elderly Tokyo residents remember the time of *iki jigoku* ("hell on earth"), but it is otherwise mostly lost in the mists of distant time.

A group of Tokyo air raid survivors tried to collect damages from the Japanese government for negligence in not properly preparing for air attack, but their class-action suit was rejected in 2013 by the Japanese Supreme Court.

Today, a modest, privately funded museum devoted to the victims of the air raids exists on a quiet side street of eastern Tokyo, near what was the epicenter of the March 9–10 attack. Elderly survivors, scholars, and schoolchildren gather there to hear lectures, hold discussions, and view artifacts of the raids, including photos and maps of the horrors that occurred and napalm canisters that fell from the sky. When you enter the museum's photo gallery section, you are first confronted not by photos of the American bombing of Tokyo but by photos of Chinese cities and civilians wounded and destroyed by Japanese bombs in the preceding years, which provides a full context for the Tokyo firebombing.

In 2015, on the seventieth anniversary of what is sometimes called the Great Tokyo Air Raid, the Japanese government sponsored a visit of reconciliation by five B-29 veterans who took part in the firebombing. They visited places where they crashed and prisons where they were tortured. At the Tokyo Air Raid Museum, ninety-five-year-old Fiske Hanley, a B-29 engineer, met seventy-nine-year-old Haruyo Nihei, who, as a girl, survived the firestorm at the bottom of a pile of bodies that sheltered her from the fire.

The American man and the Japanese woman walked through the museum together and reflected on the horrors of war. "I wonder if they had thought of the people on the ground when they dropped the bombs," she said to a reporter. "But I'm more thrilled by the fact that we, who were witnesses of that moment in history, are reunited at this place seventy years later. They must have had mixed feelings about coming here, so I'm so glad they came."

One man who could not forget the firebombing of Tokyo was Vannevar Bush, the former dean of engineering at the Massachusetts Institute of Technology and head of the US Office of Scientific Research and Development during World War II, which oversaw the development of napalm incendiary bombs. According to a friend, "For years after the war, Van Bush would wake up screaming in the night because he burned Tokyo. Even the atomic bomb didn't bother him as much as jellied gasoline."

———

The Medal of Honor casts a long shadow.

It is a rare honor, and when a person receives the nation's highest honor, they are catapulted, often from obscurity, to stardom. There is an unwritten tradition that generals, admirals, and even presidents should salute the medal worn by a recipient. Invitations to parades, speeches, autograph signings, and public events tumble into a recipient's in-box for the rest of their life. Not everyone can handle the pressure. But Red Erwin did, and admirably so.

How did Red manage the public recognition and demands of the medal? The Veterans Day parades, the Memorial Day speeches, the Fourth of July picnics, the thousands of people over the years wanting to shake his hand (until they realized at the last moment that his right hand was immobile), and the thousands who recoiled at his appearance when first meeting him? How did he do this and at the same time remain a modest, private person who was mainly concerned with being a good husband, father, and grandfather?

I knew him for a relatively short time as a grandfather. What was he like as a father? Who was this man?

After Red died, I began asking these questions to one of the people who knew him best: my father, Hank Jr. My father is a lot like Red. He's loving, supportive, enthusiastic, dependable, devoted to his family, a man of God, and also very much his own man. Like Red and me, he is a story-teller. He had a long career as a television broadcaster, and he served as a state senator. When my brother, Andrew, and I were eleven years old, he gave us some video equipment to experiment with, and we went on to become filmmakers. So you could say he set us on our path. Over many long father-and-son conversations across the years, Hank Jr. shared with me his memories and reflections on Red's life and legacy.

"The true measure of a hero is really not necessarily the gallantry of his action, but essentially how he lives out the rest of his life after all the attention and glory have faded away," my father told me. "When the bands quit playing and life has moved on, how does he or she grapple with everyday problems. That test really reveals the person's depth of courage and essential character."

He added, "Your grandfather was a man of immense integrity. His whole life revolved around integrity. He kept his nose clean and he hon-ored the Lord. He embodied all the ideals of the Medal of Honor. He wore them like a well-pressed suit. He was honest, thrifty, and patriotic. He never owed a debt, never was sued. He obeyed the law, attended church, and treated everyone with courtesy and respect."

My father explained that Red's main struggle was adapting to his broken body. "He had to learn to cope with a useless right arm, limited eye-sight, and visible burns. But he took it in stride. He never let it bother him. His philosophy was, 'Make the best out of what you have.' He never let his injuries get in his way and he never worried about it. He never complained about it. He was thankful for whatever he got. His left side was normal and intact, so he thanked the Lord for that. I was born after the burns, and I never had a before-and-after image of my dad. He was always dad to me, and it didn't matter to me whether he was burned. He never complained or griped about his wounds. He never expressed bitterness or remorse for his injuries. He never blamed God for his plight. He made the best of it."

Slowly, I was beginning to understand my dad, and through him, my grandfather. My father and his siblings watched their father live out the daily life of a war hero. He was always gracious and always available for interviews.

In 1978, Red and Betty had saved enough money for their dream home and moved out to Leeds, Alabama, to a five-acre plot of land with a split-level ranch-style home and a beautiful garden that became Red's pride and joy. This would be their retreat for the golden years of life.

An American love story: Red and Betty Erwin (Erwin Family Collection)

It also meant a new connection with the small city of Leeds. Now this community would gain the distinction of having three Medal of Honor recipients among its residents: Col. Bill Lawley, Sgt. Alford L. McGlaughlin, and Red.

Red and Betty lived quietly among the tall pine trees and appreciated the simple things of life. Red planted a vegetable garden in the backyard and worked hard in the soil, evoking boyhood memories of plowing farmland for fifty cents a day. Flowers were everywhere. Red was always working in the yard, keeping it neat and clean, ready for a white-glove inspection and a gardening competition. He was "Mister Yard Man." Every Saturday he would spend at least two hours mowing the grass and trimming the hedges. His house was air force spotless.

"When I was a boy, he spent many an hour at the Little League field hitting flies and skinners for the kids," Hank Jr. remembered. "It was a true art form. He would clinch the bat to his stomach under his bad arm, toss the ball into the air with his left hand, and then snatch the bat just in time to hit a lazy, majestic fly ball into the outfield. He was fair as an umpire and even called me out when I stepped off the bag in a game. He loved it and the kids respected him. Dad rarely got angry. I never saw him scream or curse anyone. In a few tense situations that I observed, he would rather lower the tone of his voice and forcefully express his point of view."

———

For a half century after his injury, Red Erwin loved life. He thrived personally and professionally. He taught himself to be left-handed in all his actions. He learned to write left-handed and how to dress one-handed. His penmanship was remarkable. He lifted, carried, and pushed everything with his one good arm. He kept his front lawn spotless. He devoured newspapers. He became a walking encyclopedia of American history and current events.

He paid the bills and managed the family affairs. He loved to drive—with one hand—and his daughter Nancy recalled how he "drove like a racecar driver over hills and through sharp turns, leading us kids in the back seat, in the years before seat belts, to hold on for dear life." He never had an accident. But he had a special knob placed on the steering wheel to help him guide the car. He never received a speeding ticket or even a parking ticket. He paid cash for each family car over the years. He despised debt.

He learned to work himself up a ladder with one hand so he could putter around on his roof when it needed repair. Nancy would gaze out the living room window, expecting to see him come crashing down at any moment, but he never did. Red learned to see himself in the mirror every day appearing the way he did and to charge into life.

Red didn't mind having his picture taken—in fact, he loved it. If there was a camera nearby, chances are he would maneuver himself into the photo, discreetly favoring the left side of his face.

He loved giving speeches to school assemblies and civic meetings across Alabama and beyond.

Red enjoyed meeting presidents. In 1963, he met President Kennedy, a fellow combat veteran of the Pacific theater, who, as a US Navy lieutenant, had saved eleven men, including himself, after the Japanese destroyer *Amagiri* rammed his PT-109 boat in 1943 off the Solomon Islands, creating a 100-foot-high fireball and gasoline fire that severely burned one of his crewmen. In a photo of their encounter in the White House Rose Garden at a ceremony for Medal of Honor recipients, JFK is shaking Red's left hand, and the two men share a look of camaraderie and brotherhood that perhaps can be felt only by those whose lives have been forged in courage and combat.

On May 2, 1963, Red Erwin met President John F. Kennedy during a ceremony in the White House Rose Garden. Gen. David M. Shoup (wearing glasses), commandant of the Marine Corps, stands to the right of President Kennedy. (Erwin Family Collection)

In his work for the Veterans Administration, Red ushered tens of thousands of American veterans through the sometimes Byzantine process of getting their benefits and proper medical care. Every workday, he got up around 4:30 a.m. to get an early start, drove himself to the hospital, made his rounds of checking in on all the patients in the hospital, took notes to pass on to the medical team, then grabbed breakfast in the hospital cafeteria before starting his regular day. The rest of the day he spent greeting new patients, troubleshooting claims and paperwork with the regional VA office, and making more rounds with his patients.

Red didn't advertise his Medal of Honor status at the hospital, and he wore the medal only on special occasions. But his award was commonly known among many patients, and upon first meeting him, they could tell he'd been through tough times himself. They often felt comforted and reassured by his presence. They knew he was on their side and would fight for what they deserved.

One of his coworkers at the hospital, Dakota Robinson, recalled that on the rare occasions Red couldn't deliver what a patient needed because of some irrevocable VA technicality, Red would take it personally and sometimes appear emotionally devastated himself.

For countless veterans over the decades, Red was able to come through for them, as he came through for the crew of the *City of Los Angeles* during those twenty-two fateful seconds over the Pacific Ocean on April 12, 1945.

He was, you could say, a guardian angel for all of them.

In the years that followed, Red thought many times about the idea of God saying, "Call on Me and I will answer."

It was expressed many times in the Bible, and Red never doubted that it was true. God can answer your prayers, as the Bible explains, even in the worst moment of your life:

Call to me and I will answer you and tell you great and unsearchable things you do not know. (Jer. 33:3)

In my distress I called to the LORD, and he answered me. From deep in the realm of the dead I called for help, and you listened to my cry. (Jonah 2:2)

And everyone who calls on the name of the Lord will be saved. (Acts 2:21)

Then you will call, and the LORD will answer; you will cry for help, and he will say: Here am I. (Isa. 58:9)

Before they call I will answer; while they are still speaking I will hear. (Isa. 65:24)

In my distress I called to the LORD; I cried to my God for help. From his temple he heard my voice; my cry came before him, into his ears. (Ps. 18:6)

As for me, I call to God, and the LORD saves me. (Ps. 55:16)

I call on the LORD in my distress, and he answers me. (Ps. 120:1)

Perhaps these Bible passages explain how Red Erwin survived his ordeal with death in 1945.

Chapter Nine

LEGACY IN THE CLOUDS

TODAY THERE ARE ONLY TWO B-29S IN THE WORLD that remain airworthy.

You can arrange to take a flight in either of them. *FiFi* is based in Fort Worth, Texas, and *Doc* is based in Wichita, Kansas. Neither of them saw combat, but with the exceptions of some rebuilt pieces and parts, they are in many ways the same planes flown during the war by airmen like my grandfather.

Not long ago, I took a flight in *FiFi*, a meticulously restored airplane that was discovered and rescued by aviation enthusiasts while being used, inexplicably, as a target at the Naval Air Weapons Station China Lake, in California. The aircraft is now maintained and operated by volunteers and aviation experts at the Texas-based Commemorative Air Force. In the most recent renovation of *FiFi*, the radio operator's position has been completely and painstakingly restored—and named after my grandfather.

When I first saw *FiFi*, I was amazed at its size, and, despite the horrors of the war the B-29s participated in, by its aerodynamic beauty.

I climbed into the plane and spent time in the windowless radio operator's shack, where my grandfather would have been stationed, and where he spent so many hours in communion with the Lord. In there is a plaque in Red Erwin's honor.

I spotted the area on the deck where the phosphorus flares would have been dropped, and I found it incredible to believe how Red could have bear-hugged a flaming phosphorus bomb to his chest, maneuvered himself through a cluttered plane and past a locked-down navigator's table, all the way up to the copilot's window to eject the bomb and save the crew. To him, in those moments, it may have been a reflex action to save everyone, but I simply couldn't imagine how he did it.

Red often explained how the intervention of God made it possible, and that's the only explanation that makes sense to me.

To get the best view, I climbed into the plane's Plexiglas nose, below the pilot's and the copilot's positions.

I braced myself for takeoff. The engines roared to life, the pilots carefully throttled forward, and the old plane groaned and lumbered down the runway, slow at first, then faster and faster. The ground raced by at increasing speed. The rattle was intense, the sound deafening, the moment surreal. *Come on, come on*, I half prayed.

When the plane climbed into the air, I was in awe, and alone with my thoughts as we pushed into the clouds.

———

For a long time, I ran away from my grandfather's story as a Medal of Honor recipient. I didn't want to be overshadowed by it. It was too spectacular and too distant for me to connect with. He had his life and I had mine, and I didn't see much connection between the two. It was as if there were a voice at the back of my head saying, "Okay, your grandfather is a big war hero. Now what are you going to do?"

But after Red died, his story began to inspire me.

I am a professional storyteller, and my earliest memories are of Red's telling me stories. Perhaps in doing so he helped set me on a path toward my destiny.

I spent years searching out my grandfather's story. The quest took me, my brother, and my coauthor across the United States, the Pacific, and Japan. I spoke with the woman he loved, with the crewmates he saved, and with the friends and family who shaped his life. I unearthed much of his voice through the memories of my father and in letters, scrapbooks, and archives scattered across the country. I learned a lot.

But there was one thing I didn't understand. Why and how did Henry Eugene "Red" Erwin do what he did that day in April 1945 in the sky over the Pacific Ocean?

There was one man who might know the answer.

I had to see him.

My quest took me to Charleston, South Carolina, to meet Medal of Honor recipient Gary L. Littrell, a Vietnam-era veteran who serves as president of the Congressional Medal of Honor Society. He knows the history of the medal, the people who have received the award, and the experience of it as well as any person.

Gary's office is in the USS *Yorktown*, an Essex-class aircraft carrier that saw action across the Pacific theater during World War II and is now permanently berthed at the Patriots Point Naval and Maritime Museum at Charleston Harbor. It is a magnificent ship, rich with history, and it houses the Medal of Honor Museum. It was the tenth aircraft carrier to serve in the US Navy, and it was renamed in honor of the original *Yorktown* carrier that was sunk during the epic 1942 Battle of Midway. It was known as the Fighting Lady, and it joined in the Pacific offensive beginning in late 1943 and ending with the defeat of Japan, after earning the Presidential Unit Citation and eleven battle stars.

The offices of the Congressional Medal of Honor Society are below-decks, nestled at the far end of the Medal of Honor Museum. I walked through exhibit after exhibit displaying images of Americans performing acts of courage, sacrifice, and valor. Each face stared back at me, reminding me of Hebrews 12:1: "Therefore, since we are surrounded by such a great cloud of witnesses, . . . let us run with perseverance the race marked out for us." Each story seemed more incredible than the previous one, acts of superhuman and self-sacrificial courage that awed and inspired me. I kept thinking, *What unites these people and people like my grandfather? How are they able to summon such reservoirs of courage?* Finally, I had a chance to get an answer.

As I reached the end of the exhibits and entered the offices of the Medal of Honor Society, Gary Littrell greeted me like a long-lost friend, sat me down, and talked to me like the strong, humble, funny, and folksy man he is. He described himself as an old army sergeant from Spottsville, Kentucky, which he explained was "in between Poopy Holler and Pee Ridge." I asked him about the Medal of Honor and all it represented. He told me his story, which over the years he has shared with veterans, schoolchildren, journalists, and historians alike.

In 1970, Sgt. Gary Littrell was stationed in Kontum Province in South Vietnam, serving as a light weapons advisor with the South Vietnamese Twenty-Third Battalion, Second Ranger Group.

"We had four American advisors," he recalled. "We were moving toward the Cambodian border to find the enemy, identify their location, back off, and call in air strikes on them. We moved up on top of this one hill to spend the night. We were surrounded by two North Vietnamese regiments and a sapper battalion, consisting of about five thousand of North Vietnam's finest."

He continued, "It started with an artillery barrage, which killed the South Vietnamese commander, killed one of our lieutenants, filled the other one's liver full of shrapnel, and busted the eardrums of the third sergeant. So I was the only American left after I evacuated those three. Didn't seem like anyone else wanted to come in and help me. I couldn't get any air support at all, no US artillery. All we could do was evacuate the wounded by helicopter. We finally gave that up. Because the fighting was so heavy they didn't want to come in and evacuate anyone else. They did try to make two or three high-speed, low-level runs and kick some ammunition out to us, but they couldn't land. So my primary job was just command and control, trying to get the South Vietnamese to stand and fight.

"It was a twenty-four-hour, four-day fight," Gary explained, remembering how fatigue overwhelmed him but he somehow kept fighting and leading the South Vietnamese troops, who were like brothers to him.

"I fought with the Vietnamese rangers, and they were warriors to the end," he remembered. "Most of them were vengeance, grudge fighters. They'd lost their wife, their kids, their mothers, their fathers. The life expectancy of a ranger was about eight months. And depending on their religion, most of them believed if they died honorably they'd come back a better person; hence they weren't afraid of death. Me, I didn't believe that. I didn't want to get killed. I didn't want to be reborn the next day a better person. I wanted to stay the person I was. I kind of liked me. But they were vengeance fighters. They were hard core."

The incredible story is described in Gary's Medal of Honor citation:

His dauntless will instilled in the men of the 23d Battalion a deep desire to resist. Assault after assault was repulsed as the battalion responded to the extraordinary leadership and personal example exhibited by Sfc. Littrell as he continuously moved to those points most seriously threatened by the enemy, redistributed ammunition, strengthened faltering defenses, cared for the wounded and shouted encouragement to the Vietnamese in their own language. When the beleaguered battalion was finally ordered to withdraw, numerous ambushes were encountered. Sfc. Littrell repeatedly prevented widespread disorder by directing air strikes to within 50 meters of their position. Through his indomitable courage and complete disregard for his safety, he averted excessive loss of life and injury to the members of the battalion.

I thought about those words: *dauntless will*. Is that a characteristic I possessed? Was it learned, inherited, in my DNA?

Gary continued, "You'll never find an atheist in a foxhole being fired at. I've never run across one. I've been in a lot of foxholes with a lot of soldiers, with a lot of fire, a lot of ammunition popping around their head. Never been in a foxhole with an atheist yet. On the fourth night, I pretty much had come to the conclusion that I was dead. It was over. A very quiet, peaceful, tranquil feeling came over me. God and I have our own thing going. We understand each other. That night, I knew that I would probably never see the sun shine again. It was a quiet, peaceful, tranquil feeling. Thank God he didn't take me. He left me here for a reason. I'm not sure I found that reason yet. But there's a reason I'm here.

"It was kick butt or die," he explained simply. "It was not much of a choice. You know, it was fish or cut bait. And I prefer to fish. Finally, I walked off the hill four days later with approximately forty-one walking wounded and myself."

After the evacuation, Gary radioed to the nearest American position, where an officer said, "Hey, you're getting close to my perimeter. How bad off are you?"

"I'm physically okay," replied Gary.

"What can I do for you?" the American asked.

"I want a cold drink of water and a cigarette."

When Gary and his men broke through the American perimeter, there was his new friend, waiting for him with a cup of cold water and a cigarette.

I asked Gary how the Medal of Honor affected his life.

He admitted, "All of a sudden, everybody's bowing, the ladies are curtsying, and everybody's shaking my hand, and I go to the White House to meet the president. I go over to the Pentagon and meet all the generals. Then I come back to Fort Campbell, Kentucky, back to my real job, and I had placed myself up on a pedestal a little bit.

"And one night, Sgt. Maj. Joe Feeney, a good friend of mine, looked at me and said, 'You know, I used to like you. I don't like you anymore. You've been shot in the butt with the Glory Gun. Now come on down off that damn pedestal you placed yourself on and get back down here with the guys that know you and love you.' I didn't have a response for that. I talked to a few of my other friends. They said, 'Yeah, you're not as likable as you used to be.'

"So I had to self-evaluate myself. And I said, 'Hey, what happened, happened.' Now we're back in the real world. And so, yeah, it affected me for a while. I was shot in the butt with the Glory Gun. It doesn't affect me now. I realize that I'm wearing this medal for the four hundred people who died those four days. I'm their representative. They won this medal. I was selected to wear it for them."

Finally, I asked him the question that had perplexed me for so long. "How did you do it? How did you lead those men through that battle? How does a man throw himself on a grenade? How does a man embrace and carry a phosphorus bomb burning at over a thousand degrees? How do you decide in an instant to sacrifice yourself? How did my grandfather make the choice to grab a burning bomb?"

He replied, "It's not a choice really. Not a conscious one at least. You don't have time to make a decision. You just do it. You love the men beside you. You'll do anything to save them."

It's really not a choice. Whatever is in your character simply manifests itself in that moment. I began to rethink my grandfather's story, and it all began to make sense. The very idea of words like *courage* and *valor* began to make sense.

Gary Littrell and my grandfather helped me realize that heroism isn't born in a moment but in the lifetime leading up to that moment. Whatever is in the character of these heroes manifests itself in moments of extreme pressure, and acts of courage, like Medal of Honor actions, are often acts of pure self-sacrifice and love.

I realized that, in the case of my grandfather, he had been doing this all his life. He was accustomed to sacrificing himself to the needs of other people. He started work at the age of ten and became the head of a household consisting of a widow and seven brothers and sisters. He quit high school to feed his family. He turned down a stint at Yale so he could more quickly put his life on the line for his country. He spent every Sunday morning of his life in church, in deep reflection on the fundamental Christian messages of love, compassion, charity, and self-sacrifice.

That was his life ethos, to sacrifice your own needs and your own comfort to care for those you love. It was so ingrained in him that in a moment of crisis, when his life and the lives of many others were on the line, he instantly did what he always did. It was a moment of instinct that was a lifetime in the making. When the moment came, he did the same thing for his crew that he did for his family.

What lies beyond courage and beyond valor is love. These Medal of Honor recipients don't necessarily make their ultimate decisions as acts of courage, but more as reflex actions of love for those beside them. Time and time again, story after story, the phrase "I did it for the men beside me" comes up.

They didn't want to let down the men beside them, and they didn't want them to die. These most extreme acts of courage on the battlefield are actually extreme acts of love. As Jesus said in John 15:13 (KJV), "Greater love hath no man than this, that a man lay down his life for his friends." Perhaps the more you love those around you, the more courage you can summon when it counts.

As I prepared to leave, Gary told me one last thing.

"There are only about seventy Medal of Honor recipients who are alive today. My fear is that your generation is losing sight of what the Medal of Honor means and why it matters. You should tell them that story. Tell them that the idea of doing more than is required of you is part of the American ethos, and it is exemplified in the Medal of Honor. It's part of what makes us Americans. You don't have to be a soldier on the field of battle to go above and beyond the call of duty."

I thought about that, about the idea that the essence of the Medal of Honor reaches far beyond the military. Its story and its meaning should reach into the heart of every American. After all, our country is bound together, not by geography or race, but by ideas and common dreams. We are a land of immigrant dreamers. We are diverse, as our national motto reminds us, "out of many, one." What binds us together is a set of ideas and ideals. Common virtues unite us. And to the extent that we forget those virtues, to the extent we do not pass them down through stories, we lose the ties that bind us.

One of the greatest virtues that makes us Americans is the simple idea of going above and beyond. The simple virtue of doing things others would consider unwise or impossible, all for the sake of those you love. As Jesus said, "If anyone forces you to go one mile, go with them two miles" (Matt. 5:41). My grandfather did more than what was required of him, as did all those who received the same award. And this is a concept we can all remember and we can all apply. And we can remember that beyond courage is love.

Today, I am inspired by Red Erwin's devotion to his wife, his family, and his brothers in arms and how he dedicated his life to the service of others. I am inspired by how he embodied the medal's heritage of honor, self-sacrifice, and going further, above and beyond the call of duty.

I am inspired by his love for the United States. He always said the great thing about our country is that it is imperfect, and that we have the power to make it better and leave it a better place for our children. He loved America and all it stands for, with all its problems and imperfections, and he often noted that freedom isn't free.

One of the things I love about America is that it is imperfect. And we are free to point that out, argue over it, and try to make it better. I believe America is the greatest idea in the history of nations, the idea that we can choose a government for ourselves, that we can find unity in the face of our diversity. What a radical thought, that we can be bound together by our differences, since so many of us, in the scheme of things, are from fairly recent immigrant families. America is one vast, unfinished work. It was built that way.

The Founding Fathers' idea of "all men are created equal" was such a radical idea for its time. We can't take the next step in reaching for those ideals unless we understand our own story and understand our legacy and understand our heritage and understand the lessons of our ancestors. If we don't take the time to look in the rearview mirror and study the generations that came before us and the history of the country, we are in danger of becoming a rudderless ship.

I am inspired by Red Erwin's faith in God. I am a believer in Jesus Christ, and I find great meaning, purpose, direction, and spiritual nourishment from that belief. I'm not someone who claims to understand it all, because I don't think we can fully understand the divine, but I've thrown my lot in with the words in red, namely, Jesus's words in the Bible, on a very personal level. You don't have to totally understand something to believe it. I've chosen to believe it.

I think sometimes, as Christians, we need to be witnesses more than judges, and I can only witness. I got this from my grandfather and father, two very devout men. Jesus is a huge part of the life of my family, and I believe Red embodied many of the lessons that Jesus taught.

As my father explained to me, "There's a lot of pressure that comes with a Medal of Honor, and a lot of guys couldn't handle it. Because once you get it, it's yours for your life, and you can either choose to adapt to the pressure, and it molds your character, or you can fight it all of your life. Dad chose to embrace it and live up to all the ideals that were expected of it. He chose to represent the military with respect and with dignity and that you would distinguish yourself as an American citizen wearing that medal. And so he practiced that all his life, to live up to the idea of honor. He always told the truth. He always talked highly of America. He would always say America is the greatest nation on the face of the earth. He was always giving and sacrificing and always trying to promote and take care of veterans. He became a walking embodiment of what the Medal of

Honor was all about. He remained a lifelong believer in Jesus. He always credited God for saving his life."

These days, whenever I'm faced with a difficulty in my life or my business, I think to myself, *Well, this can't be harder than carrying a detonating phosphorus bomb under my arm, saving twelve people's lives, being of service to tens of thousands of sick and wounded veterans, and living with the aftermath of massive burn injuries for fifty-seven years.* I just keep going! Red's story shows that you can push yourself and do things that people say you can't do, things that may seem impossible.

Today my brother and I are partners in a thriving entertainment business, and we strive to be of service to others by telling stories that have the power to uplift and inspire people. In our day-to-day work, the memory and lessons of Red Erwin inspire us with the ideals of endurance and perseverance, of pushing ourselves toward something that we believe is right and worth fighting for. The difference between success and failure can be when an individual chooses to quit. And I've found that the people who are successful are the people who can go above and beyond. I learned that from my grandfather.

And finally, Red's story teaches me of the true, limitless power of prayer. No matter who you are—a president of the United States, a regular mom, a dad, or a twenty-three-year-old soldier who wants nothing more than to come home to be with your true love—in the absolute darkest moments of your life, a prayer to God can create a miracle.

As for me, I've learned that the Medal of Honor given to my grandfather is his and his alone. It will never be mine, and I don't have to live under its shadow. But all the things the medal stands for—courage, self-sacrifice, faith, love, honor—form the legacy that my grandfather Red Erwin and grandmother Betty have given to me.

And I accept it gladly.

AFTERWORD

In His Own Words

[THIS IS HOW RED RECALLED HIS POSTWAR LIFE *in his own words that I found in notes, interviews, and oral histories over the years during my fifteen-year quest to research his life.*]

I went to work for the Veterans Administration in January 1948 when I got out of the military. Harry Truman had issued an executive order that any Medal of Honor recipient otherwise qualified was eligible for a veterans benefits job. I knew that the TCI company would never give me my job back at the steel plant due to the loss of my arm. I went to work for the Veterans Administration as a veterans benefits counselor. I did that for thirty-seven years, and I retired with forty-three and a half years of combined federal service. I loved the military. Even though I was severely burned, if they had retained me, I would have stayed in.

I handled all veterans claims, informing them of their rights and benefits and privileges under the laws that were passed by the Congress concerning compensation, pension, GI loans, housing, schooling, automobiles, hospitalization, outpatient treatment, you name it, and I was familiar with all of it. In fact, I enjoyed it very well. I would leave my house at 4:30 in the morning and I would be working at 5:00, even though I was my own boss for the last twenty-five years.

Having the Medal of Honor, which says "above and beyond," I always felt that I wanted to excel at my job. And I will be very frank, I'm not bragging—I did excel in it! I really enjoyed my work. I got outstanding ratings every year for the last twenty-five years.

There was deep satisfaction in helping veterans, young and old, with their problems, especially a fellow veteran, or help a widow get the benefits they are entitled to by law, to go around the obstacles and get it for them.

I have been approached by people that I know wanted to use me as a Medal of Honor recipient in their political campaigns, and I've been approached by quite a few unscrupulous individuals. But I would just tell them that the Medal of Honor is not for sale, that it was given to me by a government that I was grateful for. It's not for sale.

I'm proud of it. But being a recipient of a Medal of Honor calls for you to be in the right place at the right time. Everyone watches you, wondering if you're going to break the traditions that go along with being a recipient of the medal. You try to watch your p's and q's and try to live up to it. I hope I have.

I have made statements about the Korean and Vietnam Wars, that if we are going to kill fifty-five thousand American boys, and we are going to injure three hundred thousand more, we shouldn't have these type wars. If we are going to go to war, we should declare war and go end it, get it over with. In World War II we had the leaders, we had the logistics, and we had brave men in the right place at the right time, the kind of men who won the war for us in World War II.

The flyboys got all the credit, but actually you couldn't get that aircraft off the ground or get it back safely unless you had good ground crews. And we had crews that were just superb. Just think, in forty-eight hours they were loading bombs, putting in about 5,000 or 6,000 gallons of gasoline, checking the machine guns and everything. It was just a superb accomplishment. It was to me, probably one of the best activities in the war, how the maintenance crews and everybody else worked together in unison to get this war over as quickly as possible and get home.

Leadership is one of these things that is set by example. In other words, it's like a father-son relationship. You've got to live that life before them that will convince them you are valid, and not a hypocrite.

I have a son who was a minister and a son-in-law who is a minister and a brother who was a minister. I know my son is one of the best individuals and God-fearing men I know. He is a truly dedicated Christian. I have had four children, all of them have finished college, two of them have master's degrees. This is something I've tried to give them that I wasn't able to get during my coming-up years.

They made a fuss about my being a hero. It didn't occur to me at the time. I knew the flare was burning and I had to get it out of there!

I am not a hero. The real heroes are those who have given the ultimate sacrifice for this country, those who have given their lives. They're the ones who deserve the medals. I am only a survivor. I don't wear the Medal of Honor for what I did, I wear it for *everyone* who served.

We should take care of America because it's a great nation, and it deserves to be protected, loved, cherished, and passed on. We have more freedoms in this country than we realize. But if the youngsters will look and see what price has been paid, they'll realize freedom is not free.

I survived. So the best thing to do is always make the best of what you have. Life is what you make it. Life is beautiful.

My belief has always been if anything is worth doing, then do your best, because I believe there's a silver cloud ahead. Like a motto I once heard, "To strive, to seek, to find, and not to yield."

Jesus is my savior. He got me through, and He never lets me down.

Henry Eugene "Red" Erwin (Erwin Family Collection)

ACKNOWLEDGMENTS

THE AUTHORS WISH TO THANK HENRY E. ERWIN, Betty Erwin, Henry E. Erwin Jr., Andrew Erwin, Ray Erwin, Karen Erwin Brown, Nancy Erwin Herndon, Bette Erwin Cobb, Mark Ray, Webster Younce, Sujin Hong, Mel Berger, David Hinds, Naomi Moriyama, Brendan Doyle, Marie Louise Doyle, Pershing Youngkin, Herb Schnipper, Hap Halloran, Orville Blackburn, Ray Clanton, Carl Barthold, Shizuyo Takeuchi, Jeffrey Hester, Geneva Robinson, David Barillo, James Holmes, Randy Kearns, Alan Dimick, and Uri Aviv.

APPENDIX

Seven Prayers

PRAYER WAS THE FOUNDATION OF MY GRAND-
father's life, and today prayer is the pillar of my family's life.

America has always been a land that is nourished and guided by
prayer on the part of citizens, patriots, clergy, children, warriors, and
presidents. These prayers have been made in our houses of worship,
homes, cities, and villages, as well as on distant battlefields.

America itself is a prayer, a fervent hope by humanity for freedom,
peace, and prosperity in a world of dangers, unknowns, and boundless
possibilities. The Native Americans who tended the land for centuries
were sustained by countless forms of personal prayers and group prayer
ceremonies. The first European settlers to arrive on these shores often fell
to their knees with prayers of thanks and inspiration. Then and now, the
spiritual lifeblood of our nation is constantly renewed with the prayers of
Americans from every corner of the earth.

Prayer, in fact, has played a vital role not only in the daily lives of
countless Americans but, it has, on several occasions, helped shape history during some of our greatest national turning points, when presidents
have turned to the ultimate source for help: God.

In each of these seven critical moments, when the life and death of
nations hung in the balance, God delivered nothing less than a miracle.
America is, in a sense, the story of seven prayers.

The First Prayer

The American Revolution was a desperate seven-year prayer for miraculous deliverance through biblical-scale trials and catastrophes, orchestrated by "prayer-in-chief" George Washington.

At the dawn of the Revolution, when colonial troops faced starvation, despair, multiple defeats, and hopeless odds, General Washington prayed to God for deliverance and urged his men to do so. He declared June 12, 1775, as a national day of fasting, humiliation, and prayer, and that proclamation was endorsed by the Continental Congress under its president, John Hancock.

On May 15, 1776, Washington publicly asked God to "pardon all our manifold sins and transgressions, and to prosper the arms of the United Colonies, and finally establish the peace and freedom of America upon a solid and lasting foundation."

In the depths of the winter of 1777, Washington and his army, suffering great misfortunes, prayed to God for deliverance at Valley Forge, Pennsylvania.

In time, their prayers were answered. The ragtag armies of the fledgling thirteen colonies eventually won a miraculous victory over the vastly superior British Army. The United States was literally a "republic of miracles." Moments after General Washington announced the end of hostilities with Great Britain on April 18, 1783, he directed all the military chaplains of the new nation to "render thanks to almighty God."

The Second Prayer

In 1787, when George Washington presided over a stormy Constitutional Convention at Philadelphia that seemed on the verge of collapsing, Benjamin Franklin announced, "Gentlemen, I suggest that we have a word of prayer."

Franklin reminded the delegates, "In the beginning of the Contest with Great Britain, when we were sensible of danger, we had daily prayer in this room for Divine protection." According to Dwight Eisenhower, "Strangely enough, after a bit of prayer the problems began to smooth out and the convention moved to the great triumph that we enjoy today—the writing of our Constitution."

At the moment Washington was inaugurated as president on April 30, 1789, he announced, "My fervent supplications to that Almighty Being who rules over the universe, who presides in the councils of nations, and whose providential aids can supply every human defect, that His benediction may consecrate to the liberties and happiness of the people of the United States a government instituted by themselves for these essential purposes, and may enable every instrument employed in its administration to execute with success the functions allotted to His charge."

Since the birth of America, this nation has been built, shaped, and inspired by moments when American presidents have begged for divine intervention and relied on the power of prayer. Many of these presidents were not overtly religious, but they often harbored strong spiritual beliefs.

Many of the Founding Fathers and the presidents who followed were careful to separate church and state, while simultaneously relying on their own spiritual beliefs and values in steering our government. During his presidency, for example, Thomas Jefferson cut, pasted, and rewrote standard Bible passages into a text more to his liking, one that left out Jesus's virgin birth, resurrection, and supernatural miracles, while keeping the ethical teachings and the power of prayer.

The Third Prayer

Abraham Lincoln endowed the Civil War with sacred meaning, and he prayed for God's help in winning the war and for signs of God's will on the issue of emancipating America's slaves.

Before the war, on a freezing February day in 1861, as he boarded a train to Washington, President-elect Lincoln told a crowd in his hometown of Springfield, Illinois: "I now leave, not knowing when, or whether ever, I may return, with a task before me greater than that which rested upon Washington. Without the assistance of that Divine Being who ever attended him, I cannot succeed. With that assistance, I cannot fail."

In September 1862, after Union forces drove the Southern army from Antietam Creek in Maryland back into Virginia, Lincoln gathered his cabinet and made a startling announcement: "God had decided this question in favor of the slaves." Lincoln took the victory at Antietam as the divine signal he'd been searching for. On New Year's Day 1863, he signed the Emancipation Proclamation, freeing those slaves within the borders of the Confederacy. Lincoln explained, "I've been driven many times to my knees by the overwhelming conviction that I have nowhere else to go."

On March 30, 1863, Lincoln proclaimed a "National Day of Humiliation, Fasting and Prayer." He feared "the awful calamity of civil war" may have been "a punishment inflicted upon us for our presumptuous sins to the needful end of our national reformation as a whole people." He bluntly declared, "We have forgotten God." Three months after Lincoln and millions of other Americans heeded this presidential call to prayer, the Union army won the Battle of Gettysburg and the siege of Vicksburg, turning the tide of the war. Later that year, Lincoln revived what is now an annual tradition of issuing a presidential proclamation of thanksgiving. He asked God to "heal the wounds of the nation and to restore it as soon as may be consistent with the Divine purposes to the full enjoyment of peace, harmony, tranquility, and Union."

Lincoln's second inaugural address on March 4, 1865, was itself an intense prayer for peace: "With malice toward none, with charity for all, with firmness in the right as God gives us to see the right, let us finish the work we are in, to bind up the nation's wounds . . . and cherish a just and a lasting peace among ourselves and with all nations."

Lincoln accomplished his sacred mission, but he died on the eve of peace between the armies of the North and South.

The Fourth Prayer

In 1918, President Woodrow Wilson faced a critical moment in World War I, an industrial-scale slaughter that had been grinding on for four years and caused over forty million casualties. Russia had abandoned the Allied cause, enabling Germany to launch a spring offensive on the western front, and German troops were breaking through Allied lines and flooding into Western Europe, threatening, it seemed, the fall of Paris.

Wilson, who practiced a lifelong study of religion and consulted the Bible every night before bed, proclaimed May 30, 1918, as a national day of prayer and fasting, and exhorted all Americans "of all faiths and creeds to assemble on that day in their several places of worship and there, as well as in their homes, to pray Almighty God that He may forgive our sins and shortcomings as a people and purify our hearts to see and love the truth."

Wilson declared that prayers should be given "beseeching Him that He will give victory to our armies as they fight for freedom, wisdom to those who take counsel on our behalf in these days of dark struggle and perplexity, and steadfastness to our people to make sacrifice to the utmost in support of what is just and true, bringing us at last the peace in which men's hearts can be at rest because it is founded upon mercy, justice and good will."

Exactly one day later, a miracle occurred.

On June 1, US Marines launched their first major operation of the war: the Battle of Belleau Wood, near the Marne River in France. It was a twenty-six-day battle that climaxed in a stunning victory that blocked and stopped the Germans on the road to Paris, saved the French capital, and set the stage for the Allied victory a few months later.

Once again, a president's battle prayer was answered with a history-shaping miracle.

APPENDIX

The Fifth Prayer

As American troops prepared for one of the greatest turning points in twentieth-century history, the D-day landings on June 6, 1944, President Franklin D. Roosevelt united the nation in an epic, fervent prayer that he broadcast to the nation. "Almighty God," Roosevelt intoned, "our sons, pride of our Nation, this day have set upon a mighty endeavor, a struggle to preserve our Republic, our religion, and our civilization, and to set free a suffering humanity. Lead them straight and true. Give strength to their arms, stoutness to their hearts, steadfastness in their faith." He added, "Some shall never return. Embrace these, Father, and receive them, Thy heroic servants, into Thy kingdom."

FDR mentioned God in each of his inaugural addresses, asking for divine guidance through difficult times. Like Lincoln, FDR died on the eve of peace.

When World War II ended, President Harry S. Truman declared a day of prayer on August 16, 1945, stating that global victory "has come with the help of God, Who was with us in the early days of adversity and disaster, and Who has now brought us to this glorious day of triumph. Let us give thanks to Him, and remember that we have now dedicated ourselves to follow in His ways to a lasting and just peace and to a better world." In 1952, Truman made the National Day of Prayer an annual event. "In times of national crisis when we are striving to strengthen the foundations of peace," he explained, "we stand in special need of Divine support."

Truman relied on a single personal prayer all through his adult life: "Oh! Almighty and Everlasting God, Creator of Heaven, Earth and the Universe: Help me to be, to think, to act what is right, because it is right; make me truthful, honest and honorable in all things; make me intellectually honest for the sake of right and honor and without thought of reward to me. Give me the ability to be charitable, forgiving and patient with my fellowmen—help me to understand their motives and their shortcomings—even as Thou understandest mine!"

"I am the most intensely religious man I know," said D-day commander Dwight Eisenhower, explaining that "nobody goes through six years of war without faith." Eisenhower became the first and only president to write and read his own prayer at his inaugural ceremony in 1953, and weeks later, he became the first president to be baptized while in office.

The Sixth Prayer

In January 1961, President John F. Kennedy, a Catholic, a man of quiet faith and a regular churchgoer who rarely missed church on Sunday or a holy day of obligation, ended his inaugural address with these words: "Let us go forth to lead the land we love, asking His blessing and His help, but knowing that here on earth, God's work must truly be our own."

The following year Kennedy asked for God's help during one of the most dangerous crises the world had ever faced: the thirteen-day Cuban Missile Crisis.

Twenty-four hours after the crisis began on October 17, 1962, an apocalyptic showdown loomed with the Soviet Union that threatened to kill tens of millions of people worldwide in a nuclear war. Only a handful of people beyond Kennedy knew of the impending showdown.

At that moment, President Kennedy decided to slip away to pray at St. Matthew's Cathedral, a few blocks from the White House. It happened to be the same day as the National Day of Prayer he had proclaimed six days earlier.

Kennedy knew an old tradition among his tribe of Boston Irish Catholics, that those who visit a church for the first time are entitled to three wishes. Kennedy had been to this church many times before, but on the way to the cathedral, aide Dave Powers joked softly to his boss, "Don't forget the three wishes." Kennedy replied with deadly seriousness, "I only have one wish today." It was, Powers recalled, a prayer that a nuclear war might be averted, with God's help. In fact, according to Powers, every night before going to bed during his time in the White House, JFK got on his knees to pray.

Having made his prayer in the cathedral, and informed by the possibility of divine intervention through his lifetime of personal prayer, John F. Kennedy navigated the world to a peaceful resolution of the missile crisis, a miracle that saved the lives of at least one hundred million civilians around the world.

A decade later, in the darkest days of the Watergate scandal that torpedoed his presidency, Richard M. Nixon, raised as a Quaker, got on his knees to pray with Henry Kissinger, a Jew, inside the White House.

The day he pardoned former president Nixon, Gerald R. Ford walked to church to pray. "I felt very strongly I was about to make a monumental decision, and I wanted the feeling that I had prayed and hoped for the best," Ford remembered. Ford prayed again during the *Mayaguez* rescue operation in Cambodia in the spring of 1975, and he prayed before a summit with the Soviets at Helsinki the same year.

During the 1978 Camp David negotiations, when Egyptian president Anwar Sadat angrily threatened to leave the talks, President Jimmy Carter, a devout Baptist and a Sunday school teacher, fell to his knees and said "a long, silent prayer" that he could rescue the Middle East peace process. He then rushed to Sadat's cabin and convinced him to stay and reach a peace agreement with Israel.

The Seventh Prayer

Ronald Reagan earnestly believed he was on a mission from God to prevent a nuclear war with the Soviet Union. And in what could be considered a completely unexpected miracle, he did exactly that.

Reagan, a man of quiet personal faith who kept a prayer card in his Oval Office desk and was the son of a devout Christian mother, confessed to a friend in 1971 that he feared "for the first time ever, everything is in place for the battle of Armageddon and the second coming of Christ." He added, "It can't be long now. Ezekiel says that fire and brimstone will be rained upon the enemies of God's people. That must mean that they'll be destroyed by nuclear weapons."

Five years later, when he first ran for president in 1976, Reagan yearned for divine guidance to discover his ultimate mission. "I have to realize that whatever I do has meaning only if I ask that it serves His purpose," he said. "I believe that in my present undertaking, whatever the outcome, it will be His doing. I will pray for understanding of what it is He would have me do."

When he accepted the Republican nomination in 1980, Reagan ended his speech with a dramatic moment of hesitation and a call for God's help. "I have thought of something that is not part of my speech. And I'm worried over whether I should do it." He asked, "Can we begin our crusade, joined together, in a moment of silent prayer?" After his public prayer, he concluded with a phrase that has since become commonplace in political oratory: "God bless America."

Early in his presidency, in a letter to a friend, Reagan wrote: "My daily prayer is that God will help me to use this position so as to serve Him."

On March 30, 1981, just two months and ten days into Reagan's first term, a gunman fired a bullet into his chest that landed a quarter of an inch from his heart. The razor-close brush with death deepened Reagan's faith and clarified what the final great mission of his life would be. He recalled, "Having come so close to death made me feel I should do whatever I could in the years God had given me to reduce the threat of nuclear war; perhaps there was a reason I had been spared." Reagan told one of his Secret Service agents, "God wanted that assassination attempt to happen. He gave me a wake-up call. Everything I do from now on, I owe to God."

Throughout his life, Reagan believed there was a divine plan that God had for every human being. And late in his life, when he saw his own death narrowly averted, he finally grasped what it was: to move the world away from Armageddon and toward a more peaceful future.

The final great Oval Office prayer began in 1985, when Reagan sent a warm letter to new Soviet leader Mikhail Gorbachev, a message in which he practically pleaded for warmer relations and an end to the arms race. And in a head-spinning series of events over the next three years, Reagan and Gorbachev largely achieved those goals. Gorbachev, the last leader of the Soviet Union, was himself baptized as a child into the Russian Orthodox Church, and later revealed he was a lifelong believing Christian.

In the American Revolution, the writing of the Constitution, the Civil War and Emancipation, victory in World War I, the D-day landings, and the peaceful resolution of the Cuban Missile Crisis and the Cold War, a series of miracles shaped American history. Our greatness as a nation was achieved with divine help, one could truly believe, and through the power of prayer, invoked by leaders who held in their hands the power to save lives, just as Red Erwin did.

AUTHOR NOTE

RED ERWIN'S MEMORIES AND QUOTES IN THIS book are primarily from his oral histories, correspondence, and press interviews, and from Erwin family correspondence, scrapbooks, and interviews with and written accounts by Erwin family members, particularly Hank Erwin Jr. Unless otherwise indicated, quotations by others in this book are from author interviews.

Some accounts of Red Erwin's Medal of Honor action incorrectly assert it took place during a Japanese aerial attack over the Japanese mainland, when in fact it occurred in the area over Aogashima, a small volcanic island 220 miles south of Tokyo in the Philippine Sea and administered by the Tokyo Metropolis prefecture of Japan, which has a current population of less than two hundred Japanese citizens.

In an article titled "Medal of Honor Recipient: Henry 'Red' Erwin" by Robert F. Dorr, in the *WWII Quarterly* dated November 20, 2018, and posted online at https://warfarehistorynetwork.com/daily/wwii/medal-of-honor-recipient-henry-red-erwin/, Dorr describes the moments before the phosphorus bomb exploded:

> A yellow, twin-engined Japanese fighter known as a Nick was descending off to their right. Meatball red circles were painted on its wings, and muzzle flashes appeared at its nose.
>
> "I got 'em," said top turret gunner Sergeant Howard Stubstad. "There's also four Zekes circling off to the left."

"We're at the assembly point—" Erwin stammered.

"Four of them!" a voice garbled out the others. "Four Zekes closing
on our left!"

Dorr quoted an unnamed crew member as recalling the "Japanese
fighters were like yellowjackets swarming out of a disturbed nest." He
sourced his article to "quotes from Henry E. 'Red' Erwin Sr., gathered in
interviews conducted by the author over several decades, beginning in
1961." No other accounts sourced to Red Erwin or anybody else mention
such an aerial attack. Dorr died in 2016.

Similarly, some accounts of the emergency landing of the *City of Los
Angeles* at Iwo Jima have it occurring during a Japanese aerial attack on
the island. In accounts years later, Red said he was told after the fact that
Iwo Jima was under attack as the *City of Los Angeles* made the emergency
landing, including an air battle where sixteen Mitsubishi G4M "Betty"
bombers were shot down by P-51s over or near Iwo Jima. However, the
authors of this book have not found any documentation that either the
Medal of Honor action or the emergency landing at Iwo Jima occurred
under direct enemy fire.

In 2018 and 2019, gunner Herb Schnipper, the last surviving member of
the *City of Los Angeles* crew, had no memory of any attack that day at either
location and doubted such attacks happened. On April 12, 1945, there were
Japanese stragglers remaining in the hills and caves on Iwo Jima, and it is
possible they were active with small arms or mortar fire, but if they were,
or if enemy air attacks occurred around Iwo Jima that day, they did not
appear to have interfered with Red's evacuation and treatment at Iwo Jima.

Multiple accounts from Red and other crew members in the months
and years after the Medal of Honor action have William Loesch and/or
Herb Schnipper administering a shot of plasma and/or a shot of morphine
to Red inside the aircraft, minutes after his injury. In 2019, Schnipper had
no memory of administering any shots and said he wouldn't have known
how to do it, although he said he and Loesch ministered to Red as best they

could. Other accounts, including Red's, have Red instructing crewmen on how to administer morphine to him. Schnipper was stationed in the rear of the plane and had to crawl through a long tunnel to get to the front, so Loesch may have already given a shot or shots before Schnipper got there. There are also disagreements in various accounts about whether Eugene Strouse or Roy Stables was sitting in the copilot's seat at the time of the incident and about who forced the window open so Red could flip the bomb out. It was probably a group effort. The narrative in this book is our best effort to navigate the available evidence on these and other points.

The exact percentage of Red Erwin's body that sustained severe burns is not known, but following medical guidelines for such estimates, it was 20 percent at a very bare minimum, and probably significantly more. The burned areas comprised the entire right hand and arm and parts of the left hand and arm, right ear, eyelids, lips, nose, scalp, and parts of the face and neck.

Additionally, according to Hank Jr., "Dad's torso was pretty torn up. Not merely the burns but the use of his stomach area to supply flesh for building his arm back. At one time I understand his damaged arm was sewn to his side for up to a year to grow tissue and skin. He never went around with his shirt off. He was too sensitive about the sight. He never griped about it, but he never showed us the scars." Hank Jr. estimates that some 50 percent of Red's body was burned in total.

Information on the history of burn care and white phosphorus injuries was obtained through interviews with David Barillo, former chief of the US Army's Burn Flight Team; James H. Holmes IV, professor of surgery and director of the Wake Forest Baptist Medical Center Burn Center of the Wake Forest University School of Medicine; Randy D. Kearns, assistant professor of healthcare management at the University of New Orleans; Alan Dimick, founder and former director of the burn unit at the University of Alabama at Birmingham; and Uri Aviv, Plastic and Reconstructive Surgery Department, Chaim Sheba Medical Center, Ramat Gan, Israel.

NOTES

Chapter 2: To End This Business of War

p. 12　"We could hardly believe our eyes": Ernest Pickett and K. P. Burke, *Proof Through the Night: A B-29 Pilot Captive in Japan* (Salem, OR: Opal Creek Press, 2004), 19.

p. 13　"Every day from morning to night, B-29s": Quoted in Warren Kozak, *LeMay: The Life and Wars of General Curtis LeMay* (Washington, DC: Regnery, 2011), 194.

p. 13　"I was scared! It was known that the B-29 was a huge plane": Barrett Tillman, *Whirlwind: The Air War Against Japan, 1942–1945* (New York: Simon & Schuster, 2010), 51.

p. 17　"so chaotic that it was obvious upon my arrival": R. Ray Ortensie, "Flashback: The 'Battle of Kansas' and the Birth of the Superfortress," *Elgin Air Force News*, August 14, 2018, https://www.eglin.af.mil/News /Article-Display/Article/1602130/flashback-battle-of-kansas-and-the -birth-of-the-superfortress/.

p. 18　"Although it replaced the B-17": Robert O. Bigelow, "The Beginning of the End: The First Firebombing of Tokyo, 9–10 March 1945," Virginia Aeronautical Historical Society, *Virginia Eagles Newsletter*, July 2007.

p. 19　"The B-29 was the best airplane made at the time": Ed Shahinian, interview, December 5, 2003, Library of Congress, American Folklife Center, Veterans History Project, https://memory.loc.gov/diglib/vhp /story/loc.natlib.afc2001001.11156/transcript?ID=sr0001. Note: On B-29 crews, technically, the pilot was called the air commander and the copilot was called the pilot. In this book, we use the more familiar designations of pilot and copilot. According to John Correll, "A Brave Man at the Right Time," *Air Force Magazine*, August 2007: "The B-29 standard crew had 11 members. Of these, five crewmen—four gunners and a radar observer—were in the back, aft of the bomb bays. The other six were in the forward section of the Superfort. The pilot, copilot, and bombardier (who also served as nose gunner) were up front on the flight deck. The flight engineer's position was just back of the copilot, beside the nose wheel door."

p. 20   "You go ahead and get results with the B-29": A. J. Baime, *The Accidental President: Harry S. Truman and the Four Months That Changed the World* (New York: Houghton Mifflin Harcourt, 2017), 147.

p. 21   "utter absolute complete and irreversible lack of competence": Robert F. Dorr, *Mission to Tokyo: The American Airmen Who Took the War to the Heart of Japan* (St. Paul: MBI, 2012), 202.

p. 21   "After working with that man": Gene Gurney, *B-29 Superfortress: The Plane That Won the War* (Morrisville, NC: Lulu Press, 2019), 150.

p. 22   "With his jowly, scowling face": Robert M. Neer, *Napalm: An American Biography* (Cambridge, MA: Belknap Press of Harvard University Press, 2013), 69.

p. 22   "I'm not here to win friends": Gurney, *B-29 Superfortress*, 155.

p. 23   "I sat up nights": Richard Rhodes, *Dark Sun: The Making of the Hydrogen Bomb* (New York: Simon & Schuster, 1995), 21.

p. 23   "He was around a few days, said almost nothing to anybody": Thomas Coffey, *Iron Eagle: The Turbulent Life of General Curtis LeMay* (New York: Crown, 1986), 134.

p. 23   "In a war, you've got to try to keep at least one punch ahead": Coffey, *Iron Eagle*, 163.

p. 23   "I'll tell you what war is about": Richard Rhodes, "The General and World War III," *New Yorker*, June 12, 1995, https://www.newyorker.com/magazine/1995/06/19/the-general-and-world-war-iii.

p. 24   "so cold, hard and demanding": Rhodes, *Dark Sun*, 451.

p. 25   "He was. He was sort of an autocratic bastard": Rhodes, *Dark Sun*, 451.

p. 25   "I used to worry that General Power was not stable": Scott D. Sagan, *The Limits of Safety: Organizations, Accidents, and Nuclear Weapons* (Princeton, NJ: Princeton University Press, 1993), 150, citing Air Force Oral History interviews with Wade.

p. 25   Ed Shahinian, a B-29 gunner: Shahinian, interview, December 5, 2003, Library of Congress, American Folklife Center, Veterans History Project, https://memory.loc.gov/diglib/vhp/story/loc.natlib.afc2001001.11156/transcript?ID=sr0001.

p. 27   "I had to do something": William Ralph, "Improvised Destruction: Arnold, LeMay, and the Firebombing of Japan," *War in History* 13, no. 4 (October 2006).

p. 27   "Large sections of Japanese cities": G. Scott Gorman, *Endgame in the Pacific: Complexity, Strategy, and the B-29* (Montgomery, AL: Air University Press, 2000), 36.

p. 27   "Cities made of wood and paper": Gorman, *Endgame in the Pacific*, 36.

p. 28   "If war with the Japanese does come": Quoted in David Fromkin, *In the Time of the Americans: FDR, Truman, Eisenhower, Marshall, MacArthur— The Generation That Changed America's Role in the World* (New York: Vintage, 1995), 554.

p. 29   "No matter how you slice it": Kozak, *LeMay*, 215.

p. 29   "Dropped in loose clusters of 14": Lily Rothman, "Behind the World War II Fire Bombing Attack of Tokyo," *Time*, March 9, 2015, https://time.com/3718981/tokyo-fire/.

p. 31   "I wish there were some other way to bring Japan's leaders to their senses": Wilbur Morrison, *Birds from Hell: History of the B-29* (Central Point, OR: Hellgate Press, 2001), 162.

Chapter 3: Journey to the Apocalypse

p. 33   "You're going to deliver the biggest firecracker": Richard Rhodes, "The General and World War III," *New Yorker*, June 12, 1995, https://www.newyorker.com/magazine/1995/06/19/the-general-and-world-war-iii.

p. 35   Another B-29er described the crew briefing: Robert O. Bigelow, "The Beginning of the End: The First Firebombing of Tokyo, 9–10 March 1945," Virginia Aeronautical Historical Society, *Virginia Eagles Newsletter*, July 2007.

p. 36   "Looking down the long line of silver airplanes": Bigelow, "The Beginning of the End."

p. 37   "If I am sending these men to die, they will string me up": Robert F. Dorr, *Mission to Tokyo: The American Airmen Who Took the War to the Heart of Japan* (St. Paul: MBI, 2012), 72.

p. 39 "We appeared to be floating above a pure white carpet": Barrett Tillman, *Whirlwind: The Air War Against Japan, 1942–1945* (New York: Simon & Schuster, 2010), 120.

p. 40 "Amid the hours of tedious routine": Tillman, *Whirlwind*, 81.

p. 40 "A lot could go wrong": Donald L. Miller, *D-Days in the Pacific* (New York: Simon & Schuster, 2008), 227.

p. 40 LeMay drank from a six-ounce bottle of Coca-Cola: Dorr, *Mission to Tokyo*, 140.

p. 41 "Their long, glinting wings, sharp as blades": Michael S. Sherry, *The Rise of American Air Power: The Creation of Armageddon* (New Haven, CT: Yale University Press, 1987), 274.

p. 41 "Poor bastards": Wilbur Morrison, *Birds from Hell: History of the B-29* (Central Point, OR: Hellgate Press, 2001), 163.

p. 42 "We looked upon a ghastly scene": Kenneth P. Werrell, *Blankets of Fire: U.S. Bombers over Japan During World War II* (Washington, DC: Smithsonian Institution Press, 1996), 161.

p. 42 "When we got over the target it was like a thousand Christmas trees": Austin Hoyt, producer, *American Experience: Victory in the Pacific*, PBS, 2005.

p. 42 "Smoke Gets in Your Eyes," "My Old Flame," and "I Don't Want to Set the World on Fire": Robert M. Neer, *Napalm: An American Biography* (Cambridge, MA: Belknap Press of Harvard University Press, 2013), 80.

p. 42 "From my front-row seat in the nose": David Venditta, "Hellertown High Grad Flew on Tokyo Firebomb Raid," *Morning Call* (Allentown, PA), March 7, 2015, https://www.mcall.com/news/local/bethlehem /mc-tokyo-firebombing-anniversary-manone-20150307-story.html.

p. 43 "Hundreds of B-29s were all in the same general area": Charles L. Phillips Jr., *Rain of Fire: B-29s over Japan* (Moreno Valley, CA: Nijuku Publishing, 1995).

p. 46 "As we approached, the conflagration was such": Phillips, *Rain of Fire*.

p. 46 "It almost cost us our life": Phillips, *Rain of Fire*.

p. 47 "Bright flashes illuminate the sky's shadows": Tillman, *Whirlwind*, 148.

p. 48 "The heat from the conflagration": John W. Dower, *War Without Mercy: Race and Power in the Pacific War* (New York: Pantheon, 1986), 41.

p. 48 "Other B-29s around us were outlined in orange": Neer, *Napalm*, 81.

p. 49 Saotome Katsumoto, Ishikawa Koyo, Hashimoto Yoshiko, and Kokubo

Takako quotes: Saotome Katsumoto and Richard Sams, "Saotome Katsumoto and the Firebombing of Tokyo: Introducing the Great Tokyo Air Raid," *The Asia-Pacific Journal* 13, no. 1, March 9, 2015, https://apjjf .org/2015/13/9/Saotome-Katsumoto/4293.html.

p. 51 "They came in majesty": Warren Kozak, *LeMay: The Life and Wars of General Curtis LeMay* (Washington, DC: Regnery, 2011), 224.

p. 52 "I could hear the sound of houses burning": John Burgess, "The Night the War Came Home to Tokyo," *Washington Post*, March 10, 1985, https://www .washingtonpost.com/archive/politics/1985/03/10/the-night-the-war-came -home-to-tokyo/ee04329b-4f79-449d-9803-a3fffbe5948b/.

p. 52 "seized by the firestorm, whipped and twisted in the air": Neer, *Napalm*, 79.

p. 53 "like a cascade of silvery water": Sherry, *Rise of American Air Power*, 274.

p. 53 "We were caught between the people pushing us": Katsumoto and Sams, "Saotome Katsumoto and the Firebombing of Tokyo."

p. 53 "On a bridge spanning the Kototoi River": Neer, *Napalm*, 81.

p. 53 "A fully developed firestorm is a horrifically mesmerizing sight": Tillman, *Whirlwind*, 141.

p. 54 "fire-winds filled with burning particles": Bill Gilbert, *Air Power: Heroes and Heroism in American Flight Missions* (New York: Citadel Press, 2004), 120.

p. 57 "sadistic goons, especially picked for their brutality": Fiske Hanley II, *Accused American War Criminal* (Brattleboro, VT: Echo Point, 2016), ix.

p. 58 "Bombs away—General conflagration": Gene Gurney, *B-29 Superfortress: The Plane That Won the War* (Morrisville, NC: Lulu Press, 2019), 161.

p. 59 "It was a hell of a good mission": Thomas Coffey, *Iron Eagle: The Turbulent Life of General Curtis LeMay* (New York: Crown, 1986), 164.

p. 59 "Congratulations. This mission shows your crews have the guts": Neer, *Napalm*, 82.

p. 60 "That fire raid was the most destructive single military action": Sarel Eimerl, *The American Heritage History of Flight* (New York: Golden Press, 1964), 366.

p. 60 "because of the horrifying conditions beyond imagination": Waldo H. Heinrichs and Marc S. Gallicchio, *Implacable Foes: War in the Pacific, 1944–1945* (New York: Oxford University Press, 2017), 284. Estimates of the total number of people, mostly civilians, who died in Tokyo air raids from November 24, 1944, until the March 9–10, 1945, raid range from a low of 1,300 to a high of 2,525.

p. 60 "The great city of Tokyo—third largest in the world": Dorr, *Mission to Tokyo*, 317.

p. 61 "Neither the Army nor the Navy can possibly draw up a plan": John Toland, *The Rising Sun: The Decline and Fall of the Japanese Empire, 1936–1945* (New York: Random House, 2014), 446.

p. 62 "never considered as to whether I was killing": Shahinian, interview, December 5, 2003, Library of Congress, American Folklife Center, Veterans History Project, https://memory.loc.gov/diglib/vhp/story/loc .natlib.afc2001001.11156/transcript?ID=sr0001.

p. 62 "I'm sort of a religious person": Austin Hoyt, producer, *American Experience: Victory in the Pacific*, PBS, 2005.

p. 62 "one of the most ruthless and barbaric killings of noncombatants": John W. Dower, *Embracing Defeat: Japan in the Wake of World War II* (New York: Norton, 1999), 285.

p. 62 "scorched and boiled and baked to death": Kyoko Selden and Mark Selden, *The Atomic Bomb: Voices from Hiroshima and Nagasaki* (Armonk, NY: M. E. Sharpe, 1990), xxvii.

p. 62 "Killing Japanese didn't bother me very much": Richard Rhodes, *Dark Sun: The Making of the Hydrogen Bomb* (New York: Simon & Schuster, 1995), 21.

p. 62 "a child lying in bed with a whole ton of masonry": E. Bartlett Kerr, *Flames over Tokyo: The U.S. Army Air Forces' Incendiary Campaign Against Japan, 1944–1945* (New York: D. I. Fine, 1991), 154.

p. 64 "Once the war started like that": "Family," *The War*, PBS, 2007, https://www .pbs.org/thewar/at_home_family.htm.

p. 64 "Following that war was the best history lesson": "Family," *The War*, PBS.

p. 64 "There was a sense of urgency": "Family," *The War*, PBS.

p. 65 "became proficient cooks and housekeepers, managed the finances": Stephen E. Ambrose, *Americans at War* (New York: Berkley, 1998), 145.

p. 65 "I think for girls and women": Sharon H. Hartman Strom and Linda P. Wood, "Women and World War II," What Did You Do in the War, Grandma? An Oral History of Rhode Island Women During World War II, 1995, http://cds.library.brown.edu/projects/WWII_Women /WomenInWWII.html. Note: During this period, the *City of Los*

Angeles also took part in bombing missions against Nagoya, Tokyo, Osaka, and Kobe. On March 30–31, the aircraft took part in a mass attack by 137 B-29s against the Tachiarai machine works and Omura Airfield on Kyushu Island, in which 49 tons of bombs were dropped on the target area and fourteen enemy aircraft were shot down. The crew of the *City of Los Angeles* and the crews of the other B-29s were awarded the Distinguished Unit Citation for the mission.

Chapter 4: Day of Destiny

p. 72   Red Erwin's burn injuries: Seventy-five years after the phosphorus bomb exploded inside Red's B-29, a team of leading burn doctors and specialists in military injuries examined the available evidence, details, and photos of Red's wounds, and compared them to their own surgical experience and research. In total, these doctors had treated thousands of military and civilian burn victims and conducted extensive research into white phosphorus burns. Through their opinions and observations, a compelling picture emerges of what was happening to Red's body during these desperate hours inside the *City of Los Angeles* and in the months beyond. The medical details in this chapter are based on interviews with these medical experts.

p. 72   "There's no other injury that has such a devastating effect": Joan Hollobon, "Burn Centre: Helping Body's Largest Organ to Rebuild Infection Shield," *Globe and Mail*, May 14, 1984.

Chapter 5: Race Against Time

p. 78   "When skin, an organ about as thick as a sheet of paper toweling": Douglas Hand, "Saving Burn Victims," *New York Times*, September 15, 1985, https://www.nytimes.com/1985/09/15/magazine/saving-burn-victims.html.

p. 82   "He discarded the accepted approach": Kat Eschner, "Three Medical Breakthroughs That Can Be Traced Back to a Tragic Nightclub Fire," *Smithsonian*, November 28, 2017, https://www.smithsonianmag.com/smart-news/three-medical-breakthroughs-can-be-traced-back-tragic-cocoanut-grove-fire-180967323/#OJiUBfRr5Zp9YWMA.99.

p. 82   "a sullen sense of evil": "Island Seemed Like a Beachhead on Hell," *Life*, April 9, 1945.

p. 82   They were accompanied by shiploads of ammunition and supplies: Sid Moody, "It Was the Bloodiest Battle of the Pacific During World War," *Associated Press*, January 30, 1995.

p. 83   "the last country in the world that Japan should fight": William B. Hopkins, *The Pacific War: The Strategy, Politics, and Players That Won the War* (Beverly, MA: Voyageur, 2010), 292.

p. 83   "Mortars fell in cascade from hundreds of concealed pits": Bill D. Ross, *Iwo Jima: Legacy of Valor* (New York: Vanguard Press, 1985), 67.

p. 83   Quotes by Col. Frank Caldwell: Ken Ringle, "The Uphill Battle," *Washington Post*, February 19, 1995, https://www.washingtonpost.com /archive/lifestyle/1995/02/19/the-uphill-battle/f5265c77-b6fc-42cd -b2e1-eea6ca4d4677/.

p. 84   "Iwo Jima can only be described as a nightmare": Richard F. Newcomb, *Iwo Jima: The Dramatic Account of the Epic Battle That Turned the Tide of World War II* (New York: Henry Holt, 1965), 136.

p. 84   "uncommon valor was a common virtue": James H. Hallas, *Uncommon Valor on Iwo Jima: The Stories of the Medal of Honor Recipients in the Marine Corps' Bloodiest Battle of World War II* (Lanham, MD: Rowman & Littlefield, 2016), xiii. Note: Red Erwin was probably treated by recently arrived army medical staff at Iwo Jima. According to US Marine Corps veteran and historian John Butler in an email to the authors, "By April 12 the Marines and their corpsmen had left the island. US forces on Iwo at that time were 147th US Infantry Regiment and two squadrons of US Army Air Corps P-51s, plus likely other US Army support troops, including US Army doctors and medics."

p. 84   "the most savage and the most costly battle": Holland McTyeire Smith and Percy Finch, *Coral and Brass* (Morrisville, NC: Lulu Press, 2017), 236.

p. 85   "Of the 2,251 touchdowns popularized": Robert S. Burrell, *The Ghosts of Iwo Jima* (College Station: Texas A&M University Press, 2011), 124.

p. 87   Story of Patton's prayer: James H. O'Neill, "The True Story of the Patton Prayer," *Review of the News*, October 6, 1971, http://pattonhq.com /prayer.html.

p. 91   "conspicuous gallantry and intrepidity": US Department of Defense, "Description of Medals," https://valor.defense.gov/Description-of-Awards.

p. 91   "to be bestowed upon such petty officers, seamen, landsmen, and Marines": "National Archives Exhibit Highlights Medal of Honor

Recipients," National Archives Press Release, April 4, 2005, https://www.archives.gov/press/press-releases/2005/nr05-52.html.

p. 94   "A gold five-pointed star": Defense Standardization Program Office, "Medal of Honor History," Nebraska Medal of Honor Foundation, https://nebraskamedalofhonorfoundation.org/history/.

p. 95   "Some talked of entering a zone of slow-motion invulnerability": Peter Collier, "American Honor," *Wall Street Journal*, May 26, 2007, https://www.wsj.com/articles/SB118014402282815483.

p. 95   "When you're in a combat situation": Quoted in "Book Profiles US Medal of Honor Winners," *Voice of America News*, October 30, 2009, https://www.voanews.com/archive/book-profiles-us-medal-honor-winners-2003-11-11.

p. 96   *Dear God, please let me get just one more man*: Collier, "American Honor."

p. 96   "For those who earn it, the medal is a loaded gift": Michael Phillips, "'It's a Lifelong Burden': The Mixed Blessing of the Medal of Honor," *Wall Street Journal*, May 24, 2019, https://www.wsj.com/articles/its-a-lifelong-burden-the-mixed-blessing-of-the-medal-of-honor-11558695600.

p. 96   "I cannot eat them": Eric Grossarth, "We Are East Idaho: Sugar City," *EastIdahoNews.com*, April 29, 2019, https://www.eastidahonews.com/2019/04/we-are-east-idaho-sugar-city/.

p. 97   "I look at that medal and I could throw up": Jeff Schogol, "Dakota Meyer Explains Why He Hates His Medal of Honor," *Business Insider*, March 29, 2019, https://www.businessinsider.com/dakota-meyer-explains-why-he-hates-his-medal-of-honor-2019-3.

Chapter 6: The Gates of Eternity

p. 99   "I have a terrific pain in the back of my head": Doris Kearns Goodwin, *No Ordinary Time: Franklin and Eleanor Roosevelt: The Home Front in World War II* (New York: Simon & Schuster, 1994), 602.

p. 100   "Jesus Christ and General Jackson!": David McCullough, *Truman* (New York: Simon & Schuster, 1992), 424.

p. 100   "Harry, the president is dead": David Oshinsky, "The Strength of His Weakness," *New York Times*, October 29, 1995, https://www.nytimes.com/1995/10/29/books/the-strength-of-his-weaknesses.html.

p. 100   "I felt like the moon, the stars, and all the planets": Bert Cochran, *Harry Truman and the Crisis Presidency* (New York: Funk & Wagnalls, 1973), 118.

NOTES

p. 100 "I was handicapped by lack of knowledge": Jeffrey Frank, "How FDR's Death Changed the Vice-Presidency," *New Yorker*, April 17, 2015.

p. 100 Truman later privately asserted: Cochran, *Harry Truman and the Crisis Presidency*, 120; Alonzo L. Hamby, *Man of the People: A Life of Harry S. Truman* (New York: Oxford University Press, 1995), 313.

p. 101 "Truman probably had the human touch": William J. Hopkins, "Oral History Interview," JFK #1, June 3, 1964, John F. Kennedy Presidential Library and Museum, https://www.jfklibrary.org/asset-viewer/archives /JFKOH/Hopkins%2C%20William%20J/JFKOH-WIJH-01/JFKOH -WIJH-01.

p. 101 "Each and every one of us": William Doyle, *Inside the Oval Office: The White House Tapes from FDR to Clinton* (New York: Kodansha, 1999), 58.

p. 102 "Well, this is the kind of person that one can adore": McCullough, *Truman*, 755.

p. 102 "The first thing you find out is that he calls you by name": Ken Hechler, *Working with Truman: A Personal Memoir of the White House Years* (New York: Putnam, 1982), 20.

p. 102 "When a butler or doorman or usher would enter the room": Robert J. Donovan, *Conflict and Crisis: The Presidency of Harry S. Truman, 1945–1948* (New York: Norton, 1977), 148.

p. 102 "He always made everybody feel they were a part of a great team": Doyle, *Inside the Oval Office*, 58.

p. 102 On his first full day as president: Doyle, *Inside the Oval Office*, 46–61.

p. 102 "I'm not big enough for this job": Donovan, *Conflict and Crisis*, 15.

p. 103 "magnified his eyes enormously": R. Gordon Hoxie, *Command Decision and the Presidency: A Study in National Security Policy and Organization* (New York: Reader's Digest Press, 1977), 79.

p. 103 "He was the best in the world": Doyle, *Inside the Oval Office*, 47.

p. 103 "There are a great many different factors": Hoxie, *Command Decision and the Presidency*, 79.

p. 104 "As a veteran of the First World War": Richard F. Haynes, *The Awesome Power: Harry S. Truman as Commander in Chief* (Baton Rouge, LA: LSU Press, 1999), 15.

p. 104 "His personal and professional experience": Hamby, *Man of the People*, 484.

p. 104 "I get up at five-thirty every morning": John Hersey, "Mr. President, Quite a Head of Steam," *New Yorker*, April 7, 1950.

p. 105 After his morning walk: Doyle, *Inside the Oval Office*, 46–61.

p. 105 "I discovered that being a president is like riding a tiger": Harry S. Truman, *Memoirs of Harry S. Truman: Years of Trial and Hope, 1946–1952* (Garden City, NY: Doubleday, 1956), 1.

p. 105 "You could go into his office with a question": Robert J. Donovan, *Tumultuous Years: The Presidency of Harry S. Truman, 1949–1953* (New York: Norton, 1982), 24.

p. 105 "Truman was a dirt farmer": Doyle, *Inside the Oval Office*, 59.

p. 105 "We hadn't expected very much": Doyle, *Inside the Oval Office*, 59.

p. 106 "I'd rather wear that medal than be president": James H. Willbanks, ed., *America's Heroes: Medal of Honor Recipients from the Civil War to Afghanistan* (Santa Barbara, CA: ABC-CLIO, 2011), xv.

Chapter 7: Homecoming

p. 116 "I cannot endure the thought of letting my people suffer": Takeshi Suzuki, *The Rhetoric of Emperor Hirohito: Continuity and Rupture in Japan's Dramas of Modernity* (Newcastle upon Tyne, UK: Cambridge Scholars Publishing, 2017), 91.

p. 117 "Fundamentally the thing that brought about the determination to make peace": Robert M. Neer, *Napalm: An American Biography* (Cambridge, MA: Belknap Press of Harvard University Press, 2013), 85.

p. 117 "I, myself, on the basis of the B-29 raids": E. Bartlett Kerr, *Flames over Tokyo: The U.S. Army Air Forces' Incendiary Campaign Against Japan, 1944–1945* (New York: D. I. Fine, 1991), 293.

p. 117 "The war was lost when the Marianas were taken": US Army Air Forces, *Mission Accomplished: Interrogations of Japanese Industrial, Military and Civil Leaders of World War II* (Washington, DC: Government Printing Office, 1946).

p. 117 "The firebombing probably led to an earlier end of the war": Nicholas Kristof, "Tokyo Journal; Stoically, Japan Looks Back on the Flames of War," *New York Times*, March 9, 1995, https://www.nytimes.com/1995/03/09/world/tokyo-journal-stoically-japan-looks-back-on-the-flames-of-war.html.

p. 118 "Brother, I hope those are my discharge papers": Donald L. Miller, *D-Days in the Pacific* (New York: Simon & Schuster, 2008), 370.

p. 119 "I watched Shigemitsu limp forward": John Rich, "On the Deck of a Battleship, Men of Peace," *Christian Science Monitor*, September 1, 1995, https://www.csmonitor.com/1995/0901/01091.html.

p. 120 "that so lately belched forth their crashing battle": Quoted in William Manchester, *American Caesar: Douglas MacArthur, 1880–1964* (New York: Little, Brown, 1978), 527.

p. 120 "a solemn agreement whereby peace may be restored": *Congressional Record* 91, part 7 (Washington, DC: Government Printing Office, 1945), 8915.

p. 120 Toshikazu Kase memories of surrender ceremony: *Eclipse of the Rising Sun* (London: Jonathan Cape, 1951), 7–13.

p. 121 "Was the day beclouded by mists or trailing clouds?": Donald Wallace White, *The American Century: The Rise and Decline of the United States as a World Power* (New Haven, CT: Yale University Press, 1999), 39.

p. 122 Cushing General Hospital details: Nicholas Paganella, "Remembering Cushing Hospital, 70 Years Later," *Metro West Daily News* (Framingham, MA), January 25, 2014, https://www.metrowestdailynews.com/article /20140125/OPINION/140127304.

p. 123 "The effort to save it involved one particularly excruciating operation": Sidney Shalett, "What Happens to a War Hero," *Saturday Evening Post*, September 4, 1948.

p. 127 "The disorder is widespread among aging veterans of World War II": Associated Press, "Fifty Years Later, War Stress Ambushes WWII Vets," *Daily Courier* (Yavapai County, AZ), August 1, 1995, https://news .google.com/newspapers?nid=894&dat=19950801&id=kCYOAAAAIBAJ &sjid=lX0DAAAAIBAJ&pg=6953,97195&hl=en.

p. 128 "In many studies PTG and PTSD are found to stem from similar traumatic events": S. Moran, J. Schmidt, and E. Burker, "Posttraumatic Growth and Posttraumatic Stress Disorder in Veterans," *Journal of Rehabilitation* 79, no. 2 (April 2013): 34–43.

p. 128 Richard Tedeschi and Lawrence Calhoun first described the concept of PTG: Richard G. Tedeschi and Lawrence G. Calhoun, "The Posttraumatic Growth Inventory: Measuring the Positive Legacy of Trauma," *Journal of Traumatic Stress* 9, no. 3 (July 1996): 455–71.

p. 128 "People develop new understandings of themselves": Quoted in Lorna Collier, "Growth After Trauma: Why Are Some People More Resilient Than Others—and Can It Be Taught?" *Monitor on Psychology*, November 2016, https://www.apa.org/monitor/2016/11/growth-trauma.

p. 128 50 percent of all contemporary veterans: J. Tsai, N. Mota, S. Southwick, and R. Pietrzak, "What Doesn't Kill You Makes You Stronger: A National Study of U.S. Military Veterans," *Journal of Affective Disorders* 189 (2014): 269–71, http://dx.doi.org.ezproxy.stthomas.edu/10.1016/j.jad.2015.08.076.

p. 132 "He was bedridden, but our reunion was a wonderful occasion": William H. Stewart, "Time Heals Everything—Almost," *Saipan Tribune*, July 26, 2005, https://www.saipantribune.com/index.php/a41e8eba-1dfb-11e4 -aedf-250bc8c9958e/.

Chapter 8: Guardian Angel

p. 133 Crewmembers after the war: Ruth Orkin, "We Are the Living: Twelve Men in a Superfort," *Coronet*, August 1948, and notes and letters from crewmen in Erwin family collection.

p. 134 Fate of Eugene Strouse: Gregory Liefer, *Broken Wings: Aviation Disasters in Alaska* (Anchorage, AK: Publication Consultants, 2014), 134–38.

p. 135 Soviet tactical nuclear weapons in Cuba: Robert McNamara on ABC's *Nightline*, October 24, 1996. According to former CIA analyst Dino Brugioni, the SS-4 missiles in Cuba, which had the range to hit Washington, had warheads at their launch sites and could have been fired within a few hours of an order from Moscow. *Newsweek*, October 26, 1992, 39.

p. 136 JFK thought the chances of nuclear war were "fifty/fifty": Theodore Sorensen, interview by Carol Fleisher, *Secret White House Tapes*, A&E, 1997.

p. 136 "the government had disregarded the feelings of the people": "Honor to LeMay by Japan Stirs Parliament Debate," *New York Times*, December 8, 1964, https://www.nytimes.com/1964/12/08/archives/honor-to-lemay -by-japan-stirs-parliament-debate.html.

p. 136 "Bygones are bygones": "Honor to LeMay by Japan Stirs Parliament Debate."

p. 136 "as far as the Defense Agency knows": "Honor to LeMay by Japan Stirs Parliament Debate."

p. 137 "My solution to the problem would be to tell them": Thomas Coffey, *Iron Eagle: The Turbulent Life of General Curtis LeMay* (New York: Crown, 1986), 356, 357.

p. 138 "I used to worry about the fact that he had control": Scott D. Sagan, *The Limits of Safety: Organizations, Accidents, and Nuclear Weapons* (Princeton, NJ: Princeton University Press, 1993), 150, citing Air Force Oral History with Wade.

NOTES

p. 138   "Restraint? Why are you so concerned with saving their lives?": Gerard DeGroot, *The Bomb: A Life* (New York: Random House, 2011), 208.

p. 138   Power and LeMay rushing bomb into service: Sagan, *The Limits of Safety*, 72, 73.

p. 138   Eisenhower nuclear contingency plan: Bruce G. Blair, *The Logic of Accidental Nuclear War* (Washington, DC: Brookings Institution, 1993), 48, 49.

p. 138   "certifiably off the deep end": Bruce Blair, interview by Carol Fleisher.

p. 138   October 23, 1962, events: "Foreign Relations: The Backdown," *Time*, November 2, 1962, 27, 29.

p. 139   "Can we, maybe before we invade, evacuate these cities?": Evan Thomas, *Robert Kennedy: His Life* (New York: Simon & Schuster, 2013), 223.

p. 139   The air force dispersed hundreds of B-47 Sratojet bombers: Raymond Garthoff, *Reflections on the Cuban Missile Crisis* (Washington, DC: Brookings Institution Press, 2011), 61.

p. 139   U-2 straying into Soviet airspace: Sagan, *The Limits of Safety*, 136, 137; Dean Rusk, *As I Saw It*, ed. Daniel S. Papp (New York: Norton, 1990), 242.

p. 139   October 27, incident at New Jersey radar post: Sagan, *The Limits of Safety*, 6.

p. 139   Power and DEFCON alert: Blair, *The Logic of Accidental Nuclear War*, 24; Garthoff, *Reflections on the Cuban Missile Crisis*, 37; Sagan, *The Limits of Safety*, 62, 63, 65, 72, 73; "The U.S. Air Force Response to the Cuban Crisis" (undated Air Force document, presumably soon after crisis), National Security Archive, 1998, 18, 19; Bruce Blair and Raymond Garthoff, interviews by Carol Fleisher.

p. 142   Sullenberger inspired by Erwin: Chesley B. Sullenberger III, *Sully: My Search for What Really Matters* (New York: HarperCollins, 2016), 146.

p. 144   "For some reason the story of the Tokyo air raid was not talked about": Richard Lloyd Parry, "Tokyo Chooses to Forget the Night 100,000 Perished," *Times*, March 11, 2005, https://www.thetimes.co.uk/article /tokyo-chooses-to-forget-the-night-100000-perished-m2hjmfwqh0t.

p. 145   "I think Japanese just wanted to forget": Ben Hills, "Tokyo's Hell on Earth: The Night a City Died," *Sydney Morning Herald*, March 4, 1995.

p. 145   "I wonder if they had thought of the people on the ground": Mari Yamaguchi, "US Veterans Who Firebombed Japan in WWII Meet Survivor," *Associated Press*, December 9, 2005, https://apnews.com /42af0571c88e4f1c85c78d619801b70e/us-veterans-who-firebombed -japan-meet-survivor.

p. 146   "For years after the war, Van Bush would wake up screaming": Hills, "Tokyo's Hell on Earth."

Chapter 9: Legacy in the Clouds

p. 156   Gary Littrell's comments are reconstructed by Jon Erwin from memory and from Littrell's interview with the Library of Congress Veterans History Project, https://memory.loc.gov/diglib/vhp-stories/loc.natlib .afc2001001.89725/transcript?ID=mv0001.

Appendix: Seven Prayers

p. 172   "pardon all our manifold sins": National Archives, "General Orders, 15 May 1776," https://founders.archives.gov/documents/Washington /03-04-02-0243.

p. 172   "Gentlemen, I suggest that we have a word of prayer": Gregory Corte, "How Presidents Pray," *USA Today*, February 4, 2016, https://www .usatoday.com/story/news/politics/theoval/2016/02/04/how-presidents -pray-prayer-breakfast-eisenhower-obama/79786384/.

p. 173   "In the beginning of the Contest with Great Britain": 155 Cong. Rec. (2009), part 9, 11843, https://www.govinfo.gov/content/pkg/CRECB -2009-pt9/html/CRECB-2009-pt9-Pg11843.htm.

p. 173   "Strangely enough, after a bit of prayer": *U.S. President, Public Papers of the Presidents of the United States* (Washington, DC: Government Printing Office, 1953), 9.

p. 173   At the moment Washington was inaugurated: "Washington's Inaugural Address of 1789: A Transcription," National Archives and Records Administration, https://www.archives.gov/exhibits/american_originals /inaugtxt.html.

p. 174   "I now leave, not knowing when": Abraham Lincoln, "Farewell Address," from *Collected Works of Abraham Lincoln*, 9 vols., ed. Roy P. Basler (New Brunswick, NJ: Rutgers University Press, 1953–55), https://www.nps.gov /liho/learn/historyculture/farewell.htm.

p. 174   "God had decided this question in favor of the slaves": Allen C. Guelzo, "Emancipation and the Quest for Freedom," National Park Service, n.d., https://www.nps.gov/articles/emancipation-and-the-quest-for-freedom.htm.

p. 174   "I've been driven many times to my knees": Gregory Corte, "How Presidents Pray."

NOTES

p. 175   "beseeching Him that He will give victory to our armies": *Congressional Record* 75, part 13 (Washington, DC: Government Printing Office, 1932).

p. 176   "our sons, pride of our Nation": *Congressional Record* 154, part 8 (Washington, DC: Government Printing Office, 2008), 11503.

p. 176   "has come with the help of God": "Victory, Day of Prayer," Harry S. Truman Presidential Library and Museum, https://www.trumanlibrary .gov/library/proclamations/2660/victory-day-prayer.

p. 176   "In times of national crisis": "National Day of Prayer, 1952," Harry S. Truman Presidential Library and Museum, https://www.trumanlibrary .gov/library/proclamations/2978/national-day-prayer-1952.

p. 176   "Oh! Almighty and Everlasting God": Harry S. Truman, "A Prayer Said Over and Over All My Life from Eighteen Years Old and Younger," Notes of August 15, 1950, Harry S. Truman Library and Museum, https://www.trumanlibrary.gov/node/404492.

p. 177   "I am the most intensely religious man I know": Joseph Hartropp, "God and the Presidency: The Faith of Dwight D. Eisenhower," *Christianity Today*, October 27, 2016, https://www.christiantoday.com/article/god .the.presidency.the.faith.of.dwight.d.eisenhower/99103.htm.

p. 177   "Let us go forth to lead the land we love": "Inaugural Address: Transcript," John F. Kennedy Presidential Library, https://www.jfklibrary.org/learn /about-jfk/historic-speeches/inaugural-address.

p. 177   The following year Kennedy asked for God's help: "War and Peace in the Nuclear Age; Europe Goes Nuclear; Interview with David Powers, 1986," February 28, 1986, WGBH Media Library and Archives, http://openvault .wgbh.org/catalog/V_8946E771A345459DA076BD20131B96CB.

p. 178   Prayers by Nixon: William Safire, "Nixon on His Knees," *New York Times*, March 29, 1976, https://www.nytimes.com/1976/03/29/archives /nixon-on-his-knees.html.

p. 178   Prayers by Ford: David M. Shribman, "Prayer and the Presidency," *Buffalo News*, January 21, 1995, https://buffalonews.com/1995/01/21 /prayer-and-the-presidency/.

p. 178   Prayers by Carter: Shribman, "Prayer and the Presidency."

p. 179   Prayers by Reagan: Daniel Schorr, "Reagan Recants: His Path from Armageddon to Détente," *Los Angeles Times*, January 3, 1998, https://www .latimes.com/archives/la-xpm-1988-01-03-op-32475-story.html.

p. 179   "I have to realize that whatever I do has meaning": Richard Land, *The*

Divided States of America: What Liberals and Conservatives Get Wrong About Faith and Politics (Nashville: Thomas Nelson, 2011), 99.

p. 179 "I have thought of something that is not part of my speech": "Republican National Convention Acceptance Speech, July 17, 1980," Ronald Reagan Presidential Library and Museum, https://www.reaganlibrary.gov/7-17-80.

p. 179 "My daily prayer is that God will help me": Kiron K. Skinner, Annelise Anderson, and Martin Anderson, *Reagan: A Life in Letters* (New York: Simon and Schuster, 2004), 654.

p. 179 "Having come so close to death": Paul Vorbeck Lettow, *Ronald Reagan and His Quest to Abolish Nuclear Weapons* (New York: Random House, 2006), 50.

p. 179 "God wanted that assassination attempt to happen": John R. Barletta and Rochelle Schweizer, *Riding with Reagan: From the White House to the Ranch* (New York: Citadel Press, 2006), 56.

BIBLIOGRAPHY

Author Interviews

Interviews conducted from 2004 to 2019 by Jon Erwin, Andrew Erwin, and William Doyle, with family members Henry E. Erwin Jr., Betty Erwin, Ray Erwin, Karen Erwin Brown, Nancy Erwin Herndon, Bette Erwin Cobb, and Mark Ray; Red Erwin's crewmates on the *City of Los Angeles*, Pershing Youngkin and Herb Schnipper; B-29 veterans Hap Halloran, Orville Blackburn, Ray Clanton, and Carl Barthold; survivor of the March 9–10, 1945, Tokyo air raid Shizuyo Takeuchi; and Jeffrey Hester and Geneva Robinson of the Veterans Administration Hospital of Birmingham.

Archives and Private Collections

Author inspections of World War II–era B-29s *FiFi* (Fort Worth, Texas) and *Sentimental Journey* (Pima Air and Space Museum, Tucson, Arizona).
B-29 technical manuals and research files, Pima Air and Space Museum, Tucson, Arizona.
Henry E. Erwin correspondence, historical clippings, files and scrapbooks, autobiographical notes, Erwin Family Collection.
Henry E. Erwin Oral History interview with Maj. Judd Katz, March 5, 1986; Henry E. Erwin Oral History interview, 1974; Erwin exhibits and historical file, Enlisted Heritage Hall, Air Force Historical Research Agency, Maxwell Air Force Base, Montgomery, Alabama.
Museum exhibits and historical files, Center of the Tokyo Raids and War Damage, Tokyo, Japan.

"Prepared to Die: Henry 'Red' Erwin and the Low-Level Bombing of Japan," Oral History Interview with Henry E. Erwin, Tony Simeral, and Harry Mitchell by George Hicks, director of Airmen's Memorial Museum, Suitland, Maryland, October 6, 1989, Air Force Historical Research Agency, Maxwell Air Force Base, Montgomery, Alabama.

Robert St. John, script for *Facts and Faces* broadcast on Henry E. Erwin, National Broadcasting Company, August 1, 1946, Erwin Family Collection.

Transcript of Decoration Ceremony on Guam, Medal of Honor for S/Sgt Henry Erwin, April 19, 1945, for shortwave relay to Blue network, San Francisco, for "Fighting AAF" program, Erwin Family Collection.

Twenty-Ninth Bomb Group historical files, B-29 Museum, Pratt, Kansas, including material from the National Archives.

William Doyle interviews for *Inside the Oval Office: The White House Tapes from FDR to Clinton* (New York: Kodansha, 1999); Carol Fleisher interviews for companion A&E special.

Books

Ambrose, Stephen E. *Americans at War.* New York: Berkley, 1998.

Arnold, Henry Harley "Hap." *Global Mission.* New York: Harper, 1949.

Baime, A. J. *The Accidental President: Harry S. Truman and the Four Months That Changed the World.* New York: Houghton Mifflin Harcourt, 2017.

Barletta, John R., and Rochelle Schweizer. *Riding with Reagan: From the White House to the Ranch.* New York: Citadel Press, 2006.

Blair, Bruce G. *The Logic of Accidental Nuclear War.* Washington, DC: Brookings Institution, 1993.

Burrell, Robert S. *The Ghosts of Iwo Jima.* College Station: Texas A&M University Press, 2011.

Clanton, Raymond. *Fire, Fear and Guts: The B-29 and Her Gallant Crewmen.* Camp Verde, AZ: Ray/Jan Publishers, 2005.

Cochran, Bert. *Harry Truman and the Crisis Presidency.* New York: Funk & Wagnalls, 1973.

Coffey, Thomas. *Iron Eagle: The Turbulent Life of General Curtis LeMay.* New York: Crown, 1986.

DeGroot, Gerard. *The Bomb: A Life.* New York: Random House, 2011.

Donovan, Robert J. *Conflict and Crisis: The Presidency of Harry S. Truman, 1945–1948.* New York: Norton, 1977.

———. *Tumultuous Years: The Presidency of Harry S. Truman, 1949–1953.* New York: Norton, 1982.

Dorr, Robert F. *Mission to Tokyo: The American Airmen Who Took the War to the Heart of Japan.* St. Paul, MN: MBI, 2012.

Dower, John W. *Embracing Defeat: Japan in the Wake of World War II.* New York: Norton, 1999.

———. *War Without Mercy: Race and Power in the Pacific War.* New York: Pantheon, 1986.

Doyle, William. *Inside the Oval Office: The White House Tapes from FDR to Clinton.* New York: Kodansha, 1999.

Edoin, Hoito. *The Night Tokyo Burned.* New York: St. Martin's, 1987.

Eimerl, Sarel, *The American Heritage History of Flight.* New York: Golden Press, 1964.

Erwin, Henry E., Jr. *When Courage Calls: The Red Erwin Story.* iBooks, 2006.

Fromkin, David. *In the Time of the Americans: FDR, Truman, Eisenhower, Marshall, MacArthur—The Generation That Changed America's Role in the World.* New York: Vintage, 1995.

Garthoff, Raymond. *Reflections on the Cuban Missile Crisis.* Washington, DC: Brookings Institution Press, 2011.

Gilbert, Bill. *Air Power: Heroes and Heroism in American Flight Missions, 1916 to Today.* New York: Citadel Press, 2004.

Goodwin, Doris Kearns. *No Ordinary Time: Franklin and Eleanor Roosevelt: The Home Front in World War II.* New York: Simon & Schuster, 1994.

Gurney, Gene. *B-29 Superfortress: The Plane That Won the War.* Morrisville, NC: Lulu Press, 2019.

Hallas, James H. *Uncommon Valor on Iwo Jima: The Stories of the Medal of Honor Recipients in the Marine Corps' Bloodiest Battle of World War II.* Lanham, MD: Rowman & Littlefield, 2016.

Hamby, Alonzo L. *Man of the People: A Life of Harry S. Truman.* New York: Oxford University Press, 1995.

Hanley, Fiske, II. *Accused American War Criminal.* Brattleboro, VT: Echo Point, 2016.

Hastings, Max. *Nemesis: The Battle for Japan, 1944–45.* New York: Harper Perennial, 2008.

———. *Retribution: The Battle for Japan, 1944–1945.* New York: Knopf, 2008.

Hechler, Ken. *Working with Truman: A Personal Memoir of the White House Years*. New York: Putnam, 1982.

Heinrichs, Waldo H., and Marc S. Gallicchio. *Implacable Foes: War in the Pacific, 1944–1945*. New York: Oxford University Press, 2017.

Herbert, Kevin. *Maximum Effort: The B-29s Against Japan*. Manhattan, KS: Sunflower University Press, 1983.

Hopkins, William B. *The Pacific War: The Strategy, Politics, and Players That Won the War*. Beverly, MA: Voyageur, 2010.

Hoxie, R. Gordon. *Command Decision and the Presidency: A Study in National Security Policy and Organization*. New York: Reader's Digest Press, 1977.

Hoyt, Edwin P. *Inferno: The Firebombing of Japan, March 9–August 15, 1945*. Lanham, MD: Madison Books, 2000.

Kase, Toshikazu. *Eclipse of the Rising Sun*. London: Jonathan Cape, 1951.

Kerr, E. Bartlett. *Flames over Tokyo: The U.S. Army Air Forces' Incendiary Campaign Against Japan, 1944–1945*. New York: D. I. Fine, 1991.

Kozak, Warren. *LeMay: The Life and Wars of General Curtis LeMay*. Washington, DC: Regnery, 2011.

Land, Richard. *The Divided States of America: What Liberals and Conservatives Get Wrong About Faith and Politics*. Nashville: Thomas Nelson, 2011.

LeMay, Curtis E. *Mission with LeMay: My Story*. Garden City, NY: Doubleday, 1965.

———, and Bill Yenne. *Superfortress: The Story of the B-29 and American Air Power*. New York: McGraw-Hill, 1988.

Lettow, Paul Vorbeck. *Ronald Reagan and His Quest to Abolish Nuclear Weapons*. New York: Random House, 2006.

Liefer, Gregory. *Broken Wings: Aviation Disasters in Alaska*. Anchorage, AK: Publication Consultants, 2014.

Manchester, William. *American Caesar: Douglas MacArthur, 1880–1964*. New York: Little, Brown, 1978.

McCullough, David. *Truman*. New York: Simon & Schuster, 1992.

Miller, Donald L. *D-Days in the Pacific*. New York: Simon & Schuster, 2008.

Morrison, Wilbur. *Birds from Hell: History of the B-29*. Central Point, OR: Hellgate Press, 2001.

———. *Hellbirds: The Story of the B-29s in Combat*. New York: Duell, Sloane & Pearce, 1960.

Neer, Robert M. *Napalm: An American Biography*. Cambridge, MA: Belknap Press of Harvard University Press, 2013.

Newcomb, Richard F. *Iwo Jima: The Dramatic Account of the Epic Battle That Turned the Tide of World War II*. New York: Henry Holt, 1965.

Phillips, Charles L., Jr. *Rain of Fire: B-29s over Japan*. Moreno Valley, CA: Nijuku Publishing, 1995.

Pickett, Ernest, and K. P. Burke. *Proof Through the Night: A B-29 Pilot Captive in Japan*. Salem, OR: Opal Creek Press, 2004.

Rhodes, Richard. *Dark Sun: The Making of the Hydrogen Bomb*. New York: Simon & Schuster, 1995.

Ross, Bill D. *Iwo Jima: Legacy of Valor*. New York: Vanguard Press, 1985.

Rusk, Dean. *As I Saw It*. Edited by Daniel S. Papp. New York: Norton, 1990.

Sagan, Scott D. *The Limits of Safety: Organizations, Accidents, and Nuclear Weapons*. Princeton, NJ: Princeton University Press, 1993.

Sherry, Michael S. *The Rise of American Air Power: The Creation of Armageddon*. New Haven, CT: Yale University Press, 1987.

Skinner, Kiron K., Annelise Anderson, and Martin Anderson. *Reagan: A Life in Letters*. New York: Simon and Schuster, 2004.

Smith, Holland McTyeire, and Percy Finch. *Coral and Brass*. Morrisville, NC: Lulu Press, 2017.

Spector, Ronald H. *Eagle Against the Sun: The American War with Japan*. New York: Vintage Books, 1985.

Sullenberger, Chesley B., III. *Sully: My Search for What Really Matters*. New York: HarperCollins, 2016.

Suzuki, Takeshi. *The Rhetoric of Emperor Hirohito: Continuity and Rupture in Japan's Dramas of Modernity*. Newcastle upon Tyne, UK: Cambridge Scholars Publishing, 2017.

Thomas, Evan. *Robert Kennedy: His Life*. New York: Simon & Schuster, 2013.

Tillman, Barrett. *Whirlwind: The Air War Against Japan, 1942–1945*. New York: Simon & Schuster, 2010.

Toland, John. *The Rising Sun: The Decline and Fall of the Japanese Empire, 1936–1945*. New York: Random House, 2014.

Truman, Harry S. *Memoirs, Vol. 2: 1946–1952 Years of Trial and Hope*. Garden City, NY: Doubleday, 1956.

Werrell, Kenneth P. *Blankets of Fire: U.S. Bombers over Japan During World War II*. Washington, DC: Smithsonian Institution Press, 1996.

Wheeler, Keith, and the editors of Time-Life Books. *Bombers over Japan*. Alexandria, VA: Time-Life Books, 1982.

White, Donald Wallace. *The American Century: The Rise and Decline of the United States as a World Power.* New Haven, CT: Yale University Press, 1999.

Willbanks, James H., ed. *America's Heroes: Medal of Honor Recipients from the Civil War to Afghanistan.* Santa Barbara, CA: ABC-CLIO, 2011.

Wölk, Herman S. *Cataclysm: General Hap Arnold and the Defeat of Japan.* Denton: University of North Texas Press, 2012.

Articles, Programs, and Websites

Associated Press. "Fifty Years Later, War Stress Ambushes WWII Vets." *Daily Courier* (Yavapai County, AZ), August 1, 1995. https://news.google.com /newspapers?nid=894&dat=19950801&id=kCYOAAAAIBAJ&sjid =lX0DAAAAIBAJ&pg=6953,97195&hl=en.

Aviv, Uri, et al. "The Burning Issue of White Phosphorus: A Case Report and Review of the Literature." *Disaster and Military Medicine* 3, no. 6, August 30, 2017. https://www.ncbi.nlm.nih.gov/pmc/articles /PMC5577774/.

Bigelow, Robert O. "The Beginning of the End: The First Firebombing of Tokyo, 9–10 March 1945." Virginia Aeronautical Historical Society. *Virginia Eagles Newsletter,* July 2007.

"Book Profiles US Medal of Honor Winners." *Voice of America News,* October 30, 2009. https://www.voanews.com/archive/book-profiles-us-medal-honor -winners-2003-11-11.

Burgess, John. "The Night the War Came Home to Tokyo." *Washington Post,* March 10, 1985. https://www.washingtonpost.com/archive/politics /1985/03/10/the-night-the-war-came-home-to-tokyo/ee04329b-4f79 -449d-9803-a3fffbe5948b/.

Coffey, Patrick. "A Reporter at Wit's End: The Firebombing of Japan: 'The New Yorker,' and St. Clair McKelway." *Los Angeles Review of Books,* September 3, 2015. https://lareviewofbooks.org/article/a-reporter-at-wits-end-the -firebombing-of-japan-the-new-yorker-and-st-clair-mckelway/#!46fr.

Collier, Lorna. "Growth After Trauma: Why Are Some People More Resilient Than Others—and Can It Be Taught?" *Monitor on Psychology,* November 2016. https://www.apa.org/monitor/2016/11/growth-trauma.

Collier, Peter. "American Honor." *Wall Street Journal,* May 26, 2007. https:// www.wsj.com/articles/SB118014402282815483.

Correll, John. "A Brave Man at the Right Time." *Air Force Magazine*, May 4, 2008. https://www.airforcemag.com/article/0607erwin/.

Corte, Gregory. "How Presidents Pray." *USA Today*, February 4, 2016. https://www.usatoday.com/story/news/politics/theoval/2016/02/04/how -presidents-pray-prayer-breakfast-eisenhower-obama/79786384/.

Dorr, Robert. "B-29s over Tokyo: The Firestorm That Helped End the War." Warfare History Network, n.d. https://warfarehistorynetwork.com /2018/12/27/b-29s-over-tokyo-the-firestorm-that-helped-end-the-war/.

———. "Medal of Honor Recipient: Henry 'Red' Erwin." *WWII Quarterly*, November 20, 2018. https://warfarehistorynetwork.com/daily/wwii/medal -of-honor-recipient-henry-red-erwin/.

Eagles, Virginia. *Virginia Aeronautical Historical Society Newsletter*, July 2007.

Erwin, Henry, Jr. Interview of Henry "Red" Erwin. Red Erwin Story Archives. July 31, 2012. YouTube video. https://www.youtube.com/watch?v=wtPc9 _teMgY.

Eschner, Kat. "Three Medical Breakthroughs That Can Be Traced Back to a Tragic Nightclub Fire." *Smithsonian*, November 28, 2017. https://www .smithsonianmag.com/smart-news/three-medical-breakthroughs-can-be -traced-back-tragic-cocoanut-grove-fire-180967323/.

Ford, Corey. "Sergeant Erwin and the Blazing Bomb." Reprinted "Stories in Uniform: A Look at the Heroics, Laughs, Sorrows, and Tragedies of Our Soldiers." *Reader's Digest*, 2013.

"Foreign Relations: The Backdown." *Time*, November 2, 1962.

Frank, Jeffrey. "How FDR's Death Changed the Vice-Presidency." *New Yorker*, April 17, 2015.

Frisbee, John. "Valor: Missions Accomplished." *Air Force Magazine*, January 1, 1994. https://www.airforcemag.com/article/valor-missions-accomplished/.

———. "Valor: Red Erwin's Personal Purgatory." *Air Force Magazine*, October 1, 1989. https://www.airforcemag.com/article/valor-red-erwins-personal -purgatory/.

Grossarth, Eric. "We Are East Idaho: Sugar City." *EastIdahoNews.com*, April 29, 2019. https://www.eastidahonews.com/2019/04/we-are-east-idaho-sugar-city/.

Guelzo, Allen C. "Emancipation and the Quest for Freedom." National Park Service, n.d. https://www.nps.gov/articles/emancipation-and-the-quest -for-freedom.htm.

Hand, Douglas. "Saving Burn Victims." *New York Times*, September 15, 1985. https://www.nytimes.com/1985/09/15/magazine/saving-burn-victims.html.

Hartropp, Joseph. "God and the Presidency: The Faith of Dwight D. Eisenhower." *Christianity Today*, October 27, 2016. https://www.christiantoday.com /article/god.the.presidency.the.faith.of.dwight.d.eisenhower/99103.htm.

"Henry 'Red' Erwin." Medal of Honor Society. September 27, 2011. YouTube video. https://www.youtube.com/watch?v=tzx8BkSwwWk.

Hills, Ben. "Tokyo's Hell on Earth: The Night a City Died." *Sydney Morning Herald*, March 4, 1995.

Hollobon, Joan. "Burn Centre: Helping Body's Largest Organ to Rebuild Infection Shield." *Globe and Mail*, May 14, 1984.

"Honor to LeMay by Japan Stirs Parliament Debate." *New York Times*, December 8, 1964. https://www.nytimes.com/1964/12/08/archives/honor -to-lemay-by-japan-stirs-parliament-debate.html.

Hopkins, William J. "Oral History Interview," JFK #1, June 3, 1964. John F. Kennedy Presidential Library and Museum. https://www.jfklibrary.org /asset-viewer/archives/JFKOH/Hopkins%2C%20William%20J/JFKOH -WIJH-01/JFKOH-WIJH-01.

Hoyt, Austin, producer. *American Experience: Victory in the Pacific*. PBS, 2005.

"Island Seemed Like a Beachhead on Hell," *Life*, April 9, 1945.

Japan Air Raids.org: A Bilingual Historical Archive. http://www.japanairraids.org.

Katsumoto, Saotome, and Richard Sams. "Saotome Katsumoto and the Firebombing of Tokyo: Introducing the Great Tokyo Air Raid." *Asia-Pacific Journal* 13, no. 1, March 9, 2015. https://apjjf.org/2015/13/9/Saotome -Katsumoto/4293.html.

Katz, Judd A. "Red Erwin and the Medal of Honor." *Alabama Heritage* 39, Winter 1996.

Kearns, Randy D. "Blast Injuries and Burn Care." *EMS World*, May 2013. https://www.emsworld.com/article/10913345/blast-injuries-and-burn-care.

Kristof, Nicholas. "Tokyo Journal; Stoically, Japan Looks Back on the Flames of War." *New York Times*, March 9, 1995. https://www.nytimes.com/1995/03/09 /world/tokyo-journal-stoically-japan-looks-back-on-the-flames-of-war.html.

Lincoln, Abraham. "Farewell Address." From *Collected Works of Abraham Lincoln*, 9 vols., edited by Roy P. Basler. New Brunswick, NJ: Rutgers University Press, 1953–55. https://www.nps.gov/liho/learn/historyculture/farewell.htm.

Moody, Sid. "It Was the Bloodiest Battle of the Pacific During World War." *Associated Press*, January 30, 1995.

O'Neill, James H. "The True Story of the Patton Prayer." *Review of the News*, October 6, 1971. http://pattonhq.com/prayer.html.

Orkin, Ruth. "We Are the Living: Twelve Men in a Superfort." *Coronet*, August 1948.

Ortensie, R. Ray. "Flashback: The 'Battle of Kansas' and the Birth of the Superfortress." *Elgin Air Force News*, August 14, 2018. https://www.eglin .af.mil/News/Article-Display/Article/1602130/flashback-battle-of-kansas -and-the-birth-of-the-superfortress/.

Oshinsky, David. "The Strength of His Weakness." *New York Times*, October 29, 1995. https://www.nytimes.com/1995/10/29/books/the-strength-of-his -weaknesses.html.

Paganella, Nicholas. "Remembering Cushing Hospital, 70 Years Later." *Metro West Daily News* (Framingham, MA), January 25, 2014. https://www .metrowestdailynews.com/article/20140125/OPINION/140127304.

Parry, Richard Lloyd. "Tokyo Chooses to Forget the Night 100,000 Perished." *Times*, March 11, 2005. https://www.thetimes.co.uk/article/tokyo-chooses -to-forget-the-night-100000-perished-m2hjmfwqh0t.

Phillips, Michael. "'It's a Lifelong Burden': The Mixed Blessing of the Medal of Honor." *Wall Street Journal*, May 24, 2019. https://www.wsj.com/articles /its-a-lifelong-burden-the-mixed-blessing-of-the-medal-of-honor -11558695600.

Rich, John. "On the Deck of a Battleship, Men of Peace." *Christian Science Monitor*, September 1, 1995. https://www.csmonitor.com/1995/0901/01091.html.

Ringle, Ken. "The Uphill Battle." *Washington Post*, February 19, 1995. https://www.washingtonpost.com/archive/lifestyle/1995/02/19/the-uphill -battle/f5265c77-b6fc-42cd-b2e1-eea6ca4d4677/.

Rothman, Lily. "Behind the World War II Fire Bombing Attack of Tokyo." *Time*, March 9, 2015. https://time.com/3718981/tokyo-fire/.

Safire, William. "Nixon on His Knees." *New York Times*, March 29, 1976. https://www.nytimes.com/1976/03/29/archives/nixon-on-his-knees.html.

Schogol, Jeff. "Dakota Meyer Explains Why He Hates His Medal of Honor." *Business Insider*, March 29, 2019. https://www.businessinsider.com /dakota-meyer-explains-why-he-hates-his-medal-of-honor-2019-3.

Schorr, Daniel. "Reagan Recants: His Path from Armageddon to Détente." *Los Angeles Times*, January 3, 1998. https://www.latimes.com/archives/la-xpm -1988-01-03-op-32475-story.html.

Shahinian, Ed. Interview, December 5, 2003. Library of Congress. American Folklife Center. Veterans History Project. https://memory.loc.gov/diglib /vhp/story/loc.natlib.afc2001001.11156/transcript?ID=sr0001.

Shalett, Sidney. "What Happens to a War Hero." *Saturday Evening Post*, September 4, 1948.

Shribman, David M. "Prayer and the Presidency." *Buffalo News*, January 21, 1995. https://buffalonews.com/1995/01/21/prayer-and-the-presidency/.

Stewart, William H. "Time Heals Everything—Almost." *Saipan Tribune*, July 26, 2005. https://www.saipantribune.com/index.php/a41e8eba-1dfb-11e4-aedf-250bc8c9958e/.

Strom, Sharon H. Hartman, and Linda P. Wood. "Women and World War II." What Did You Do in the War, Grandma? An Oral History of Rhode Island Women During World War II, 1995. http://cds.library.brown.edu/projects/WWII_Women/WomenInWWII.html.

Swopes, Bryan R. "Tag Archives: City of Los Angeles, 12 April 1945." This Day in Aviation: Important Dates in Aviation History, 2018. https://www.thisdayinaviation.com/tag/city-of-los-angeles/.

Tedeschi, Richard G., and Lawrence G. Calhoun. "The Posttraumatic Growth Inventory: Measuring the Positive Legacy of Trauma." *Journal of Traumatic Stress* 9, no. 3 (July 1996): 455–71.

Truman, Harry S. "A Prayer Said Over and Over All My Life from Eighteen Years Old and Younger." Notes of August 15, 1950. Harry S. Truman Library and Museum. https://www.trumanlibrary.gov/node/404492.

Tsai, Jack, et al. "Post-traumatic Growth Among Veterans in the USA: Results from the National Health and Resilience in Veterans Study." *Psychological Medicine* 45, no. 1 (January 2015): 165–79. https://www.ncbi.nlm.nih.gov/pubmed/25065450.

Venditta, David. "Hellertown High Grad Flew on Tokyo Firebomb Raid." *Morning Call* (Allentown, PA), March 7, 2015. https://www.mcall.com/news/local/bethlehem/mc-tokyo-firebombing-anniversary-manone-20150307-story.html.

"Voices of the WW2 Veterans." *Air & Space Magazine*, May 2015. https://www.airspacemag.com/articles/voices-of-veterans-180954673/.

Windham, Ben. "Southern Lights: One Heroic Moment—But It Didn't End There." *Tuscaloosa News*, January 27, 2002. https://www.tuscaloosanews.com/article/DA/20020127/Opinion/606128591/TL/.

Yamaguchi, Mari. "US Veterans Who Firebombed Japan in WWII Meet Survivor." *Associated Press*, December 9, 2005. https://apnews.com/42af0571c88e4f1c85c78d619801b70e/us-veterans-who-firebombed-japan-meet-survivor.

ABOUT THE AUTHORS

JON ERWIN IS THE GRANDSON OF MEDAL OF
Honor recipient Henry E. "Red" Erwin. Jon and his brother, Andrew, are
film directors and producers whose four feature films have all opened in
the top ten movies in America and collectively grossed more than $100
million at the US box office. They are also among only eight directors to
receive the incredibly rare A+ Cinemascore not once but twice, joining a
list that includes Steven Spielberg and Robert Zemeckis.

Their film *I Can Only Imagine* shocked the entertainment industry
to become the #1 independent movie of 2018, and it is the highest gross-
ing film in the history of its distributor, Roadside Attractions, collecting
more than $83 million in box office revenue on a production budget of
just $7 million.

Jon and Andrew seek to tell stories through a variety of platforms that
appeal to the American heartland faith-and-values audience and show-
case themes of hope, heroism, faith, and redemption. Currently, the team
has a multiyear film and television deal at Lionsgate.

WILLIAM DOYLE IS AN AWARD-WINNING *NEW
York Times* bestselling author, and has produced television shows for
HBO, the History Channel, and PBS. He is the coauthor of *American*

Gun: A History of the U.S. in Ten Firearms (with Chris Kyle), *Navy SEALs: Their Untold Story* (with Dick Couch), and *Let the Children Play: How More Play Will Save Our Schools and Help Children Thrive* (with Pasi Sahlberg), and the author of the highly acclaimed 2015 book *PT 109: An American Epic of War, Survival, and the Destiny of John F. Kennedy*. William is a Fulbright Scholar and the son of a US Army veteran who served in the Pacific theater during World War II.